Destroying the Village

Eisenhower and Dulles, 1956

Destroying the Village

Eisenhower and Thermonuclear War

Campbell Craig

COLUMBIA UNIVERSITY PRESS   NEW YORK

COLUMBIA UNIVERSITY PRESS
Publishers Since 1893
New York Chichester, West Sussex
Copyright © 1998 Columbia University Press

Library of Congress Cataloging-in-Publication Data

Craig, Campbell
    Destroying the village : Eisenhower and thermonuclear war /
Campbell Craig.
        p.   cm.
    Includes bibliographical references (p. 197) and index.
    ISBN 978-0-231-11123-2 (pbk. : alk. paper)

    1. Nuclear warfare—Government policy—United States—History.
    2. United States—Politics and government—1953–1961.
    3. Eisenhower, Dwight D. (Dwight David), 1890–1969.   I. Title.
UA23.C67224 1998
355.02′17′097309045—dc21   98–11023
                                                                                          CIP

Casebound editions of Columbia University Press books
are printed on permanent and durable acid-free paper.
Printed in the United States of America

For Christine, Sylvie and Elise
Ma Belle Famille

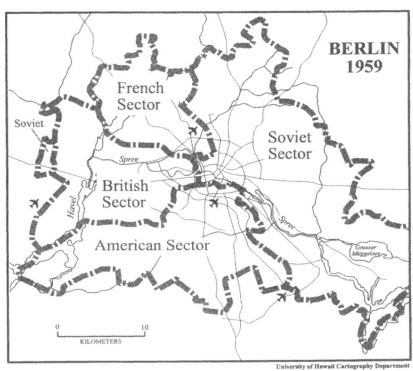

BERLIN
1959

French
Sector

Soviet

Soviet
Sector

Spree

British
Sector

Havel

American Sector

Grosser
Müggelsee

Spree

0   10
KILOMETERS

Contents

Preface

Up until the mid-1950s President Dwight D. Eisenhower believed that waging all-out war against an enemy threatening to end your national existence was right, natural, and necessary. In the wake of World War Two this was hardly a controversial position, as memories of Munich, Pearl Harbor, and Adolf Hitler had made the notion of just total war unobjectionable to all but a very few Americans. For Eisenhower, however, to defend what America had done during World War II was not simply a matter of abstract justification, but rather one of direct personal responsibility. He had been the American who authorized the total destruction of Nazi Germany: the violent elimination of the *Wehrmacht*, the fire-bombing of German cities. Perhaps no one in history is more properly associated with the phenomenon of total war than he.

Yet in 1955 and 1956, Eisenhower looked at the megaton thermonuclear weapons that the United States and the Soviet Union were building and threw this belief away. He had begun to realize that a general war waged to preserve the United States would not simply be immensely destructive — as the architect of the obliteration of Germany, he could accept that. Instead, a total thermonuclear war between the two Cold War superpowers would put a permanent end to everything it was being fought to protect. It would destroy America in order to save it. Like the burning down of Vietnamese villages to save them from communism, this was not just lamentable, or even criminal: it was absurd.

The prospect of being responsible for the purposeless, cataclysmic destruction of an all-out thermonuclear war horrified Eisenhower in a modern, existential sense. If World War Three would annihilate everything he believed to be important and worthwhile, then permitting it to happen for such a traditional reason as national security would be ridiculous, not only because by killing all Americans it would fail to preserve American security, but also because such a war would repudiate any claim Eisenhower and his nation might make to be on the side of reason or justice. Whatever moral distinctions there were between the United States and its twentieth-century adversaries would be quite meaningless to any survivors of World War Three: words like "democracy," "security," and "Eisenhower" would mean the same things to anyone left alive after a thermonuclear war that "national socialism" or "Hitler" mean to a survivor of the Holocaust.

But even if Eisenhower could abstractly permit himself to believe that general war was no longer acceptable, how could he renounce the idea of American national security during the height of the Cold War? There was simply no way that he could straightforwardly suggest to his military and civilian advisers, the nation as a whole, and America's allies around the world that the advent of intercontinental thermonuclear weaponry meant that the United States would no longer wage all-out war. To do so would convulse the international order, unleash political chaos at home, and lead immediately to his removal from office. It was not an option.

To resolve this dilemma, Eisenhower decided in 1955 and 1956 that his primary mission as president must be to develop a plan to prevent the outbreak of war with the Soviet Union without formally abandoning the basic national security policy of the United States. To be sure, to accomplish this it would be necessary to establish stable relations with the Soviet Union and construct a regime of nuclear deterrence. But such steps would not be sufficient. Eisenhower had known international politics and crisis for a long time, and he knew that a confrontation between the United States and the Soviet Union could occur despite the rhetoric of peaceful coexistence, despite arms control agreements, and despite both sides' deployment of retaliatory megaton nuclear weapons. If the two Cold War superpowers found themselves facing one another down over a genuine dispute, Eisenhower wanted to be sure that he could always steer the crisis toward compromise. To ensure this, Eisenhower developed a strategy to evade nuclear war. How he did that is the subject of this book.

The book is divided into three parts. The introduction and chapters 1 and 2 are really meant to define the predicament Eisenhower found himself facing after taking office: namely, the U.S. policy to defend its presence in

unresolved areas, most notably West Berlin, with the threat of general thermonuclear war. This first part is based upon secondary as well as primary
sources and is not intended to offer a new interpretation. Chapters 3 through
7 show how Eisenhower used American military policy to devise his strategy
of evading war, and how he implemented this strategy, especially during the
Quemoy-Matsu crisis of 1958 and the Berlin crisis of 1958–59. These chapters stem from the declassification of crucial documents relating to Eisenhower's making of basic national security policy and his actions during the
Quemoy-Matsu and Berlin crises. Chapters 8 and 9 provide an account of
Kennedy administration planning for a possible showdown with the Soviet
Union over Berlin during the period January–October 1961. I show how
Eisenhower's strategy to evade war extended into this period, despite the
desires of many of Kennedy's advisers to wield a more flexible and assertive
strategy on Berlin. This last section is also based upon recent declassification.
In an epilogue I compare Eisenhower's strategy to a more traditional one
conceived by Thomas Schelling during the early 1960s and embraced by
Robert S. McNamara before October 1962.

One last comment

The reader may notice a polemical tone in certain parts of the book—
especially the epilogue. This tone comes from my belief that many students
of the Cold War have taken a rather nonchalant view of the nuclear peace
attained by the superpowers since 1945. Such nonchalance reveals hypocritical and ahistorical thinking on both the traditional Cold War left and
right. On one hand, many conservatives attribute American success of the
last fifty years stems to toughness, suggesting that the primary lesson of the
Cold War is that militarism and diplomatic rigidity pays.[1] These kind of
conservatives supported military action during every single Cold War crisis,
and it was they who routinely accused American leaders able to resist the
hard-line and achieve compromise, such as Eisenhower and Kennedy, of
appeasement and even treason. Yet, looking back from the post-Cold War
world, would anyone wish to contend that it was a mistake for the United
States to cut a deal with the communists over the tiny islands of Quemoy
and Matsu, or over western occupation policy in Berlin? Does anyone wish
to argue that we really should have gone to thermonuclear war over these
stakes? It is hypocritical to denounce compromise in theory but applaud it
in fact.

Conversely, many observers of American foreign policy on the left have not seemed able to reconcile their pessimistic and sometimes even fatalistic predictions about the warlike direction of the American "national security state" with the remarkable nuclear peace achieved, at least in part, by the United States. A cynical view of aggressive American Cold War militarism, combined with the pessimistic (but theretofore historically valid) observation that weapons that are built eventually get used, made for the common presumption among many on the left that in its quest for Cold War supremacy the U.S. would inevitably blow up the world.[2] With the end of the Cold War, these leftist critics of American policy have not, as far as I have seen, conceded that the United States may have done well in preventing World War Three. Like their counterparts on the right, these critics speak of nuclear peace unremarkably, as if it happened without anyone, or at least anyone in power, really seeking it.[3] Nuclear weapons "deterred" war. Nations "of course" chose coexistence over confrontation. The critical and analytical dimension of Cold War history dies when it comes to accounting for its biggest story, replaced by the odd twentieth-century assumption that American and Russian leaders were somehow mechanistically destined to keep their rivalry from descending into war. Cold War accusations of appeasement are conveniently forgotten; so are cynical predictions of capitalist armageddon.

If this book makes only one point, it is that the American avoidance of nuclear war, like everything that takes place in history, did not just "happen." Actual people, above all Eisenhower, sought to evade nuclear war; many powerful figures at the center of decision believed that such a war was justifiable and regularly called for steps that would have begun one. In the historical struggle between these two sides during the crisis period of 1958-62, the former was barely able to prevail over the latter; had they failed we would not be able to write this history today. Those who see the demise of the Soviet Union and the end of the Cold War as an unalloyed victory of American toughness ought to recognize this. Those who are advocating a twenty-first century international order governed by nuclear deterrence ought to as well. And those of us who are thankful that the Cold War came to an end without either side resorting to its most powerful weapons should not feel embarrassed, even if it means praising a member of the power elite, about giving credit where credit is due.

Acknowledgments

My first debt is to John Gaddis, my doctoral adviser and mentor. His dedication to scholarly rigor has made itself felt on every page in this book, as has his unbending insistence upon lively writing. For their professional comments I also thank Richard Immerman, Philip Nash, Richard Harknett, and Columbia's anonymous reviewer, all of whom read the manuscript and saved me from many mistakes. For earlier direction and comments I'm grateful to Professors Alonzo Hamby, Akira Iriye, George Jewsbury, and Steve Miner, and also to Alecia Long, Joel Rosenthal, Oliver Schmidt, David Tait, Ruud Van Dijk, and Laird Wynn.

I would also like to thank Ben Frankel, for his consistent support of my scholarship, the Contemporary History Institute at Ohio University, for financial and institutional help, and Kate Wittenberg and Leslie Bialler of Columbia University Press, for their editorial guidance. Here at the University of Hawaii, Professor Idus Newby read the manuscript from beginning to end and supplied me with literally hundreds of stylistic improvements. Liz Contrades did excellent, conscientious editing. The professional staff at the University library's inter-library loan and government document departments fulfilled many last-minute requests. I also thank my colleagues here in the UH history department for their professional advice and encouragement of my work. Finally, thanks to Ev Wingert and especially Christina A. Tolosa at the UH Cartography lab.

Archivists at the Eisenhower and Kennedy presidential libraries, the Seeley Mudd library at Princeton, and the National Security Archive in Washington made this hit-and-run scholar feel welcome. Every student of American foreign policy owes a debt to the State Department's historical division, whose *Foreign Relations of the United States* series is a shining example of what government documentation can be.

I completed the bulk of this book during the summer of 1996. I would like to thank the National Endowment for the Humanities for a summer stipend that supported my writing, and Professor James Turner Johnson for encouraging me to introduce my thesis to a seminar at Rutgers on war and religion. I'm also grateful to my kind relatives in Delaware, who helped my wife and me make ends meet during our stay there. Right after we arrived my grandfather, Charles Noble Lanier Jr., died. He was a role model for me, both as a scholar and as a decent man. I hope that this book honors his memory.

My parents, Bruce and Andrea Craig, have supported my academic career with both loving support and intellectual input. My wife Christine has endured the high insecurity of being married to a young professor with seemingly limitless good humor. She has also edited this book with a skilled hand. I dedicate it to her and our two little girls.

You might as well go out and shoot everyone you see and then shoot yourself.

—Dwight D. Eisenhower, on what to do in case of war with the Soviet Union

Destroying the Village

Introduction:
Basic American Security Policy

During the summer of 1948 George Frost Kennan wrote down two "fundamental objectives" of American foreign policy. First, the United States had to "protect the security of the nation" from interference by foreign powers. Second, Americans needed to promote a world order in which the United States "can make the maximum contribution to the peaceful and orderly development of other nations and derive maximum benefit from their experiences and abilities."[1]

In this book the term basic American security policy refers to the efforts made by the U.S. government to achieve the former of these objectives—the physical defense of the United States from outside threats. However one wants to interpret the latter passage, the indisputable fact remains that the United States would have had a difficult time promoting world order and benefiting from the global economy had it ceased to exist. Basic security has to be the first requirement of any nation's foreign policy: if it is conquered and wiped out, it is no longer that nation.

For the first century and a half of its existence, however, this was a requirement the U.S. found effortless to meet. Once it had shaken off the last of British and French mercantilism, America was able to obtain a kind of physical national security unknown to the older European states. Indeed, from 1815 to 1941, speaking roughly, Americans did not really have to prepare a peacetime security policy for fear of another nation's conquest. The great European powers had been kind enough to balance one another off—when they were not actually at war—and this prevented the formation of a

European superstate that realistically could have hoped to invade and conquer the North American continent. Even if such a regime had arisen, the great oceans made the prospect of such an invasion, in the days before airplanes and ocean-floor cables, at best formidable. This happy combination delivered Americans from the collective fear and militarism that comes with chronic national insecurity.[2]

Naturally, American governments sought to sustain this situation, by staying well away from serious Old World conflict. The only president who substantially deviated from this course, Woodrow Wilson, met political and personal disaster. Most American statesmen were quite content to limit U.S. foreign policy to the search for new markets and resources for American businessmen, and the spread of American institutions and culture—the pursuit, to put it in broad terms, of Kennan's second objective.[3] While European statesmen had to worry about intricate alliance shiftings and minute military innovations, American diplomats were busy paving the way for Singer sewing machines, the United Fruit Company, and the YMCA. The United States' geographical security made it easy to emphasize this kind of diplomacy.

By December 1941 the two historical sources of American security were coming to an end. First, military technology, in the form of long-range airplanes, was making it possible to launch a surprise and sustained attack over the oceans and across American borders. Second, Adolf Hitler was on the verge of creating the very kind of superstate capable of invading America without opposition from other European powers. Moreover, Nazi Germany was a regime capable not merely of invading the North American continent and governing it remotely, like the British in 1760, but actually of dominating it directly in the totalitarian manner available to twentieth-century superpowers. Modern forms of communication, transportation, and social control made the prospect of a violent Nazi conquest fundamentally different from the old mercantile threats of Great Britain or France. These modern capabilities caused the United States to regard the Second World War far more fearfully and intensively than it had the first.

It is true that World War II did not put an end to traditional American commercial diplomacy; indeed, American officials continued to focus great effort upon economic expansion during and after the war. The destruction of the main industrial rivals of the United States provided American businessmen, working in tandem with U.S. diplomats, with an opportunity to dominate world markets and realize tremendous profits, and that was what many of them did. Nations that prevail in world wars tend to find ways to benefit materially from their success, and the United States was no exception.

American material exploitation of the postwar world would have occurred no matter who remained standing at the end of the war. What made American foreign policy different after 1945 was its simultaneous concern with the peacetime security of the United States. This new policy stemmed from two factors: American memories of the war, and an assessment of the Soviet Union. The two most visceral disasters of the war—appeasement at Munich and surprise attack at Pearl Harbor—persuaded Americans that the free security they had enjoyed was indeed gone. Hitler had demonstrated that ambitious regimes could, in the twentieth century, accumulate the kind of power sufficient to threaten North America. The Japanese had proven that modern military technology gave such regimes the capability to attack the United States.[4]

These new realities would have seemed less significant had, say, France been the other powerful nation standing at the end of the war.[5] Some sort of postwar rivalry might well have developed between the two nations, and certainly their competition for economic hegemony would have been fierce, perhaps something like the relationship between America and Britain during the 1920s. But the United States would never have regarded France after 1945 as a nation interested in threatening America directly with military conquest and totalitarian rule. The primary reason American officials instigated the Cold War was that it was possible for them to regard the Soviet Union in this way. The official ideology of the Soviet Union was to seek the eradication of capitalist regimes like the United States. The Soviet Union had cynically signed a peace treaty with Nazi Germany, its leader, Josef Stalin, had killed millions of his fellow citizens, and the Red Army, having brutally pillaged its way to Germany, continued to dominate, in violation of wartime agreements, several eastern European states. This did not mean, despite the rhetoric of American militarists, that the Soviet Union was destined to mount a Hitler-like campaign against the United States. But it was possible to believe, especially given the vivid lessons of recent history, that it might.

For the first time in its history, the United States perceived a peacetime threat to its national survival. This threat derived from the existence of military technology capable of traversing the oceans, and of a regime potentially interested in using such technology for the purposes of conquering the United States. The American government therefore was forced to develop, for the first time, a basic national security policy. This phenomenon distinguishes United States foreign policy during the years 1945–1989 from eras before and since.[6]

The Development of Basic American Security Policy

American security policy during the Cold War consisted of two basic elements. The first was the decision to contain the Soviet Union and its main allies—to prevent them from expanding into important areas of the world. This would deny them the geopolitical momentum that would have allowed them eventually to isolate and encircle the United States. The second was to ensure that the Soviet Union and its main allies did not attain a military capability so far superior to that of the United States that it could push aside these forces of geopolitical containment and threaten the United States directly. Both of these elements emerged in 1946 and 1947.

The architect of the element of American security policy dealing with containment was George F. Kennan, a career diplomat, expert on the Soviet Union, and, by 1948, head of the State Department Policy Planning Staff. In the immediate aftermath of World War II it became clear to Kennan that the Soviet Union would project its power beyond its own borders, as victorious empires are in the habit of doing. However, Kennan believed that the Soviet Union might go further; that if unchecked it could drive violently toward a worldwide empire hostile to the United States and indeed threatening to American survival. This possibility was sufficiently remote for the United States to prevail by opposing Soviet expansion with political and economic means, in a patient rather than a panicky manner. Thus in 1946 and 1947, Kennan devised a strategy of containing the Soviet Union.[7] He wanted to demonstrate that the Soviet Union was not a normal adversary, but one against which the United States needed to exercise unusual vigilance. He also contended that the United States had to concern itself with seemingly minor Soviet advancements, because the balance of power in key areas like Europe was so fragile. Both of these arguments became staples of American Cold War policy.

Kennan's Cold War career began in February 1946. The State Department, under orders from the White House, asked its embassy in Moscow to explain why the Soviets were being so hostile. Kennan, the embassy's specialist on Soviet politics, seized this opportunity to make a name for himself. On the 22nd, he issued his famous "Long Telegram," in which he warned his superiors in Washington that the Soviet threat to American survival was real and needed to be taken seriously.

The Soviet government, Kennan argued, regarded the outside world in a manner so cynical, fearful, and antagonistic as to be almost incomprehensible to the American mind. It was a long Russian tradition to view international agreements and treaties as bourgeois legalisms, to be used only to take advantage of nations naive enough to adhere to them. It was another long Russian tradition to venerate the more "civilized" West on one day and hold it in contempt the next. It was a third Russian tradition to see an adversary not as a rival to be deterred or even subdued but as a sworn enemy to be destroyed. All of these Russian characteristics were reinforced by the official Soviet ideology of Marxism-Leninism, which provided Soviet leaders with a "scientific" justification for their diplomatic emotions and imbued in them a sense of inevitable conflict.[8]

Kennan's "Long Telegram" captivated official Washington: by giving American officials a cogent explanation of the Soviet Union's strangely pugnacious postwar behavior, and by providing them as well with a series of recommendations for dealing with the USSR, Kennan decisively contributed to the commencement of the Cold War. Yet he knew that for all his provocative warnings the Soviet Union was too battered in 1946 to pose an imminent threat to the United States. How might the Soviet Union, in the future, endanger American survival? Kennan was asked in the summer of 1946 to lecture at the National War College, and it was there that he addressed this question and developed an American strategy to deal with it.

World War II had demonstrated the importance of national morale. By making their conquest of Europe appear inevitable to unstable and war-weary populations, the Nazis had easily defeated several European countries whose aggregate material power outmatched that of Germany. If the Soviet Union were someday to embark on a similar campaign, the United States, to avoid defeat, would have to ensure that the war-weary and unstable nations of Europe and East Asia would be able to stand up to it. A Soviet Union contained within its own borders could not threaten American survival. Nor could one that had expanded in a limited way, seizing control over adjacent and undeveloped nations and abetting sympathetic movements elsewhere. What the United States had to prevent was a widespread resignation to the inevitability of Soviet conquest—it had to prevent the coming of that crucial moment when the industrial nations of Europe and East Asia, observing the Soviet Union confidently expand, would begin to see the writing on the wall and would reconcile themselves to Soviet domination. There was a line somewhere—and it was impossible to know exactly where it lay as it was psychological as much as it was geographical—which the United States could not let the Soviets cross. "One of the vital facts about the international communist movement," Kennan told his students in March 1947,

> . . . is the pronounced "bandwagon" character that movement bears. By that I mean a given proportion of the adherents to the movement are drawn by no ideological enthusiasm, indeed not even in many instances by any particular illusions about its real nature. Many followers to communism are drawn primarily by the belief that it is the coming thing, the movement of the future—that it is on the make and there is no stopping it. They believe those who hope to survive let alone to thrive in the coming days when it will be the movement of the present will be the people who had the foresight to climb on the bandwagon when it was still the movement of the future.[9]

How might this "bandwagon" effect threaten American survival? Again, the question was as much psychological as geographical. To abandon "Eurasia to whatever the future might spell for it,"

> . . . we would be abandoning not only the fountainheads of most of our own culture and traditions; we would also be abandoning almost all the other areas in the world where progressive, representative government is a working proposition. We would be placing ourselves in the position of a lonely country, culturally and politically. To maintain confidence in our own traditions and institutions, we would henceforth have to whistle loudly in the dark. I'm not sure that whistling could be loud enough to do the trick.[10]

Here was the foundation of Kennan's strategy, as it related to American security. Contemporary history had shown beyond a doubt that the comfortable realities of a given international situation can change quickly. The United States, however powerful and secure its current position, had to recognize how suddenly the "bandwagon effect" could destabilize a familiar international order. Most important, Americans had to realize that continuing to survive as a "lonely, threatened power on the field of world history" would not be so easy in the twentieth century.[11] "The fact of the matter," Kennan told his students,

> is that there is a little bit of the totalitarian buried somewhere, way down deep, in each of us. It is only the cheerful light of confidence and security which keeps this evil genius down at the usual helpless and invisible depth. If confidence and security were to disappear, don't think that the totalitarian impulse would not be waiting to take their place.[12]

Kennan's point here was not simply to remind his audience that Americans were not immune to the tyrannical impulses that beset other societies,[13] but also to argue that such impulses were most likely to emerge in the climate of insecurity and panic that would accompany enemy advancements overseas. Containment was about keeping Soviet tyranny at bay, both in its physical and psychological forms.

Kennan had urged that the United States emphasize non-military forms of containment, such as economic aid and diplomatic pressure. The Soviet Union had been so devastated by the war that a confrontational, militaristic American policy not only wasted resources, but also risked making the Kremlin desperate and vengeful. Kennan opposed American plans to remilitarize central Europe and East Asia, downplaying the likelihood of a Soviet military attack against these crucial regions.[14] He supported initiatives like the Marshall Plan, which restored morale to allies and utilized American strengths. He believed that the struggle with Russia could be won without a war, and without the United States having to prevail in an arms race, provided American diplomats were skillful enough in reviving independent forms of power in Europe and Asia. Faced with a unified moral front, the Russians would eventually forget about world conquest.

Other policymakers in the Truman administration were not as sanguine. President Truman himself, for example, saw Stalin as a leader less concerned with morale or political unity, and more with tangible measures of power, like industrial capability and military might. Truman liked to relate the famous anecdote about Stalin's indifference to the opinion of the Vatican — "How many divisions did you say the Pope has?" — not only to highlight the Soviet leader's callousness, but also to remind his listeners that the United States ought not to find itself in the position of the Holy See.[15] In 1946

Truman acted upon this cynicism on several occasions. He approved of Winston Churchill's quite hard-line (for the time) "Iron Curtain" speech in March, to the dismay of many advisers still hopeful for some sort of accord with the Russians. He encouraged Bernard Baruch to toughen up the Acheson-Lilienthal plan, a complex proposal to transfer atomic energy knowhow to the United Nations, so much that the Soviet Union would never accept it. He authorized the writing of the militaristic Clifford-Elsey report on American security requirements. He eased, or pushed, doves like Henry Wallace out of power, and replaced them with hawks like James Forrestal and Fred Vinson, people who agreed more with his nuts-and-bolts measurement of power than with Kennan's moral calculus.[16]

But it would be incorrect to argue that Truman had completely abandoned Kennan's innovative diplomatic strategy by 1947 in favor of a more conventional, military one. Demobilization of the American armed forces was continuing apace, as was the diminishment of the military budget. Secretary of State George Marshall introduced the European Reconstruction Plan to the world in June; the Marshall Plan, by combining an offer to revitalize the economies of Western Europe with a gambit that the Soviet Union would not accept it (as it did not), was pure Kennan. Truman's announcement in March that the United States would henceforth come to the aid of free peoples resisting aggression, while more open-ended than Kennan's selective strategy, still was in tune with the latter's emphasis upon political morale and initiative. In his speech Truman was careful to label the enemy "totalitarianism," not the Soviet Union, and to emphasize political, not military, aid.[17]

There were reasons for Truman to maintain Kennan's nonmilitaristic approach, at least for the moment. He was himself still unsure about how to regard the Soviet Union. He had approved of Churchill's speech, but he also tried to keep his distance from its more inflammatory passages. There still was a significant wing of the Democratic party that opposed making the Soviet Union the enemy, and Truman himself wanted to continue expressing at least rhetorical support for a rapprochement with the Russians.

More important, the United States held monopoly possession over the atomic bomb. However clumsy and ineffective Secretary of State James Byrnes had been in late 1945 and early 1946 in trying to intimidate the Russians with it, the fact remained that the Soviets had to believe that if they started a war with the United States, atomic bombs would fall on their armies and cities. With this deterrent in place, American economic and diplomatic pressure became that much more effective. Ironically, Kennan's selective, nonmilitarist strategy of containment was quite well-suited to a nation that had the atomic bomb in quiet reserve.

Formalizing Early National Security Policy

By the middle of 1947, then, one can discern the early objectives of American security policy vis-à-vis the Soviet Union. A primary objective was to contain the Soviets: to keep key nations, like Japan, the oil-rich regimes of the Middle East, and especially the industrial countries in western Europe, out of the communist orbit. To accomplish this containment the United States would employ economic and diplomatic pressure, measures made more effective by the tacit presence of the atomic bomb. American officials who wanted the United States and its allies to place its first reliance upon military forces, like Secretary of Defense James Forrestal, were met by people like Kennan and Marshall, who could point to the reconstruction plan as proof the Soviets could be stopped without vast American rearmament.

Despite this elegant formula, however, the Cold War in 1947 was hardly the picture of stability. There was still contested territory, above all Germany. The defeated nation was still under the occupation of France, Great Britain, the Soviet Union, and the United States; these four powers each controlled regions in Germany, and, to make matters more contentious, they each also occupied sectors in the old capital of Berlin. Which side would get control when the occupation ended?

The stable balance created by Russian armies and the American bomb also had an uncertain future. Many American scientists were warning the Truman administration that the Soviet Union could build a bomb in several years, maybe sooner. Combined with his standing armies, the bomb would give Stalin an awesome military force. One need not have been a cynical Russophobe to worry that once he got the bomb he might be less inclined to respect the lines the West had drawn.

By early 1948 the Truman administration had begun to prepare a harder line. On March 17, the president spoke to a joint session of Congress on the "Threat to the Freedom of Europe." The enemy was no longer "totalitarianism," and its target, "free peoples," as Truman had declared a year earlier; now, the threat to freedom was the "Soviet Union and its agents," who, if unchecked, meant to extend their domination "to the remaining free nations of Europe." Czechoslovakia had fallen, Truman warned, and Finland, Greece, and Italy could soon follow.[18] Two weeks later the National Security Council (NSC), an interdepartmental body created back in July 1947, issued its first major policy statement. This new policy stated that "Stalin has come close to achieving what Hitler attempted in vain," the conquest of the European continent. The United States, to prevent Stalin from completing his quest, had to adopt a "counter-offensive" policy. The long-term objective of this policy, as the name suggested, was simple: "The defeat of the forces of Soviet-directed world communism is vital to the security of the United States." To realize this objective, the United States needed to take several "immediate steps": the first two of these were to "strengthen promptly the military establishment" and to "[m]aintain overwhelming US superiority in atomic weapons."[19] NSC-7, it is clear, did away with the generalities of the Truman doctrine, specifying quite precisely who the enemy was and how the United States would meet it.

Truman's speech and NSC-7 ran counter to the diplomatic and economic emphases of Kennan and Marshall. But as of March 1948 a speech given to Congress and a more hard-line NSC document were rhetorical declarations, not implemented policies. Congress had yet to approve the new military expenditures called for in NSC-7; Soviet conventional forces still dominated on the continent, balanced only by the (secretly minuscule) American atomic arsenal. The catalyst for a genuine toughening of American security policy would soon arrive, however, in a Soviet move that went unanticipated in NSC-7 and Truman's speech.

Part 1

The Predicament

1   *Casus Belli* in Berlin, 1948

As of March 1948 Harry Truman and his foreign policy advisers had given little thought to the continuing presence of western occupation forces in Berlin. There were more urgent matters to deal with: the Marshall Plan, the imminent Jewish victory in Palestine, communist successes in Italy and Greece, the communist *putsch* in Czechoslovakia, and, especially in the president's case, gearing up for the fall campaign. In this climate the minor question of unresolved occupation policy easily slipped toward the bottom of Truman's Cold War list. And even if some prescient staffer had managed to foresee trouble in the Prussian capital, the NSC was not yet in the habit of developing contingency plans and topical strategy papers. The intense turmoil of 1948 international politics, together with the improvisational manner with which Washington approached global crises, made the United States seriously unprepared for a confrontation in Berlin.

The western position there was objectively tenuous. In the last months of the war in Europe General Dwight D. Eisenhower, Supreme Allied Commander of the European theater of operations, decided to send his armies toward Bavaria rather than race to Berlin ahead of the Russians.[1] Upon the German surrender American, British, and free French forces occupied southern and western Germany, while the Soviet army controlled the northeastern part of the country. But the allies also established a four-power formal occupation of Berlin, as victorious armies tend to do in a vanquished capital. The problem was that instead of conveniently straddling eastern and western Germany, Berlin lay 110 miles east of the western border, well into the Soviet sector.

As the United States and the Soviet Union turned against one another in 1946 and 1947, relations among the occupying forces in Berlin predictably worsened. Metropolitan politics there turned into a forum for superpower competition, as Soviet-bankrolled parties competed for local power against American-bankrolled parties. To transport supplies to their sectors the western powers obviously had to cross Soviet-controlled territory, an awkward task that increasingly aggrieved the Soviets and their East German clients. The proximity of Soviet and western armies in Berlin led to numerous skirmishes and street confrontations, as did the tendency of both sides' top officials to travel gratuitously into the other's sector. Berlin became a microcosm of the emerging Cold War.[2]

Making matters worse were the desperate economic conditions prevailing throughout Germany. The allied policy of exercising complete control over German society, together with the Soviet Union's systematic looting of its sector (something few in the West wanted to criticize, given the Nazis' depredation of Russia during the war), stifled economic activity in the defeated nation. The economy, as Political Adviser for Germany Robert Murphy stated, was getting "steadily worse."[3] In fact the allied victors were obligated to keep the population alive, doling out 1,500-calorie food rations—more to coal miners, less to the elderly—and addressing endless power outages and housing shortages. This task, not at all attractive to nations trying themselves to recover from the war, was even less appealing to the military governors assigned to rule Germany. The heady days of shaking hands and sharing vodka in the Nazi rubble were gone.

In February 1948 delegates from the three western occupying powers convened in London, in order to arrange some sort of common political and economic reform in western Germany.[4] Despite the agreement at the Potsdam conference in July 1945 to maintain joint four-power occupation over all Germany until a final peace treaty was signed, the Soviet Union was not invited to this conference. On March 6 the London delegates issued a communique announcing their intention to reconstruct western Germany along capitalist, Marshall-Plan lines.[5] Meanwhile, American planners began to set up "Operation Bird Dog," a secret scheme to introduce a new currency throughout western Germany. Bird Dog would connect that part of Germany with the economy of western Europe, making it ready for Marshall plan aid; in so doing it would separate it cleanly from the eastern Soviet sector, just as the Plan had demarcated eastern and western Europe.[6]

The Soviet military governor in Germany, Marshal Vassily Danilovich

Sokolovsky, protested that these initiatives revealed a western intention to renege on the Potsdam agreement and divide Germany along Cold War lines.[7] As a reaction, on March 30 his forces began to interfere with western rail and road traffic within and around Berlin. More of a harassment than a confrontation, the Soviet action consisted of closer inspection of western vehicles, derailment of railroad cars, and a more obstinate attitude at Allied Control Council (ACC) meetings. It was now up to the western powers, and especially the United States, to decide whether to remain in Berlin, which meant putting up with Soviet harassment and antagonizing the Russians further, or to abandon the city, turning over its sectors there to Soviet control, and concentrating efforts upon western Germany. For almost three years the occupation of Berlin had persisted ad hoc. Now, the United States needed to come up with a policy.

To be sure, the West still had a legal right to remain in Berlin, and some American statesmen, notably Secretary of State George Marshall, initially believed that this was the best line to take.[8] No peace treaty had been signed with the Germans: whatever informal arrangements the western delegates were devising in London, the four powers still enjoyed the venerable victors' rights of occupation and control. Indeed, according to this literal perspective, as to the governing of Germany the Soviet Union and the United States were still allies. But recent events had put the lie to such legalism. President Truman's March 17 speech made the notion of Soviet-American alliance obviously specious; the March 6 London communique underscored this antagonism as far as Germany was concerned. The relations between the United States and the Soviet Union had no longer anything to do with international law. If the West was going to stay in Berlin, it needed a better justification.[9]

"Legalistic argument no longer has meaning," stated General Lucius Dubignon Clay, the American military governor in Germany, in a March 31 teleconference on the Soviet harassment. "We are now faced with a realistic and not a legalistic problem. Our reply will not be misunderstood by 42 million Germans and perhaps 200 million Western Europeans."[10] Clay had long believed that Berlin symbolized American commitment to Europe. Once the Soviets began their harassment of western commerce and travel, Clay, along with Political Adviser Robert Murphy, sought to persuade Washington that a departure under Soviet duress would demoralize Germans and lead to American defeat on the continent. Over the next several weeks Truman and his advisers gradually endorsed this position. Indeed,

Clay and Murphy ended up fulfilling their own prophecy: as Clay in particular well understood, in the absence of other information, relentless description of something as a crucial stake can make it just that.

In early April Clay and Murphy argued emotionally in communications
across the Atlantic for American resoluteness. Evacuation, in the immediate
wake of anti-communist elections in Italy and the growing success of the
Marshall Plan, was to Clay "almost unthinkable." Murphy predicted that an
American withdrawal "would have severe psychological reparations which
would, at this critical stage in European situation, extend far beyond bound-
aries of Berlin and even Germany."[11] With the Soviets backing off their
border harassment, Clay expounded his views in an April 10 teleconference
with Chairman of the Joint Chiefs of Staff Omar Bradley:

> Why are we in Europe? We have lost Czechoslovakia. We have lost
> Finland. Norway is threatened. We retreat from Berlin. . . . If we mean
> that we are to hold Europe against communism, we must not budge.
> We can take humiliation and pressure short of war in Berlin without
> losing face. If we move, our position in Europe is threatened. If Amer-
> ica does not know this, does not believe the issue is cast now, then it
> never will and communism will run rampant.[12]

Initially, diplomats in Washington were less sure. The veteran policy-
maker Robert Lovett, for example, was not convinced that Berlin was an
important Cold War stake, and he also worried that pugnacity there, especially given recent American successes in Europe, might make the Russians
desperate. On April 22 Lovett sent a personal telegram to Clay, Murphy,
and the American ambassador to Great Britain, Lewis Douglas, warning that
intransigence could provoke a "drastic Sov reaction" and recommending
instead that the three powers send a joint note to the Soviets explaining their
position.[13] Following up on this, in early May Marshall and Truman ordered
the U.S. ambassador in Moscow, Walter Bedell Smith, to hand the Kremlin
a conciliatory note calling for mutual efforts to resolve the Berlin question.
Also, Marshall and Bradley rejected Clay's plan to send an armed convoy
through eastern Germany toward Berlin; Bradley curtly reminded Clay that
he was not to escalate.[14]

One wonders then why Washington left the one real means with which
Clay could intensify the crisis entirely in his hands. On June 7, the delegates
at London announced their decision to go ahead with currency reform in

western Germany. As the American governor (the United States was providing the currency for Operation Bird Dog) Clay was given complete discretion as to the actual implementation of this reform. Given his clear opinions about western presence in Berlin it should have come as no surprise that Clay decided to initiate Bird Dog immediately, and to distribute the new currency not only in western Germany but also the western sectors of Berlin. On June 18 Clay informed Sokolovsky of his intentions; the Russian Marshal protested, proposing instead that a special currency be distributed throughout Berlin only. Clay had no problem rejecting this offer, and on June 23 American authorities began to introduce the western Deutschmark, stamped with a "B," to the three western sectors. Clay went ahead with all of this before getting approval from Washington.[15]

On June 24 Sokolovsky formally described Clay's action as a violation of the Potsdam treaty, and offered a final proposal which would evacuate all occupying forces from Germany. With no positive response from Washington, the Soviet Union on the evening of the 24th imposed around the western sectors of Berlin a complete land and water blockade, closing off as well electricity and food supplies which came from the eastern sector. With this move Stalin was clearly raising the stakes, for the West would now have to get out of Berlin once supplies ran out or confront the blockade physically. Now the United States had to decide whether to risk war to maintain a western presence in Berlin.[16]

Again, while Washington tried to come up with a coherent policy Clay pushed matters toward a confrontation. His subordinate, Colonel Frank Howley, stated publicly that his forces were not going anywhere, while Clay told his superiors in Washington that "we have to sweat it out, come what may. . . . To retreat now is to imply we are prepared to retreat further."[17] On June 26, once again without approval from his superiors, Clay initiated a small airlift to bring needed supplies from western Germany into Berlin. As Avi Shlaim writes, the political significance of this move was "paramount," because the United States was engaging in military action to signify a determination to stay in Berlin and to stand up to the Soviet challenge.[18]

Would Washington back up Clay's action? Murphy sent his opinion in a midnight telegram. The "presence in Berlin of Western occupants became a symbol of resistance to eastern expansionism," Murphy wrote.

It is unquestionably an index of our prestige in central and eastern Europe. As far as Germany is concerned, it is a test of US ability in

Europe. If we docilely withdraw now, Germans and other Europeans would conclude that our retreat from western Germany is just a question of time. US position in Europe would be gravely weakened, and like a cat on a sloping tin roof.[19]

On June 28 Truman met with his main advisers to reach a formal decision. The president was asked: What was the long-term American policy regarding Berlin? There was to be "no discussion on that point," he answered: "we were going to stay period." As Truman put it in hindsight:

> What was at stake in Berlin was not a contest over legal rights, although our position was entirely sound in international law, but a struggle over Germany and, in a larger sense, over Europe. . . . the Kremlin tried to mislead the people of Europe into believing that our interest and support would not extend beyond economic matters and that we would back away from any military risks.[20]

That evening Marshall sent a telegram to Douglas, who had earlier reported that the British were unsure about how serious the American commitment to the Prussian capital actually was. Marshall's order reflected Truman's unambiguity: "We stay in Berlin," he wired to London.[21] On the 30th Marshall, with Truman's concurrence, announced publicly that the United States and its two allies intended to stay in Berlin indefinitely. Marshall hinted that airlift capability could be increased significantly so as to supply Berlin for the indefinite future (a suggestion that became reality with the opening of a new airstrip that fall). On July 6 the western powers delivered a formal note protesting the blockade,[22] but this was after Clay, together with Air Force Chief of Staff Hoyt Vandenberg, had already begun to put in place a full-time airlift that could keep West Berlin alive. Using C-47 and C-54 transport planes the U.S. and British air forces began to ferry food, coal, and medical supplies to airstrips in western Berlin, eventually bringing 2.3 million tons of material to the beleaguered city.

The United States decided to stay in Berlin, even at the risk of war, because Clay and Murphy had persuaded Washington that the "bandwagon" model that the Truman administration had applied to the rest of Western Europe applied to Berlin as well. American policymakers agreed with Kennan that the struggle with the Soviet Union for Western Europe was as much psychological as it was economic or military: the United States had to prevent the fall of Berlin not for its inherent geopolitical value, but because an American departure under Soviet duress would cause Western Europeans to doubt the commitment of the United States. Ambassador to Great Britain Douglas, in a passage that (were it more eloquent) Kennan might have written, laid out his opinion to Lovett in July: Warning that to abandon Berlin would be "a calamity of the first order," he stressed that "Western European confidence in us, in the light of our repeated statements that we intend to remain in Berlin, would be so shattered that we would, with reasonable expectancy [sic], progressively lose Western Germany, if not Western Europe."[23]

But few in the Truman administration had even thought about the importance of Berlin before the spring of 1948. The German capital was hardly at the center of the American sphere; indeed, it was the last place on the continent that the West could plausibly claim as its own whose political affiliation had yet to be firmly decided. This was why the actions of Clay and Murphy were so decisive: these two agitators saw to it that their "repeated statements" transformed Berlin, in the minds of busy Washington officials, into a Cold War stake more like France than Finland. As Richard Betts has put it: "[p]sychological symbolism became strategic determinism."[24]

NSC-30

Once the United States committed fully to supplying West Berlin with resources (Truman made the formal decision to maintain the airlift indefinitely on July 22) the crisis there stabilized. The Russians, aware of the American bomb, did not want to escalate the confrontation into war. Truman was equally cautious: in his July 22 order he expressly ruled out a hawkish plan to break down the Soviet blockade. Most important, the Soviet expectation that the airlift would falter during the winter proved to be incorrect. The American and British air forces got into high gear by the fall of 1948, transporting thousands of tons of basic supplies to Berlin every day. Providentially the winter of 1948–49 turned out to be remarkably mild, allowing the airlift crews to maintain sortie rates unheard of for winter flying. At the same time the West Berliners, by defiantly enduring the blockade's privations, frustrated Soviet hopes that the winter's misery would destroy their morale.

In the late summer and fall of 1948, therefore, the crisis evolved from a volatile confrontation into another Cold War dispute that neither side was going to go to war over. Through the second half of 1948 delegates from all four nations met to argue about the Berlin blockade at Council of Foreign Ministers' meetings in Paris and during United Nations Security Council meetings; by the end of the year the western powers were concerning themselves more with the development of a West German "Basic Law" and federal political system, and with the inauguration of the North Atlantic Treaty Organization. As a consequence the Russians responded positively to subtle American overtures to begin negotiations on ending the blockade, and in the spring of 1949 the American diplomat Philip Jessup met secretly with a Soviet counterpart, Yakov Malik.[25] On May 3 the two negotiators formally signed an agreement to raise the blockade, and at midnight on May 12 the East Berlin authorities began to permit traffic to cross over into the western sector. With this the Berlin blockade was over, a plain victory for the West.

But this victory was simply a tactical one of rebuffing the Soviet blockade. Berlin still lay in the Soviet sector, the East German authorities still controlled all access points around the city, there was no independent economy there, nor any Western military forces to speak of. At the Council of Foreign Ministers' meetings in early June, moreover, the four sides reached no agreement whatsoever concerning the longer-term political status of Berlin. In other words, there was nothing to prevent the Soviet Union from reviving its harassment and obstruction of commerce and movement any time it wanted to, nor anything to prevent the Russians from taking West Berlin by force once they believed that they had sufficient military power to deter American escalation. The action taken by the United States in 1948 and 1949 to maintain a Western presence in Berlin succeeded on its own terms but solved nothing.[26]

The Berlin blockade prompted the West to make several major changes in its Cold War policy. One conclusion that American decisionmakers, especially Secretary Forrestal and the Joint Chiefs of Staff, reached was that the United States military needed much more money. This led to an intense budget battle in 1948 and 1949 between the military and President Truman, a battle resolved for the time being in the form of NSC document 20/4. The blockade also contributed to the formation of NATO. It showed that the Russians were willing, despite the American atomic monopoly, to move against vulnerable western positions. European politicians wanted formal assurance that the United States would come to their aid should the Soviet Union try its luck elsewhere. Both of these stories have been expertly treated by other historians.[27]

A third consequence of the Berlin blockade was less immediate, but equally important. Berlin gave Forrestal and the chiefs the opportunity to demand that Truman decide whether the United States would be willing to wage general war to defend that city. Ever since the early confrontations they naturally saw in the airlift a possible prelude to a wider European war. Alarmed by the weak Western military position in Berlin and in Germany generally, they had argued that the American policy on Berlin could lead to disaster. If the airlift escalated into actual warfare the immense Soviet army could overwhelm the local forces and move rapidly westward. Western European nations—in particular, France—were in no condition to fight in the first place and especially not in a war triggered by a dispute over occupation rights in the faraway Prussian city and erstwhile Nazi capital. Like all major crises, Berlin forced policymakers to make difficult decisions previously avoidable.[28]

Indeed, early planning on Berlin had indicated the administration's desire to avoid the subject. If the United States were to go to war with the Soviet Union, argued Secretary Royall on May 19, the United States needed to decide whether it would use atomic weapons.[29] On the 21st Truman asked the Joint Chiefs to prepare a plan "envisaging that we will not use atomic weapons." The NSC debated this proposal, and for the moment "deferred action on this subject."[30]

In the summer of 1948 Truman's military advisers insisted that it was a poor idea to continue deferring this subject, and an even poorer one to envisage a war with the Soviet Union in which the United States would not use its atomic weapons. In early July Forrestal met with the Joint Chiefs of Staff to discuss a rumor that the Soviets would launch balloons to frustrate the nascent airlift. At this meeting the Joint Chiefs agreed that if a war broke out in Berlin this would escalate into a war for Europe. As deployments currently stood the United States would have to use atomic weapons in this war if it were to have any hope of winning it. The chiefs all agreed that the NSC needed to develop an atomic policy that specified under what political circumstances the United States would initiate atomic war.[31]

Truman hinted at an answer to this question two weeks later, when he set into motion a plan to deploy several B-29 bombers to Britain. B-29s could carry atomic bombs, and the Russians were quite aware of this.[32] Quietly but not indetectably, several of these aircraft were deployed to Britain in mid-July.

But the B-29 deployment was a bluff; there were no atomic bombs aboard the planes, nor were they even fitted for them, something of which we now know Stalin was probably aware.[33] Moreover, control of atomic weapons still was formally held in the Atomic Energy Commission's (AEC) civilian hands. Forrestal and the JCS wanted to know what the United States would actually do if the Soviets initiated war in Berlin.[34] On July 22 and 23 the NSC met to discuss this problem. Truman stated his position: the defense of Berlin was a matter of utmost national security, and it would not do to modify that objective because the Pentagon thought that military forces in Europe were inadequate. "If we move out of Berlin," he asserted, "we have lost everything we have been fighting for." Truman found an ally in General Clay, who described the good morale among West Berliners and downplayed the like-lihood of a Soviet escalation of the crisis.[35] The point was to defend western rights in Berlin first and worry about the unlikely chances of a war breaking out second. Truman, worrying about the difficult election battle that fall, wanted the Berlin airlift to go smoothly while avoiding new defense spending.

Forrestal and the Joint Chiefs could not accept this. On July 26 and 28 they articulated their opposition to Truman's stance on Berlin. Forrestal stated in a letter to Marshall that should the Soviets move against the airlift, neither he nor the JCS could recommend an expansion of the war, due "to the risk of war involved and the inadequacy of United States preparation for global conflict."[36] If defending Berlin were really a matter of defending "ev-erything we have fought for," why did the AEC still control atomic bombs? Why had the administration developed no atomic strategy? From the mili-tary perspective atomic bombs would be necessary to win a war over Berlin.[37]

Truman wanted to satisfy the demands of Forrestal and the JCS. In Sep-tember he signed on to NSC-30, the first formal expression of American atomic policy.[38] NSC-30 was a brief against the proposition that the United States should refrain from waging atomic war for moral reasons. It was "futile to hope or to suggest that the imposition of limitations on the use of certain military weapons can prevent their use in war." The novel nature of atomic war nevertheless made it advisable to refrain from openly declaring an Amer-ican atomic strategy, because that would alarm the American public, trig-gering a moral debate that would lend comfort to the Russians. The Soviets, according to the new document, "should in fact never be given the slightest reason to believe that the U.S. would even consider not to use atomic weap-ons against them if necessary."[39]

NSC-30 did not contain a specific atomic strategy, at least in the sense that "strategy" came to have in the more meticulous 1950s and 1960s. It contained no targeting doctrines, deterrence theories, battlefield tactics, or sociological studies.[40] Indeed, insofar as the authors of NSC-30 worried about the actual conduct of an atomic war, it was to bring up the point that the destructiveness of such a war might make its political objectives harder to attain. It was necessary therefore to ensure that an atomic attack indeed "advances the fundamental and lasting aims of US policy." One of the reasons, of course, for this lack of specificity was that the Soviet Union had not yet gotten its own bomb, making concerns over deterrence or counterforce targeting premature. But more important than this was the overriding purpose of NSC-30, which was not to decide how to wage an atomic war but whether to do so in the first place. Hiroshima had bothered American decision-makers, not least President Truman himself, despite his public pose of gruff pragmatism.[41] For three years the United States government had avoided squarely deciding whether it would wage atomic war to avoid defeat at the hands of the Soviet Union. NSC-30 was, above all, a policy meant to answer this question.

Soon after the NSC meeting at which NSC-30 was unveiled the president made a point of assuring his military advisers that he was determined to adhere to this new policy. Truman "prayed that he would never have to make such a decision," Forrestal recalled the president saying, "but that if it became necessary no one need have a misgiving but what we would do so."[42]

With this endorsement basic American security policy formally evolved.[43] Before 1948 the United States had no direct policy regarding general atomic warfare: there was no statement indicating over exactly which stakes the United States would wage general war, nor was there a strategy that specified under what circumstances the United States would use atomic weapons. There were several reasons for this imprecision, but probably the most important of them was Truman's preference to avoid the question. Berlin made him confront it. With his plain endorsement of NSC-30 he had concluded that the United States must wage general war to maintain a western presence in Berlin, and by general war he meant atomic war.

2 General War Becomes Thermonuclear War, 1948–1952

The only question left to resolve regarding atomic weapons and American security policy, now that Truman had signed on to NSC-30, seemed to be the bitter, but in the larger picture unimportant, question of who exactly in the U.S. military would be in charge of waging atomic war. Truman's unexpected and dramatic victory in the November election had encouraged him during budget negotiations in early 1949 to stick to his policy of low defense spending. Everyone in Washington knew that with Truman's $14 billion defense allocation the United States armed forces would not be able to do much in a general war other than launch the atomic arsenal, so the branch given primary responsibility for that job would have unquestionably triumphed in the interservice wars and could rightly be seen to dominate the American military. While American and British pilots continued to fly back and forth across eastern Germany in late 1948 and early 1949, Army, Navy, and Air Force representatives in Washington went after one another's throats in their struggle for money and strategic sway.[1]

A weapon in this latter war was the Harmon report, a study on the likely outcome of an atomic war completed by Lt. General Hubert Harmon of the Air Force in May 1949. This report was remarkably pessimistic. Harmon and his committee concluded that a general war against the Soviet Union, despite the American atomic monopoly, would be difficult for the United States to win. Lessons from the previous war suggested that a unilateral atomic attack upon Russian cities could well stiffen, not break, the resistance of the Russian people, and by escalating the war into this new realm the

United States risked making the Soviet government desperate and its fighting forces vengeful, something against which memories of the previous war also cautioned. It would be very bad for America to lose a war into which it had introduced atomic weapons. Despite these fundamental problems, however, there was no alternative in the end but to maintain the current strategy of relying upon the atomic monopoly. The Soviet standing army was too big, and the American defense budget too small, to do otherwise.[2]

In retrospect the Harmon report remains a fascinating document, not least for its description of atomic war as something much less than the total, species-destroying cataclysm that a war between the United States and the Soviet Union would later connote. Moreover, the report turned out to be the first of a series of speculative studies on atomic and thermonuclear war to be written over the next decade that would come to have a decisive impact upon policymakers' considerations of general war. As far as its immediate influence upon Truman administration security policy was concerned, however, the Harmon report was of little significance. Secretary of Defense Louis Johnson, an ally of the Air Force in the interservice wars, thought the report insufficiently supportive of atomic strategy and kept it away from Truman's desk. The president therefore did not learn of the report's main points until well after it was completed, and nothing in the report found its way into approved NSC policy.

Reacting to the Soviet Bomb

But even had Truman read it and immediately set about conforming national security policy to its conclusions, the Harmon report would likely have had little lasting effect. In early September the AEC reported that its sensors had detected a significant release of radioactivity from somewhere in Soviet Asia. Immediately AEC scientists began to analyze the data, concluding by the third week of September that the level of radioactivity had to have been produced by the detonation of some sort of atomic device. The American monopoly was over.[3]

The initial American reaction to this news was, in many cases, one of denial. Secretary Johnson, and evidently President Truman as well, initially subscribed to the theory that the radioactivity detected by the AEC came not from the successful test of an atomic bomb but from some sort of accident—that the American monopoly had not ended at all. Hinting at this, Truman in his public statement of September 23 ambiguously called the test a "nuclear explosion."[4] Gradually this theory lost credence in the White House, however, and on October 10 Truman approved an NSC plan, which had been conceived by the Defense Department back in September, to assume that the Soviet Union had indeed built a bomb, and make the American response one of escalating atomic-bomb production. The American decision to rely upon atomic bombardment in a general war—the basis of NSC-30—did not necessarily require an atomic monopoly, but it certainly required atomic predominance. There was simply no way to win a war to stay in Berlin, for example, if the Soviets had an atomic arsenal comparable to the American one. Truman approved the NSC plan quickly and the AEC began work building more bombs.[5]

But this initiative, like the Berlin airlift, would provide only temporary reprieve. The West could regain a numerical advantage, to be sure, but however many atomic bombs the United States built, the Soviets would in all probability eventually attain enough themselves to offset them in any likely theater. That stalemate would then make the Soviet advantage in conventional forces decisive. Almost immediately many of Truman's advisers and others in Washington began to consider another way of responding to the Soviet achievement.

Upon learning of the Soviet test two of the most influential atomic policymakers in Washington—Senator Brien McMahon, chairman of the Joint Congressional Committee on Atomic Energy, and Lewis Strauss, one of the AEC's five commissioners—began to urge Truman to move ahead quickly on a project to build a thermonuclear bomb.[6] Manhattan Project scientists had theorized during the war that an atomic fission explosion could generate enough heat to implode two nuclei, creating a thermonuclear explosion that would dwarf its atomic counterpart. After the Soviet test many of these scientists, including Ernest Lawrence, Luis Alvarez, and Edward Teller began to promote this theory more vigorously; Senator McMahon concurred, and had his principal adviser, William Borden, draft a policy statement, which the senator entered into the record on September 29. This proposal argued simply for an immediate crash program to develop the superbomb and a nuclear-powered airplane to deliver it to Soviet targets.

On September 30 Strauss sent Truman a memorandum suggesting that by building the superbomb the United States could regain its qualitative advantage in the Cold War. Thermonuclear weaponry represented a "quantum jump" in military hardware, and with it America could once again confront the Soviets with confidence and aggressiveness. Truman met with Strauss to discuss this memorandum, and, according to Hewlett and Duncan, urged its author to "force the issue up to the White House and do it quickly."[7]

Truman's order set the decisionmaking process in motion. By early October, the various bureaucracies in Washington concerned with nuclear weapons had turned their attention exclusively to the question of whether or not to build the superbomb. The AEC directed its General Advisory Committee (GAC), a group made up mostly of prominent atomic scientists, to advise on the feasibility and merit of developing thermonuclear weaponry. The Joint Chiefs and other military planners began to consider how the new bomb might fit into military planning. Secretary of State Acheson asked George Kennan to evaluate the effect of thermonuclear bombs upon the long-term interests of American foreign policy.

The GAC was led by J. Robert Oppenheimer, the "father" of the atomic bomb, and consisted largely of scientists and other civilian experts on atomic issues. Working quickly, the committee completed its final report by October 30. Its main recommendation was to urge Truman to refrain from building the superbomb. Though the GAC's formal mission was to evaluate the decision scientifically, the basis of this recommendation was not. The moral opprobrium associated with building such a weapon, together with the possibilities of international control and the poor state of Soviet thermonuclear research, the committee argued, outweighed any political or strategic use the superbomb might provide.[8] In an addendum to their report the authors (probably the main author was Oppenheimer) explained their thinking. "We base our recommendation," they stated,

> on our belief that the extreme dangers to mankind inherent in the proposal wholly outweigh any military advantage that could come from this development. Let it be clearly realized that this is a super-weapon; it is in a totally different category from an atomic bomb. . . . We believe a superbomb should never be produced.[9]

The authors of the GAC were not blind to the likely objections that would be placed against their report. In particular, they contended that the United States could continue to wage the Cold War successfully against the Soviet Union even if the Soviets, as a result of the American decision to eschew the superbomb, attained a thermonuclear monopoly. Atomic weapons were destructive enough to serve as a deterrent to war. A Soviet thermonuclear attack, they argued, could be met effectively with atomic reprisal.[10]

Seeing the GAC report as a possible obstacle to Truman's immediate

approval of the H-Bomb project—particularly given the GAC's elite repu-
tation and Truman's frequent public expressions of support for the idea of
international control—NSC officials and the Joint Chiefs turned their full
attention to defeating the GAC recommendation. These supporters of the
bomb sent urgent memoranda to the White House in November and December. One clear message emerged from their sharp testimony. The political risk inherent in allowing the Soviet Union to acquire the bomb before
the United States outweighed the "extreme dangers to mankind" of which
the GAC warned. This risk could not be described in traditional terms of
relative military power, as the GAC had tried to argue; it was more profound
than that, striking at the very core of American national survival.

Everyone clamoring for Truman's ear in late 1949 iterated this basic
point.[11] The Joint Chiefs argued simply that "[P]ossession of a thermonuclear weapon by the USSR without such possession by the United States
would be intolerable."[12] Paul Nitze, speaking for the State Department,
wrote that "it is essential that the U.S. not find itself in a position of technological inferiority in this field;" Strauss noted understatedly that "The
danger in the weapon does not reside in its physical nature but in human
behavior. Its unilateral renunciation by the United States could very easily
result in its unilateral possession by the Soviet government. I am unable to
see any satisfaction in that prospect."

"[O]ur arsenal," Strauss concluded, "must not be less well equipped than
with the most potent weapons that our technology can devise."[13] Defense
members of a NSC working group elaborated further:

> The situation today is strikingly parallel to that of a few years ago when
> this nation was engaged in a desperate race to develop a fission bomb
> before Germany. From the Soviet point of view sole possession of the
> thermonuclear weapon would place in their hands an offensive
> weapon of the greatest known power possibilities. . . . In time of war
> sole possession of the thermonuclear weapon coupled with tremen-
> dous superiority of conventional military forces would provide the So-
> viets with the necessary balance . . . to risk hostilities for the rapid
> achievement of their objectives. . . . The inevitable jeopardy to our
> position as a world power and to our democratic way of life would be
> intolerable.[14]

Attacks on the GAC report also came from Congress. Senator McMahon
led the way. In a November 21 letter to Truman he argued that the "specific

decision that you must make regarding the superbomb is one of the gravest ever to confront an American president. . . . If we let Russia get the super first," McMahon added, "catastrophe becomes all but certain — whereas, if we get it first, there exists a chance of saving ourselves."[15]

Having allowed the debate to percolate, Truman prepared to make a final decision in January. Back in November the president had created a special committee of the NSC, to be made up of Acheson, Secretary of Defense Louis Johnson, and AEC Chairman David E. Lilienthal, whose job would be to consider the various arguments and make a formal recommendation to the president on the superbomb. The special committee's mission was perfunctory, given Truman's own view that the bomb should be built, together with the adamant concurrence of the Joint Chiefs, his main advisers, and the dominant congressional authority on atomic weaponry. Moreover, all three of the special committee's members had already made their opinions known.[16] Nevertheless the three men submitted their final report to Truman on January 31, 1950. They recommended, with Lilienthal dissenting, that the United States proceed with a program to build the superbomb.[17] Truman did not need to be persuaded. The president asked: "Can the Russians do it?" All three members of the subcommittee, including Lilienthal, assented. "In that case," Truman concluded, "we have no choice. We'll go ahead."[18]

The GAC made a poor case against the bomb, for in their recommendation there can be found no effective refutation of the thesis put forth by Nitze, Strauss, the Joint Chiefs, et al. However true it was that the superbomb could kill civilians by the millions, that the Soviet Union could not possibly attain the bomb for several years, that international control was feasible, that atomic bombs could deter a thermonuclear attack — none of these arguments spoke to the simple fact that the only sure way for American national security to be put in fundamental danger in 1950 was for the Soviet Union to acquire a monopoly over thermonuclear weaponry, and the only sure way to prevent that from happening was for the United States to build a bomb first.[19] It was this simple formula that prompted the chorus of support for the superbomb in late 1949; it was this distinction that prompted McMahon to remark that the GAC report "made me sick."[20]

Kennan's Demurral

By contending that America atomic arsenal could serve as an effective deterrent to a Soviet thermonuclear attack, the GAC failed to recognize, or chose to overlook, the advantage that military predominance can provide apart from actual warfare. It was particularly surprising that they missed this since it was precisely this advantage that the United States had utilized during its atomic monopoly. The decision to build the hydrogen bomb was not a last-ditch effort to prevent an otherwise imminent Soviet attack; rather, it was to make sure that the balance of Cold War power did not tilt irretrievably toward the Soviet side.[21] To object to this line of reasoning on its own terms one would have had to advance the proposition that the "extreme dangers to mankind" inherent in thermonuclear technology should have been of greater concern to Americans than their national survival. The GAC critics of the H-Bomb decision were not willing to make that argument.

One who was willing to make that argument, or at least grope toward it, was George Kennan. Secretary of State Dean Acheson had asked Kennan, who was about to leave the State Department, to assess the superbomb decision in the light of larger American foreign policy objectives. Kennan spent his last days in Washington dedicating himself to this task, completing by January a memorandum so elaborate in form and unusual in content that Truman never came close to seeing it. Yet Kennan hit upon something that the GAC and other critics of the super had not.

The outgoing Policy Planning Staff director had been thinking about the thermonuclear bomb since 1949. Senator Edwin Johnson of Colorado had let slip in a television interview in November of that year that the United States was considering its development, and this prompted Kennan to send an anguished letter to Acheson. The following questions, Kennan insisted, "would have to be answered" if the United States were to "arrive at a rational decision" regarding the bomb. "Would our possession of the weapon as a means of creating terror," Kennan asked, "serve the interests of the United States either as a preventive of war or as a means of winning it? What would be the moral effect in the United States and throughout the world of our developing this weapon of mass destruction the ingredients of which have no peaceful applications whatever?" Kennan added that the "ultimate decision whether to develop the super-bomb will be made from the point of view of national security in its broadest sense—self-preservation or actual survival."[22] Asked for his professional opinion about whether it would be in the American interest to build the superbomb, like the GAC Kennan instead listed his moral objections to it.

In January, before Truman made his final decision, Kennan completed his last memorandum, a remarkably long essay called "International Control of Atomic Energy."[23] In this paper Kennan suggested that surrender to the

Soviet Union might well be preferable to a thermonuclear war. Warfare, he argued,

> should be a means to an end other than warfare, an end connected with the beliefs and the feelings and the attitudes of people, an end marked by submission to a new political will and perhaps to a new regime of life, but an end which at least did not negate the principle of life itself.
>
> The weapons of mass destruction do not have this quality. . . . they cannot really be reconciled with a political purpose directed to shaping, rather than destroying, the lives of the adversary.[24]

Kennan acknowledged that nuclear weapons could serve the United States temporarily as tools of deterrence. But this was to be an expedient until steps were taken to establish international control over the bomb. "In the military sphere," Kennan added in February, "we should act at once to get rid of our dependence, in our war plans, on the atomic weapon."[25]

One can discern the difference, subtle and undeveloped as it was, between Kennan's opposition to the superbomb and that of the GAC. Both sides saw in the hydrogen bomb a revolutionary military invention so potentially destructive that to use it posed dangers to humanity as a whole. Thermonuclear weapons were different from atomic ones. But the GAC tempered its objection by insisting that the United States, even after having allowed the Soviets to obtain a thermonuclear monopoly, could still win a war and preserve its security, by responding to a Soviet attack with atomic weapons. Even in the thermonuclear age, according to this view, the United States could maintain its political survival by prevailing in a world war.

Kennan disagreed. He admitted that the hydrogen bomb could deter the Soviet Union from embarking upon aggression, but he was more interested in trying to force American policymakers to think about what the new weapon could actually do for them. The more important question looked to the future: once both sides had attained thermonuclear arsenals, could the United States, or any nation, "win" a general war in the traditional sense? Could Americans really defend their national existence by fighting a war with hydrogen bombs? If not, then what other solutions were there, other than creating an airtight system of international control, or developing a new policy which in the end admitted that "submission to a new political will" was better than unleashing a general war?

Truman did not take such reasoning into consideration. Acting upon

basic national security logic, he wanted quickly and unconditionally to go
ahead with the superbomb, and objections to this decision by some scientists
and a State Department official on his way out of Washington were hardly
going to change his mind. On January 31, 1950, he made the decision to
build the hydrogen bomb.

NSC-68

The same day that he approved of the decision to go ahead with the
hydrogen bomb, President Truman also issued this order:

> I hereby direct the Secretary of State and the Secretary of Defense to
> undertake a reexamination of our objectives in peace and war and of
> the effect of these objectives on our strategic plans, in the light of the
> probable fission bomb capability and possible thermonuclear bomb
> capability of the Soviet Union.[26]

The task of officially complying with Truman's January 31 directive fell to
Paul Nitze, the State Department expert who would soon take over Kennan's
job as head of the Policy Planning Staff. Nitze completed NSC-68 on April
14, 1950.[27] In it he argued that the primary threat to American security over
the coming years would be a stronger and more confident Soviet Union,
emboldened particularly by its new weaponry. Always a fanatical regime bent
on world domination, the Kremlin had avoided confrontation in the Cold
War's early years because of the American atomic monopoly.[28] Once Stalin
obtained nuclear parity, Nitze warned, he would use it to cancel out the
American arsenal, move his vast, almost omnipotent conventional forces into
the "Eurasian land mass" and dare the Americans to risk World War III by
stopping him. If the West were to retain its moral resolve to resist totalitarianism over the long haul, it would have to prevent the Soviets from gaining
this upper hand.[29]

Breaking finally from Kennan's policy, Nitze argued in NSC-68 that the
best way to keep the Soviets at bay would be to embark upon a vast buildup
of American armed forces. Political and economic means of containment
were fine, he acknowledged, but in the crucial coming years the Kremlin
would be deterred in the end only by substantial military might. Until the
Soviets demonstrated a willingness to participate "normally" in international
politics, United States officials needed to concentrate upon the military component of American security policy.

Nitze's basic recommendation, therefore, was straightforward. Potential Soviet attainment of nuclear arsenals meant that the United States must intensify its strategy of containment. This new approach had to emphasize military power over other means of containment. Policymakers needed to forget notions of fiscal restraint and engage in Keynesian deficit spending, so as to provide larger sums for defense without stifling the domestic economy. Americans also needed to shed any illusions about Soviet intentions: the Kremlin's aim was world domination, and only the United States stood in its way.

Conspicuous in its absence from this basic national security policy was any substantial discussion of the thermonuclear weapons that prompted its writing in the first place. Nitze's argument was that the United States needed to beef up its military power so as to counteract an increasing Soviet threat. Consequently he supported significant expansion of American conventional and atomic capabilities. But as for deployment of the weapons that Truman had just decided to build, weapons that Nitze himself had urged Truman to build, on this matter Nitze was ambiguous. In fact, his recommendation regarding thermonuclear weapons was so equivocal, contrasting strongly with the assertive tone of the rest of the document, that one must wonder what was going on.[30]

"In the event of a general war with the U.S.S.R.," Nitze stated, "it must be anticipated that atomic weapons will be used by each side in the manner it deems best suited to accomplish its objectives."[31] In other words, one could not base one's policy upon the assumption that either side would refrain from using these weapons in an all-out war. This was a position consistent with that taken by Nitze and many others when demanding that Truman go ahead with the super. Yet Nitze went on to write that it

appears to follow from the above that we should produce and stockpile thermonuclear weapons in the event they prove feasible and would add significantly to our net capability. Not enough is yet known of their potentialities to warrant a judgment at this time regarding their use in war to attain our objectives.[32]

Thermonuclear weapons, as Nitze knew, would be able to destroy the enemy hundreds of times more quickly and completely than atomic bombs, a fact he alluded to in his recommendation that Truman go ahead with the bomb. So it is hard to see how Nitze could wonder whether such weapons would "add significantly to our net capability." Further along in NSC-68

Nitze elaborated on this point, but he continued to be vague. It was "mandatory," he argued, "that we enlarge upon our technical superiority by an accelerated exploitation of the scientific potential of the United States and our allies."[33] He concluded: "It is necessary to have the military power to deter, if possible, Soviet expansion, and to defeat, if necessary, aggressive Soviet or Soviet-directed actions of a limited or total character."[34]

If the United States was to exploit the West's scientific potential in order to create military forces capable of both deterring Soviet expansion and defeating the Soviet Union in any kind of war, then one has to ask what kind of military forces Nitze could possibly have had in mind other than the weapons that the United States was at that moment rushing to build.[35] Yet again Nitze left the issue unclear, not stating here or anywhere else in NSC-68 that the threat of thermonuclear war would have to become the *ultima ratio* of basic American military policy.

The Truman administration's implementation of NSC-68 had enormous consequences. Sitting on Truman's desk the day North Korean forces crossed over into South Korea, NSC-68 provided Truman and his main security advisers with both a ready-made explanation of this invasion, and a broad strategy to deal with it. It suggested that the events in Korea were not the opening salvo of a civil war in a remote part of the world but of a systematic Soviet Cold War offensive. Nitze's Keynesian argument that the United States could treble or quadruple defense spending without stifling the domestic economy provided the president with a rationale to spend far more to repel the Soviet threat than he had previously been willing to. Finally, NSC-68 replaced Kennan's emphasis upon political and economic means of resisting Soviet expansion with a new and thoroughgoing emphasis upon military power. Truman's approval of NSC-68, then, foretold his rejection of more moderate Cold War policies in favor of the all-out military crusade upon which the United States embarked after January 1950. This is a story that has been authoritatively told.[36]

The one area of national security policy which did not fit into the NSC-68 blueprint was the Truman administration's attitude toward thermonuclear weaponry. If American policy on thermonuclear war had conformed to the recommendations of NSC-68 as closely as non-nuclear policy had, then one might have expected to see in the years 1950–53 a patient attempt to build the superbomb, and at the same time an effort among American military planners to construct a general war strategy that excluded, or at least sought to avert, all-out thermonuclear attack. What actually occurred was quite the opposite, revealing a large gap between Truman administration policy and practice on the question of thermonuclear war.

All-out for the Superbomb

The arrest of Julius and Ethel Rosenberg on charges of passing nuclear secrets to the Russians in August 1950, coming in the wake of the British announcement that Klaus Fuchs, an emigré who had worked on the Manhattan project, had been caught committing a similar crime, intensified the desires of many American officials to spare no expense in building the superbomb. The logic that led Truman to make the initial decision in January had not gone away: it was by no means impossible that Fuchs or the Rosenbergs had transferred to the Russians decisive information on the development of thermonuclear weaponry, and this meant that the Soviets could still get the bomb before the Americans.[37] Added to this was the "loss" of China in late 1949, the outbreak of the Korean war, an event that seemed to conform with NSC-68's resonating depiction of the USSR as a messianic regime bent on world domination, and the shocking entrance of the Chinese communists into that war in late 1950. It was in this climate that Senator Joseph McCarthy was able to prosper, that the Congress and the president acquiesced in the quadrupling of the American defense budget, that General Douglas MacArthur publicly defied the orders of his president to popular acclaim, and that American military planners and scientists, urged on by the frenzied Senator Brien McMahon, worked to develop a thermonuclear bomb and a strategy to deploy it against the Russians.

In the late summer of 1950, as the Korean war raged, Truman moved to expedite the superbomb program. On August 2 McMahon argued in front of his joint committee that the United States needed to begin a crash program of constructing new nuclear reactors and the industrial plants needed to manufacture the Uranium 235 and heavy water necessary for successful nuclear fusion. Truman agreed, and soon AEC operatives were at work at new or rehabilitated facilities in Washington, Idaho, South Carolina, and Tennessee, and in laboratories at Los Alamos, Berkeley, and Chicago.[38] At the same time operatives overseas secured American control over raw materials in South Africa, the Belgian Congo, and Norway, and Edward Teller, now a chief scientist at Los Alamos, received funding for new laboratories and the hiring of many new scientists. Basic, theoretical research, Teller argued, was necessary if there were to be a chance of building a bomb quickly. On December 1 Truman asked Congress for an additional $16.8 billion in defense spending—a figure higher than the *total* he had wanted back in 1949 to spend for all of fiscal 1951—and $1 billion for the AEC, a sum to be dedicated entirely to thermonuclear research and production. In May of 1951 officials conducted early tests, code-named Greenhouse, in the Nevada desert, which demonstrated that it would be possible to create the heat necessary to instigate fusion with atomic explosions.[39]

On the military front, General Curtis LeMay of the U.S. Air Force transformed the Strategic Air Command (SAC), theretofore a minor Air Force agency, into the force that would be responsible for delivering thermonuclear bombs to Russian targets. LeMay's mission was to attain the capability to launch a large nuclear attack against the Soviet Union before the Soviets could respond in kind. He therefore acquired new intercontinental bombers, some with the ability to reach Russian targets and return to base without refueling. SAC commissioned new pilots and base commanders. And LeMay brought together many colleagues who had served under him in the campaign to bombard German and Japanese cities during World War II. In 1951 and 1952 this new staff developed a systematic targeting doctrine, taking from their previous campaign the idea (one rejected, among other places, in the Harmon report) that comprehensive bombardment of a nation's industrial and economic centers and its strategic forces still on the ground could lead to a quick and decisive victory. LeMay believed that intensive nuclear bombardment could win a world war pretty much by itself. His force therefore had to predominate in any military planning for World War III. SAC would not be providing support for ground troops.[40]

The effort to build the bomb only intensified after the Greenhouse tests. McMahon, believing like LeMay that a substantial arsenal of hydrogen bombs could all by itself give the United States decisive Cold War superiority, called for building "thousands and thousands" of them in the summer of 1951.[41] Following a second Soviet atomic test in late September, something that magnified fears in Washington of an imminent Soviet monopoly, Truman acceded to the demands of McMahon and other hard-line congressmen that the United States go even further to get the bomb as soon as possible. In February 1952 Congress allocated an astonishing $4.9 billion for construction of new manufacturing facilities and a state-of-the-art laboratory near the Berkeley campus at Livermore.[42]

By the summer of 1952 AEC officials were informing Truman that a thermonuclear device, code named for the moment "Alarm Clock," would probably be ready by the fall.[43] This posed a political dilemma, for it would appear strange for an outgoing president to authorize a thermonuclear test before the general election in early November. Truman apparently tried to get the test date moved back to late November or December, but clear days at the test site, the Eniwetok atoll in the South Pacific, were rare toward the end of the year.[44] As it happened AEC forecasters predicted clear weather on November 1—October 31, Halloween, in the United States—and, with Truman's go-ahead, early in the morning on that date AEC and military officials ignited "Mike," a sixty-ton apparatus designed to fuse a nucleus and thus create a thermonuclear reaction.

The ensuing explosion was measured at ten megatons, i.e., the equivalent of ten million tons of dynamite blowing up in a single instant.[45] The fire-power unleashed by Mike easily exceeded the aggregate blast and heat produced by every bomb America dropped in World War II, including the two atomic ones. Mike was detonated over the island of Elugelab in the Eniwetok atoll. After November 1, 1952, Elugelab was no more; it was vaporized out of existence.[46]

Though Mike was a prototype, at sixty tons hardly available for use as a weapon of war, the successful test at Eniwetok signified the beginning of the thermonuclear age. Mike showed that fusion could create an explosion that made fission bombs seem impotent in comparison; from November 1 onward the problem was simply a mechanical one of designing a lighter bomb, a task no one believed to be insurmountable. It did not require great vision to see that a war fought with bombs as powerful as the one that put an end to Elugelab could destroy nations whole and kill hundreds of millions or more in a matter of days or even hours. Nor did it require a particularly pessimistic opinion of international politics to see that in 1952 such a war might well occur. The United States and the Soviet Union were engaged in a hostile, worldwide struggle. The Truman administration had developed a military policy which dictated that the United States would wage general war, which meant nuclear war, over stakes it deemed vital to American national security. To be sure, many areas so deemed were quite unlikely to be attacked by the Soviet Union in any foreseeable future; the Cold War had become stable, with each superpower tacitly staying away from the other's vital interests and preferring to push matters to a conflict only in more peripheral places like Korea. An exception to this rule, however, was the continuing Western presence in Berlin.

Part 2

Eisenhower's Strategy to Evade
Nuclear War

3 The Rise and Fall of Massive Retaliation, January 1953–July 1955

The Republican candidate for president in 1952, Dwight D. Eisenhower, and his Secretary of State-in-waiting, John Foster Dulles, believed that unresolved situations like the one in Berlin signified the problem with Truman's basic Cold War policy. The tenuous American position in Berlin was simply one of the more grievous examples of the Truman administration's propensity to react, marionette-like, to communist aggression on every front. Not only had NSC-68 created an American bunker mentality in Europe, it had also led to the stalemated war in Korea and $50 billion defense budgets. Eisenhower and Dulles played up these issues in the fall campaign, offering an alternative foreign policy that would at the same time wage the Cold War more actively and demand less from the American taxpayer.

This foreign policy, which the Eisenhower campaign dubbed the "New Look," originated in the writings of John Foster Dulles. A powerful Wall Street lawyer and devout Presbyterian, Dulles had headed during the war the Federal Council of Churches' "Commission on Just and Durable Peace," an interdenominational Protestant organization set up to oppose more pacifistic Protestant groups. After 1945 the future Secretary of State effectively positioned himself as the leader of the internationalist wing of the Republican party. Dulles argued tirelessly in support of the vast involvement in overseas affairs that the Cold War entailed, especially in opposition to isolationist Republicans like the Ohio Senator Robert Taft. In books and articles, in front of Republican groups, and as an official American delegate at the United Nations and in Japan, he denounced isolationism as an immoral stance in a world of Hitlers and Stalins.

Yet Dulles opposed Truman's Cold War strategy. He sincerely viewed the Cold War as a struggle between a West that still retained spiritual values and a communist world proud to boast of its absolute materialism. Like the American religious philosopher Reinhold Niebuhr, he worried that in its necessary efforts to confront the Soviets the West would find its moral bearings overwhelmed by expedient power calculations; unlike Niebuhr and other pessimistic moralists, he believed that it was America's mission to spread good, not just resist evil.[1] Truman was waging a "nonmoral diplomacy," as Dulles put it during the 1952 campaign, because his policy, to contain potential communist aggression by deploying American military force against it, had robbed the United States of its initiative.[2] By concentrating on material resistance to the communist threat, the Democrats were allowing the Cold War to devolve into an old-style geopolitical power struggle in which outrage over the immorality of communist designs was being eclipsed by secular calculations of deterrence and balance-of-power. "Limited policies inevitably are defensive policies," Dulles wrote in 1950, "and defensive policies inevitably are losing policies."[3] A protracted policy of reactive containment would create a moral malaise in the West comparable to that found in France after the construction of the Maginot Line. America needed to assert its moral superiority by going on the offensive, by seeking unlimited, not limited, objectives.

What did an "unlimited" Cold War policy mean? In "A Policy of Boldness," a major article published in the May 19, 1952 issue of Life magazine, Dulles unveiled his approach to the American public. Much of the article, while surely original to most of Life's mass readership, reiterated points Dulles had been making for years. Current United States strategy, he wrote, was "far-flung," "erratic," and "militaristic," designed to stop emerging crises rather than achieve some longer-term objective. Not only was Truman's approach ultimately futile and unequal to the traditions of American morality, it also imperiled American prosperity with its "gigantic" defense expenditures.[4]

What made "A Policy of Boldness" significant was Dulles's decision to include a specific strategic alternative to Truman and Nitze's containment policy. Rather than reacting to Soviet moves around the globe, the United States should "retaliate instantly" to communist expansion by striking "back where it hurts, by means of our own choosing." How to retaliate effectively against the vast armies of the East? The West must develop a "community punishing force" willing to attack the communists with America's nuclear weapons. Dulles elaborated:

> So far these weapons are merely part of general arsenals for use in fighting general war when it has come. If that catastrophe occurs, it will be because we have allowed these new and awesome forces to become the ordinary killing tools of the soldier when, in the hands of statesmen, they could serve as effective political weapons in defense of the peace.[5]

In other words: instead of deploying nuclear weapons like most weapons of war, to be used in battle as military conditions demanded, why not threaten to use such weapons in order to avoid war in the first place? What this meant, although Dulles was unwilling to be so specific, was that the West should launch a nuclear attack "where it hurts" in the event of any significant communist aggression.

With such a retaliatory threat in place, Dulles concluded, the communists would not dare risk aggressive military action. The West could then confidently proceed with a dynamic political offensive against the immoral communist regimes without having to worry about getting bogged down in another Korea.

Eisenhower had his own Cold War strategy, which at the outset of his new administration seemed to correspond well with the Dulles plan. His strategic views stemmed from his experiences as a military commander during World War II, during which Eisenhower rose rapidly through the ranks to become Supreme Commander of the European theater and the Allied expeditionary forces. By 1944, put in charge of a multinational command bureaucracy that conducted the largest military operation of all time, with the aim of defeating Nazi Germany, conquering Western Europe, and transforming the balance of global power, Eisenhower had a chance to become familiar with the problem of weighing political interests against military planning.[6] Commanding an all-out military campaign to defeat Hitler unconditionally, moreover, he also had the opportunity to think about the morality of attacking German civilians. Eisenhower confronted both of these matters directly. On one hand, he deftly managed the gigantic ambitions of subordinates like General George Patton and Field Marshal Bernard Montgomery, while at the same time fending off the political maneuverings of

Winston Churchill and Franklin Roosevelt, in order to achieve without deviation his objective of taking France, defeating Hitler's armies, and winning the war in Europe.[7] On the other hand, to ensure and hasten the Nazi surrender, he also approved the strategic bombing of crowded French and German cities and hence the incineration of tens of thousands of noncombatants.

World War II confirmed for Eisenhower a lesson from the Prussian military philosopher Karl von Clausewitz's book *On War*—a work that a superior officer, General Fox Conner, had ordered him to read three times in the 1920s.[8] Clausewitz issued the famous warning in *On War* that mass military operations become increasingly difficult for political authorities to control: in spite of all reason and planning modern war escalates toward absolute violence, as even well-meaning, politically sophisticated military commanders cannot help but use their most powerful weapons rather than risk defeat.[9]

Yet Eisenhower was less concerned in 1952 than he had been in 1944 with the military side of American policy. At that moment of vast American military superiority and economic prosperity Eisenhower believed that a greater threat to United States national interest lay in excessive government spending than in potential military defeat. He repeatedly warned that the logic of NSC-68—that national security was an absolute objective to which unlimited resources should be allotted—threatened to undermine the end of national interest in the name of military security. Of course he wanted to maintain basic American Cold War military deployments, but he wanted to do so at a lower cost, and he wanted also to wean the American public away from the Keynesian (and "Nitzean") notion that the government could spend whatever it wanted to.[10]

This was why Eisenhower initially went along with Dulles's concept of massive retaliation. He preferred it over other prospectively inexpensive strategies because Dulles's apparent rejection of the idea of limited war with the Soviet Union was in accord with his Clausewitzean conviction that any war with the Soviet Union would eventually become total.[11]

The Short-Lived Policy of Massive Retaliation

Eisenhower handily beat the Democratic candidate, Adlai Stevenson, in the November election. Upon taking office in January 1953, he organized a foreign policy planning exercise, which came to be called "Operation Solarium." Eisenhower directed three task forces to draft competing approaches to national security policy.[12] Group "A," which Eisenhower appointed George Kennan to head, was charged with presenting the case for traditional containment, along the lines of the Truman administration's policy. Group "B," headed by Air Force Major General James McCormick, formulated a strategy based primarily upon nuclear weapons: communist advancement beyond a given perimeter would trigger an immediate American nuclear attack upon the Soviet Union. Group "C," headed by the Navy's Vice Admiral Richard Conolly, developed a more intricate and activist strategy designed to roll back communist bastions by employing a variety of means, including nuclear and conventional warfare, covert action, and propaganda.[13]

The National Security Council studied the alternatives provided by Solarium in the fall of 1953, and under Eisenhower's direction, blended them into the new administration's first basic security policy, NSC-162/2. A sampling from each of the three Solarium alternatives, NSC-162/2 in the end looked a lot like Dulles's "Policy of Boldness."[14] From Group C came Eisenhower's third-world policy: while the United States would not "roll back" established communist states in Europe, it would adopt active and various military initiatives against lesser adversaries. From Group A, which is to say from Kennan, NSC-162/2 took the general ideology of containment, the conviction that the Soviet Union was a moribund experiment which, if it were effectively contained, would eventually collapse. From Group B came the most obvious feature of the New Look, the emphasis on nuclear forces and the corresponding downplaying of conventional deterrence.

The nuclear strategy which emerged from Group B and found its final form in NSC-162/2 was the product of intensive debate in two NSC meetings in July and August.[15] Dulles, Secretary of Defense Charles Wilson, and Chairman of the Joint Chiefs of Staff Admiral Arthur Radford called for a liberal interpretation of Group B's recommendations, advocating the maintenance of significant conventional forces and a broader array of nuclear weaponry. Secretary of the Treasury George Humphrey and Director of the Budget Joseph Dodge—whose very presence at high-level security meetings illustrated Eisenhower's preoccupation with economy—supported a basic nuclear retaliatory force. Eisenhower sided with Humphrey and Dodge, and their position therefore prevailed. Dulles did not make this an issue during the early meetings, but that would change.

The resulting American nuclear force posture from 1953 to 1955 consisted of three main components: a small deployment of tactical nuclear weapons in Europe; a modest Civil Defense Program; and the centerpiece of the New Look, an integrated bomber force, still under the direction of LeMay's Strategic Air Command, which would carry out massive nuclear retaliation against an enemy nation that was preparing for or initiating war against the United States or its close allies.[16] By the end of 1953 the United States had adopted a policy, and was in the process of deploying military forces designed to fulfill that policy, which stipulated that any major Cold War confrontation would probably bring nuclear war.

Amid this policymaking process the Russians, again, raised the stakes of American nuclear strategy earlier than anticipated. In August 1953, four years after its atomic test, the Soviet Union successfully exploded a device that produced radioactivity comparable to a small thermonuclear blast. It appears now that the 300-kiloton explosion was that of a boosted fission bomb, but Eisenhower administration officials chose to be less skeptical about the Soviet achievement than Truman had been four years earlier. As far as Eisenhower and Dulles were concerned, the test showed that the Soviets had acquired the superbomb, or at least were about to. United States security policy now had to account for *an imminent* Soviet thermonuclear capability.

The news had an immediate effect upon American security policy. In early September, even as the NSC was developing NSC-162/2, Dulles composed a general memorandum which began, "Our collective security policies require urgent reconsideration." NATO strategy, he stated, had been based on the assumption that the American nuclear arsenal would deter the Soviets from invading Europe, but "that assumption is now shaken." The Europeans would recognize that the United States, soon to be vulnerable to a Soviet nuclear attack, might stay out of a European war. That, Dulles warned, could give rise to neutralism. He offered a potential solution to this problem: the United States should make a "spectacular effort to relax world tensions" while the Soviet arsenal was still small. Perhaps the United Nations could even establish international control of atomic weapons.[17]

"If we are to attempt real revision in policies," Eisenhower replied on September 8, ". . . we must begin now to educate our people in the fundamentals of these problems." The "problems" he was referring to were the military dilemmas created by the "capabilities now and in the near future of the H-Bomb, supplemented by the A-Bomb."

Eisenhower got to the point: if the Soviet leaders, "aware of the great destruction of these weapons," would not make "any honest effort" toward such a plan for international control, then they "must be fairly assumed to be contemplating their aggressive use." To meet this threat the United States would have to maintain a constant state of full mobilization, and if this showdown were

> to continue indefinitely, the cost would either drive us to war—or to some form of dictatorial government. In such circumstances, we would be forced to consider whether or not our duty to future generations did not require us to *initiate* war at the most propitious moment that we could designate.[18]

Thus in early September 1953, the messianic brinksman John Foster Dulles was recommending a "spectacular" détente with the Soviet Union, while the golfing Eisenhower was suggesting a nuclear attack against an adversary whose crime would have been to decline to turn over its weapons to the United Nations. But this first exchange provided a misleading, if not entirely inaccurate, picture of their emerging positions. The moralist Dulles, seeing little hope for a future just war against communism, offered, for the sake of argument, the drastic but logical alternative of "spectacular" arms control. The pessimist Eisenhower, seeing no hope for a future winnable war, replied with the extreme, but logical solution of preventive war.[19]

A month later the NSC met to discuss NSC-162/2, and after an arduous debate on military spending the discussion turned to the coming Soviet nuclear arsenal. Talk of preventive war was in the air, but Eisenhower expressed his aversion to using the "special weapons." Secretary of Defense Wilson demanded to know: "Do we intend to use weapons on which we are spending such great sums, or do we not?" Eisenhower replied that of course he would use them if "the interests of U.S. security" so dictated, but the military should not "plan to make use of these weapons in minor affairs." Dulles then "repeated his often-expressed view that somehow or other we must manage to remove the taboo from the use of these weapons." Eisenhower noted that using "these weapons" might make it appear that the "U.S. were initiating global war," and with this the discussion came to an end.[20]

The respective positions of Dulles and Eisenhower in their correspondence in early September and in the above meeting were less inconsistent than they might appear. Dulles took the "special weapons" more in stride: they could be dealt with by establishing a regime of international control or, more realistically, by removing the taboo from atomic weaponry and deciding to use the bombs as one would conventional forces. Eisenhower countered that the problem could be solved right away by launching an unprovoked attack on the Soviet Union, or, more realistically, by accepting the fact that the United States would have to avoid conflict that might lead to global war. At a private dinner with the recently re-elected British Prime Minister, Winston Churchill, his foreign Secretary Anthony Eden, and Dulles, Eisenhower promoted the idea of preemptive war one final time, suggesting that the United States could promote peace by destroying Soviet thermonuclear production.[21] On January 12, 1954 Dulles publicized his view in a speech given to the Council on Foreign Relations. The Secretary of State summarized the strategy in a single sentence: "The way to deter aggression is for the free community to be willing and able to respond vigorously at places and with means of its own choosing."[22] One of these "means," Dulles emphasized, was "the deterrent of massive retaliatory power." This expression gained widespread attention, and contemporary observers of American policy began to talk about the new official strategy of "massive retaliation."[23]

In office for only a year, Eisenhower and Dulles by early 1954 had developed a new American nuclear policy. Each of them had endorsed the unilateral, offensive use of nuclear weaponry in their private security planning, while Dulles had made the unilateral defensive use of such weaponry the public basis of American foreign policy. These strategic expressions had two effects. First, and more immediately, they served as a conspicuous signal to weaker nations whom the United States wanted to intimidate that the new American administration was not so squeamish about using atomic weapons to achieve military objectives. Putting nuclear weaponry at the center of American security policy made it easy for Eisenhower and Dulles to wage "atomic diplomacy" against North Korea and China in 1953, the North Vietnamese in 1954, and China again in 1955, in each case securing political arrangements more favorable to the United States than the military situation on the ground warranted.[24]

Second, and for the longer run, by clearly making the threat of nuclear war the basis of American Cold War policy, Eisenhower and Dulles forced themselves to consider thermonuclear war. By skirting the question of how the United States would wage all-out war, and by emphasizing conventional and atomic forms of deterrence, NSC-68 had allowed Truman and his advisers to avoid thinking about this difficult problem. This was not possible for Eisenhower or Dulles—the price of the New Look was having explicitly to face the prospect of a thermonuclear World War III. And it became obvious during secret policy debates in 1954 and 1955 that this prospect meant something very different to the president than it did to his Secretary of State.

Early Dissent

In March 1954 the NSC met to revise an old Truman policy statement, NSC-20/4, "U.S. Objectives Vis-à-Vis the USSR in the Event of War." Eisenhower at this meeting put forth some opinions about what a war with a fully-armed Soviet Union would be like. First, he said, such a war would create chaotic conditions impossible to plan for or even foresee. Second, the *only* objective of the United States would be to destroy the Soviet Union as completely as possible. His third point was a final repudiation of his earlier support for preventive war: the United States would never launch its thermonuclear arsenal "except in retaliation against a heavy attack." Fourth, in the aftermath of a general nuclear war the United States would have to become a dictatorship. Eisenhower scoffed at Radford and Cutler for even attempting to develop a list of war objectives and scenarios.[25]

Paying heed to Eisenhower's four arguments, on August 7 the NSC issued a new Basic National Security Policy (BNSP), NSC 5422/2.[26] The Soviet Union, the new document said, would likely attain a substantial nuclear weapon capability during the period 1956-59. Once it did a total war between the two superpowers "would bring about such extensive destruction as to threaten the survival of Western Civilization and the Soviet regime." Nevertheless, because limited war was not feasible the United States would wage a war against the Soviet Union "with all available weapons." NSC 5422/2 also included a skeptical paragraph on disarmament, suggesting that there was "serious question" whether any arms control regime could be developed in the near future.[27]

NSC-5422/2 was a rejection of Dulles's position. The Secretary of State had made clear his desire to remove the stigma from nuclear weapons, his support for limited nuclear wars against local communist aggression, and, for good measure, his idealistic notion that disarmament might provide an escape from the coming dilemma. Each of these wishes was explicitly ruled out in NSC-5422/2. But dealing with this rebuff was the sort of challenge at which Dulles excelled. Not a personable figure, he had risen to the top of the Republican Party's foreign policy hierarchy by sheer force of contention. In addition, he knew that there were others on the NSC who opposed Eisenhower's categorical views of nuclear war. Recognizing the breach between himself and the president, Dulles set out to provide an alternative strategy to NSC-5422/2.

In November, as the first Quemoy-Matsu crisis unfolded, Dulles proposed that the NSC consider "clarification and changes in emphasis" to the new policy. Regarding general war, he argued, the United States had to be prepared to meet hostilities "in a manner and on a scale which will not inevitably broaden them into total nuclear war." In particular, he continued, the nation needed to remember that it was "morally committed" either to use nuclear weapons in a European war or supply them to NATO allies; the West "should explore urgently" the possibility of developing a strategy flexible enough to avoid turning any war in Europe into an all-out nuclear war.[28]

Having watched Dulles jump safely into the water, other opponents of NSC-5422/2 began to send in their own criticisms of the president's strategy. The Secretary of State's brother Allen[29], who was the director of the CIA, warned in an NSC paper that unless there were "improvement in defensive measures presently contemplated," the Europeans "will show increasing reluctance to engage in diplomatic or military action which seems to involve a risk of war." Director of Defense Mobilization Arthur Flemming demanded that the United States never "adopt a defeatist or fatalistic attitude" about war once the Soviets attained their arsenal. The Joint Chiefs, with concurrence from Secretary Wilson, warned that if the United States were afraid to engage in "timely and dynamic action" it would soon become isolated from its allies and eventually face the choice between appeasement and general war.[30]

Eisenhower and his critics met for a volatile NSC meeting on November 24. Dulles, Wilson, and Flemming reiterated their fear that the coming Soviet arsenal threatened American security and alliances. Eisenhower demanded that "the critics of our current policy" be more specific. Admiral Radford stated that "soon the U.S. could no longer count on the Russians being afraid of starting general war. . . . some time or other the Soviet Union will elect to force the issue."[31]

Eisenhower, "speaking with considerable forcefulness," insisted that he was unable to see any "fundamental difference . . . among the departments, despite whatever the words spelled out."[32] But Dulles and his colleagues were determined to get rid of NSC-5422/2. After considerable argument Wilson recommended that a "high-level interdepartmental group" meet to work on a "revised basic national security policy." Relenting, Eisenhower said that he would "consider this recommendation . . . " Minutes of the meeting noted that the NSC would direct its Planning Board "to prepare for early Council consideration a restatement of basic national security policy in the light of the above-mentioned suggestions and discussions."[33]

The reasons why Eisenhower capitulated on this issue are unclear. It is possible that he felt that he could not govern effectively while holding a distinctly minority view in the NSC; certainly he did not want to wage a more conspicuous conflict with his Secretary of State. Another possibility is that it was late 1954: the Soviet Union would not be attaining "atomic plenty" for another few years, and policies could always be changed before then.[34]

On December 14 the Planning Board produced NSC 5440, which was "intended to supersede NSC 162/2 and NSC 5422/2." The new document omitted talk of waging any war "with all available weapons" and recommended instead the deployment of

> military forces with sufficient strength, flexibility and mobility to enable them to deal swiftly and severely with Communist overt aggression in its various forms and to cope successfully with general war should it develop.

NSC-5440 continued,

> The ability to apply force selectively and flexibly will become increasingly important in maintaining the morale and will of the free world to resist aggression. As the fear of nuclear war grows, the United States and its allies must never allow themselves to get into the position where they must choose between (a) not responding to local aggression and (b) applying force in a way which our own people or our allies would consider entails undue risk of nuclear devastation. However, the United States cannot afford to preclude itself from using nuclear weapons even in a local situation, if such use . . . will best advance U.S. security interests. In the last analysis, if confronted by the choice of (a) acquiescing in Communist aggression or (b) taking measures risking either general war or loss of allied support, the United States must be prepared to take these risks if necessary for its security.[35]

NSC 5440 was a fundamental revision of the earlier BNSP. Its authors (a) renounced massive retaliation, (b) precisely articulated the strategy of "flexible response" as it would become known seven years later, and (c) predicted, in the last sentence, exactly the dilemma which the Eisenhower administration would face in Berlin four years hence.

Over the ensuing year Eisenhower deferred to his Secretary of State, allowing the "clarifications" in NSC-5440 to go unchallenged. Debate over the 1955 BNSP, NSC-5501, was relatively mild and short-lived: in a meeting on the subject in January Eisenhower raised no objections to the retaining of NSC-5540's emphasis on flexibility.[36] In March the world witnessed perhaps the most conspicuous demonstration of atomic diplomacy used during the Cold War, as the president cooperated with Dulles in threatening the Chinese with nuclear war unless they backed off Quemoy and Matsu. On March 8, 1955 Dulles referred in a radio address to "new and powerful weapons of precision which can utterly destroy military targets without endangering unrelated civilian centers"; on the 16th Eisenhower declared, in response to a reporter's question, that in a combat situation the United States would use tactical nuclear weapons "just exactly as you would use a bullet or anything else."[37] The Chinese then ended their efforts to take the two islands.[38]

In 1954 and 1955 Dulles promoted to the NSC a nuclear strategy that he knew conflicted substantially with Eisenhower's views (just as it conflicted with popular perceptions that official American security policy during the Eisenhower administration was based upon massive retaliation). By vigorously pushing his ideas forward, Dulles had been able to make the basic National Security policies of those two years reflect his, not his president's, vision of war with the Soviet Union. Had there been a major crisis during this period, Eisenhower might well have ignored the Dulles strategy and acted as he saw fit. But that possibility did not make Dulles's dissent unimportant. Forced by their New Look to reckon with the prospect of thermonuclear war, the debate between Eisenhower and Dulles really was more about the future orientation of American basic security policy—about how the United States should regard general war once the Soviet Union acquired a serious arsenal—than about devising working contingency plans for an immediate crisis. By taking on the president in 1954 Dulles made it known that he opposed the all-or-nothing approach found in NSC-5422/2, and would presumably continue to oppose it as Soviet thermonuclear capability neared. Dulles, in other words, was communicating to Eisenhower, via the medium of national security planning, the message that he did not share his president's understanding of general war in the thermonuclear age. That was something Eisenhower could not dismiss.

4   Eisenhower Takes Over, July 1955–April 1957

Amid little fanfare and with no debate, Eisenhower ordered the Pentagon in the summer of 1955 to make the production of intercontinental ballistic missiles (ICBMs) an objective of the "highest national priority." The president's reasoning, like Truman's reasoning in deciding to stay in Berlin and to build the superbomb, was simple. Eisenhower had received two reports early that year indicating that the Soviet Union was likely to acquire, in the relatively near future, hundreds of megaton thermonuclear warheads and the ballistic missiles on which to deliver them to American targets. A report by the Technological Capabilities Panel (commonly known as the Killian committee), entitled "Meeting the Threat of Surprise Attack," warned of a Soviet "multimegaton capability" by as early as 1958; this was confirmed by a National Intelligence Estimate presented to the president in June.[1] Once the Russians perfected this technology they would be able to deliver a thermonuclear warhead to American cities in about thirty minutes, as opposed to the twelve hours or so needed by a manned bomber. Without the threat of American retaliation in kind the Soviets could, conceivably, launch an attack out of the blue, crippling the nation utterly and making American defeat surely inevitable. More plausibly, the mere possibility of such an attack could encourage the Soviets to go on a Cold War offensive that the West would be too terrified to obstruct. "We had simply got to achieve such missiles as promptly as possible," Eisenhower argued, "if only because of the enormous psychological and political significance of ballistic missiles."[2]

Eisenhower's decision to move quickly on ICBM production carried with it none of the drama of the Berlin and H-Bomb decisions that preceded it. An order to accelerate the development of delivery systems was not as dramatic as flying food to the people of West Berlin or going ahead with a program to develop thermonuclear fusion. But from the perspective of the history of military technology the creation of ICBMs was perhaps an even greater step. The prospect of fighting a thermonuclear war with manned bombers was gruesome, even insane, but it was, for the moment at least, *military*: pilots could panic, defect, or be ordered to turn around; American skill in evading Soviet air defense and in shooting down Russian planes could maybe make a real difference in the outcome of the war. But with the advent of ICBMs this last bit of human volition in modern war disappeared. There is no way to stop thousands of missiles from annihilating your nation absolutely. World War III, if both sides fought it in the total manner of World War II, would be an event of immediate and unstoppable holocaust, not a military phenomenon at all.

Yet this grim view of a thermonuclear war waged with intercontinental missiles did not stop the president from pushing his defense bureaucracy hard to get them built quickly. In the short run, getting missiles before the Soviets, or at least at roughly the same time, would prevent the Russians from exercising the blackmail envisioned in the worst-case analyses of the Killian report. Once in place, moreover, ICBMs would over the long haul surely deter the Soviet Union from embarking upon any aggression that could foreseeably trigger an American response. Indeed, thermonuclear missiles could create a stable Cold War deterrence, as rational nations would avoid risking general war.

Perhaps this was so, but Eisenhower was too pessimistic about the ability of statesmen to act rationally, and too unwilling to evade difficult questions, to see in the advent of ICBMs a panacea of deterrence. Yes, large thermonuclear arsenals would deter statesmen from courting World War III. But the Cold War was volatile: deterrence could fail. To avoid planning for that possibility, on the grounds that rational actors of course would never initiate a thermonuclear war, was simple abrogation. As the ultimate author of American basic national security policy, it was still his responsibility to decide under what circumstances the United States would wage war against the Soviet Union.

In response to the Soviet Union's approaching attainment of an ICBM arsenal, Eisenhower altered American military policy in three ways. First, he sought to deploy a sufficient number of long-range nuclear weapons and a

good warning system so that the United States could promise a massive nuclear retaliation in response to a Soviet attack. This would deter the Soviets
from launching such an attack in the first place, and would also prevent the
Russians from enjoying the psychological advantage that a first-strike nuclear
capability could provide. This effort at attaining a nuclear force capable of
deterring a Soviet ICBM attack began in earnest in 1955, and intensified after
the Sputnik launch in 1957. Second, Eisenhower restructured America's
conventional force posture, giving the U.S. Army primary responsibility for
dealing with smaller wars away from major regions of Cold War conflict. The
advent of mutual nuclear deterrence might encourage the Soviets to promote
local communist advancement in areas of the world which the United States
was not willing to defend with general war. Eisenhower therefore wanted
forces able to deal with the "brushfire" wars that might ensue.

Third, Eisenhower moved between 1955 and 1957 to remove limited,
non-nuclear military planning from American general war policy, so as to
ensure that any war directly between the United States and the Soviet Union
would escalate automatically into an all-out thermonuclear war. While his
reasons for making the two changes listed above are generally agreed upon,
the president's motivation in taking this third step remains unclear and dis-
puted.[3] What follows is an account of the rancorous struggle between Eisenhower and his major advisers over his efforts to banish the idea of limited
war with the Russians from American military policy, and a new interpretation of his odd decision.

The Rhetorical Offensive

On September 24, not long after the NSC formally rendered his order
for a rapid buildup of ICBMs, Eisenhower suffered a heart attack. During
his four-month period of convalescence, the president for the most part did
not participate in decisionmaking.[4]

At the beginning of 1956, Eisenhower returned to full-time duty, and on
January 12 attended his first NSC meeting since his heart attack. Among
the items on the agenda was the question of government stockpiling during
a general war, and the president took the opportunity to express some things
he may have been dwelling on privately in his sickbed. He first said that
stockpiling made sense even in the nuclear age, that "in any future war, the
U.S. would have to pick itself up from the floor and try to win through to a
successful end." Pleased to see that during his convalescence Eisenhower

had gotten rid of his earlier skepticism about winning a nuclear war, Secretary of Defense Charles E. Wilson naturally concurred, but it turned out the president had spoken tongue-in-cheek. He turned to Wilson and said, with "some warmth," that "the only thing we could really know about the nature of a future war was that it would be completely different from any wars fought in the past." Moving on to a projected study on the human effects of nuclear weapons, Eisenhower went further. These weapons, he stated, were pushing us "past the point of human endurance." He did not want "a lot of long-haired professors" to examine that problem, but "we must pause and think where we are going in the field of these weapons." Of one thing Eisenhower "was dead sure. No one was going to be the winner in such a nuclear war. The destruction might be such that we might have ultimately to go back to bows and arrows."[5]

At the next NSC meeting a week later Eisenhower continued with this theme. The council was meeting primarily to discuss a top-secret report by the retired Air Force General Harold L. George, which predicted that a war on the hypothetical date of July 1, 1956 would destroy the American economy and undermine American cultural institutions. The president expressed his "astonishment at our inability to defend ourselves better from aerial attack after a strategic warning" and later that day entered in his diary his fear that after such a calamity "it would literally be a business of digging ourselves out of ashes, starting again."[6] At another NSC meeting on February 7 Eisenhower persisted with this argument, urging his colleagues several times to remember the "transcendent consideration—namely, that nobody can win a thermonuclear war."[7]

By this time the NSC was facing the annual task of rewriting basic national security policy for 1956. The president's recent commentary suggested that his views on war with the Soviets were not in accord with current policy, yet in a preliminary memorandum attached to the 1956 version, the NSC Planning Board noted that the new BNSP would continue to emphasize "flexible capabilities to deter or defeat local aggression . . . to avoid the broadening of hostilities into general war."[8] The president and those who would maintain existing policy were on a sort of collision course, and it happened on February 27, in perhaps the richest NSC meeting on nuclear strategy during the entire Eisenhower era. On that day the NSC went over the Dulles version line by line, and Eisenhower made his opposition to it plain for everyone to see.

The participants in the meeting immediately turned to the question of nuclear strategy. The Chairman of the Joint Chiefs, Admiral Arthur M. Radford, argued strongly that nuclear weapons must be accorded conventional status. Eisenhower answered that world opinion would be repelled by the American use of such weapons in small wars. Dulles insisted that "in operations short of general war," the Planning Board language of February 13 should be retained.[9] Eisenhower's reply here perfectly demonstrated his disbelief in limited war. He

> asked that the Council imagine the position of a military commander in the field. His radar informs him that a flock of enemy bombers is on the point of attacking him. What does the military commander do in such a contingency? Does he not use every weapon at hand to defend himself and his forces?[10]

It was all well and good to speak of limited war in the abstract, Eisenhower was saying. But in a war between great powers, like World War II, no one was going to accept defeat when there were powerful weapons still at hand.

Dulles responded to Eisenhower's scenario literally, noting that it was not relevant to actual policy since the president was supposed to authorize any use of nuclear weapons anyway. Either relinquish that power, the lawyer Dulles was saying, or admit that what the "local commander" wants to do is not important. It was time to stop engaging in thought-experiments and get administration policy clear. What, he asked, should the United States do if, for example, "the Soviets impose a new blockade on Berlin?"[11]

Eisenhower was caught off guard by Dulles's response. He was trying to talk about the central problem of military instinct during the heat of war, and here was Dulles raising prosaic objections. Eisenhower asked the council to "suspend action" on the issue of revising NSC-5602's two paragraphs dealing with nuclear strategy. Dulles urged that the council instead adopt the Planning Board language, but Eisenhower insisted upon waiting.[12]

The NSC turned next to the problem of "local Communist aggression," and Eisenhower wasted no time in restating his case. The Korean War had shown that

> in the future these peripheral wars must not be permitted to drag out. We must now plan to fight peripheral wars on the same basis as we would fight a general war. After all, *there was no good reason* for drawing distinctions between peripheral and general wars.[13]

The Secretary of State thought that there was good reason indeed to distinguish between peripheral and general wars. What would the United States do, the prescient Dulles asked, "if the Vietminh undertook to attack South Vietnam? Would we proceed to drop atomic bombs on Peking?"[14]

Dulles, discerning the new direction that Eisenhower was taking, had seized upon its weakness. An all-or-nothing nuclear strategy left the United States with no options in a major crisis other than backing down or unleashing general thermonuclear war. Not only was this dangerous from a military perspective, but it also threatened to neutralize America's key allies. Could the French, Dutch, or West Berliners really be expected to believe that the Americans would come to their rescue by initiating a war that would automatically annihilate the United States? The Secretary of State thought this a fatal defect of Eisenhower's apparent strategy, pardonable perhaps in the days of bombers and Soviet inferiority but not so on the eve of the missile age.

Despite his clear and fundamental disagreement with it, Eisenhower decided, in an NSC session to sign on to the final BNSP for 1956, to leave Dulles's flexible strategy intact.[15] NSC-5602/1 stipulated, like its predecessors, that the United States must maintain a "flexible and selective nuclear capability," so as to avoid both "not responding to local aggression" and "applying force in a way which our own people or our allies would consider entails undue risks of nuclear devastation."[16] This language was in direct, plain contradiction to Eisenhower's recent statements.

There were several reasons for Eisenhower to leave the BNSP the way it was. He may have believed that what he said superseded written policy, and that it was therefore not worth the trouble to argue over words, especially as an election was coming up and it would be best to avoid disagreement among his main security advisers. He knew as well that sometime later that year NATO would be meeting to revise its military policy in the light of the Soviet Union's emerging thermonuclear capabilities. Then he would probably have to show his hand, and there would be no advantage in writing a policy now, having it leak out, and alienating his European allies. Moreover, he knew that a definitive policy decision was not yet necessary. Intelligence continued to predict that the Soviets would be without massive retaliatory capabilities until 1958 at the earliest; hence basic policy still remained an exercise, a procedure that would not constrain future action. The documentary evidence does not indicate which, if any, of these reasons really persuaded Eisenhower to leave basic policy alone. What can be said is that in

1957, when none of these considerations remained, he quickly replaced the existing policy with his own.

Dissent from the Pentagon and State Department

Eisenhower's main security advisers recognized what the president was doing, and for the rest of 1956 and early 1957 they took steps to oppose him. Dulles, as mentioned above, was especially worried about the effect an all-or-nothing nuclear policy would have on America's European allies. The Joint Chiefs disliked greatly having no guidance as to when they could use nuclear weapons other than in an all-out retaliation. Though the Suez Crisis, the Soviet invasion of Hungary, the showdown in Little Rock over school desegregation, and the election campaign diverted White House attention from nuclear policy during the summer and fall of 1956, Dulles and the Chiefs made their resistance evident enough to convince Eisenhower that he would have to impose his views more forcefully.

The Joint Chiefs' attitude toward the president in 1956 and thereafter can best be described as *suspicious*. Charged with planning for war, the chiefs wondered with increasing exasperation why Eisenhower refused to say under exactly what circumstances he would authorize the use of thermonuclear weapons. They raised the issue repeatedly.

On March 30 Eisenhower met with the four joint chiefs alone. Radford, speaking for all four, wanted to raise "basic questions on which clarification is needed." The first, Radford continued, was "whether we will use atomic weapons in war."[17] After lecturing the chiefs for awhile on the tragedy of interservice rivalry, Eisenhower got to the point. The Chiefs need not worry about any hesitancy on his part when it came to nuclear weapons—he was clear in his own mind "that in any war with the Soviets we would use them."[18] Of course, this begged the question: when, under what contingencies, would Eisenhower actually approve of their use? NSC policy stipulated clearly that the president would have final say on all decisions to use nuclear weapons. But the Chiefs had to make rough war plans. Would Eisenhower be willing to wage nuclear war flexibly? In a May 10 meeting Radford "pleaded" for a decision on this question, complaining that the NSC "could not continue to straddle it." The Chairman stated his case plainly:

The problem is not what we do in global war, but whether we can use nuclear weapons in military situations short of global war. We must

60   EISENHOWER'S STRATEGY

be clear whether or not our armed forces can use nuclear weapons in
this latter type of situation.[19]

Eisenhower responded to the Chiefs' demands over the following weeks;
during May of 1956 the president met with the Joint Chiefs more frequently
than in any other month of his presidency. In a May 14 meeting with Radford alone Eisenhower suggested that "we would not get involved in a 'small
war' extending beyond a few Marine battalions or Army units. If it grew to
anything like Korea proportions, the action would become one for use of
atomic weapons."[20] On the 24th, Eisenhower met with Radford and Army
Chief of Staff Maxwell Taylor, who argued that the inevitable advent of
thermonuclear arsenals would "deter both sides from a big war," thus com-
pelling the United States to retrain its focus on fighting smaller wars. Taylor
also suggested that talk of using atomic weapons in every kind of war "con-
travened" current NSC policy, which stipulated "flexibility" in small war
situations.
    Eisenhower's response to Taylor's queries deserves lengthy quotation.
"The president [wrote his staff secretary, Colonel Andrew J. Goodpaster],"

    said he thought General Taylor's position was dependent on an as-
    sumption that we are opposed by people who would think as we do
    with regard to the value of human life. But they do not, as shown in
    many incidents from the last war. We have no basis for thinking that
    they abhor destruction as we do. In the event they should decide to
    go to war, the pressure on them to use atomic weapons in a sudden
    blow would be extremely great. He did not see any basis for thinking
    other than that they would use these weapons at once, and in full
    force. The President went on to say that he did not care too much for
    the definition of general war as given. To him the question was simply
    one of a war between the United States and the USSR, and in this he
    felt the thinking should be based on the use of atomic weapons—that
    in his opinion it was fatuous to think that the U.S. and the USSR
    would be locked into a life and death struggle without using such
    weapons. We should therefore develop our readiness on the basis of
    use of atomic weapons by both sides.[21]

Here is a summary of Eisenhower's view of modern war. Clausewitz held
that war tends toward total war—that military commanders will always use

"every weapon at hand" rather than go down to defeat. Any tempering of this tendency by moral, religious, or chivalric limitations on violence—well, the two World Wars had ushered that right out. If the two superpowers went to war there was no reason to believe—indeed, it was *fatuous* to believe—that the tyrants in the Kremlin would moderate their attack in any way. What point was there, then, in developing limited strategies to initiate war against the Soviet Union by attacking this supply line or that tank division, when the first thing the Russians would do is propel every weapon they had toward American cities? World War III would be a spasmodic, all-out ther-monuclear war; planning for other scenarios was purposeless.[22]

Eisenhower took a similar line in his 1956 dealings with Dulles, who was also proving resistant to the president's new thinking. Their debate mani-fested itself—when the two were not otherwise occupied with the Suez Cri-sis—over the question of NATO policy. Dulles did not want to offer to his European colleagues an American strategy that would turn any war on that continent into an all-out thermonuclear war. Since Eisenhower had not officially changed the basic policy, Dulles guessed that it would be possible to propose an American position to the Europeans that did not conform to the president's wishes.

The British Prime Minister Anthony Eden wrote to Eisenhower on July 18, wondering what effect the "Radford Plan" to reduce U.S. troops in Eu-rope would have upon NATO allies edgy about being defended by ther-monuclear weaponry. Eisenhower responded nine days later by assuring Eden that the Radford plan was rumor only, and that the American position on NATO military policy would be forthcoming. "[W]e hope to be ready about the middle of August to give you our views," Eisenhower predicted.[23]

The Suez Crisis, igniting as Eisenhower penned his reply, delayed the NATO conference, and this gave Dulles an opportunity to try to persuade Eisenhower to change his mind. On October 1 he presented the president with a formal memorandum on the "United States Position of Review of NATO strategy and Force Levels." In this memorandum Dulles openly de-scribed his flexible strategy as official U.S. policy, as if Eisenhower's repeated rejections of it over the past several months had not occurred. "Our presen-tation to the Council and to the British would be based on the following," Dulles wrote:

1. The NATO military mission now includes the defense of the NATO area against all types of aggression, including any local attack.

. . . The maintenance of an effective shield for these purposes must include sufficient conventional ground forces to avoid inflexibility.

2. Accordingly, we find unacceptable any proposal which implies the adoption of a NATO strategy of total reliance on nuclear retaliation.[24]

Eisenhower couldn't have made his rejection of this, at a White House conference the next day, more plain. The United States would not remove divisions from Europe, he conceded: that would have an "unacceptably damaging" effect upon the West German president Konrad Adenauer. But from now on "we will proceed with plans and preparations on the basis that, if the Soviets attack, atomic weapons will be used."[25] Dulles had his orders for the NATO meeting, postponed by Suez but now scheduled for December.

Despite this directive, Dulles tried to dilute Eisenhower's position during the Paris meetings. The Secretary of State warned in an informal preliminary speech that the NATO allies "dare not put our eggs in one basket. There must be diversity of capability and must be flexibility." Nor, Dulles argued in the first formal session, "could the US accept the idea that there was no need for substantial manpower because any attack would set off massive retaliation and in that provide a sufficient deterrent."[26] Later in the conference he continued to fudge the issue, declaring at the last ministerial meeting that "NATO should not rely wholly on atomic weapons, though [it is] proper to say we have primary reliance upon them. Conventional forces are necessary, and [the] burden of supplying conventional forces should increasingly be assumed by Europeans."[27] Caught between his own convictions and his direct orders, Dulles equivocated.

NSC-5707/8

Eisenhower did not have an easy time of it in 1956. In addition to the fervent dissent of his Secretary of State and the Joint Chiefs, he had to face increasingly numerous and gruesome reports on what a general war would entail. Back in November several members of the Federal Civil Defense Administration presented a "Human Effects of Nuclear Weapons Development" study that Eisenhower had commissioned after the George report.[28] It concluded that an all-out war with the Soviet Union would leave fifty million Americans dead or injured and endanger basic American social institutions. A month later, after Eisenhower's return from his annual vacation at Augusta, the NSC met to consider a report submitted by General Gerald C. Thomas of the Net Evaluation Committee, a war-planning arm of the NSC. Thomas said that by 1959 an all-out Soviet nuclear attack upon an alert United States would, after the American retaliation, result in the effective destruction of both nations. Such a war, Thomas estimated, would leave forty percent of the United States' population dead and another thirteen percent injured. If the Soviets managed to launch such an attack upon an insufficiently alert America, the Soviet Union would "emerge as the dominant world power in 24 hours."[29]

If Dulles's and the Joint Chiefs' objections were not sufficient, then here was strong persuasion that Eisenhower moderate his new policy. Yet the president's reaction to these chilling scenarios was not to concede the necessity of limited-war strategies or to advocate a new program of civil defense. Instead, the president wondered, after hearing Thomas's presentation,

> why we should put a single nickel into anything but developing our capacity to diminish the enemy's capacity for nuclear attack. Rather than worry too much about the submarine menace, protecting shipping on the seas, etc., the United States should continue to concentrate on producing a force that is so good and so well distributed that the Soviets will not attack. . . .[30]

Undaunted, the next day Radford and Taylor resumed their case for a more flexible and elaborate military posture, insisting at an NSC discussion that the United States was on the verge of military overextension. Dulles responded that the Soviet Union was actually in much worse shape than America; but this could tempt Soviet leader Nikita Khrushchev to act desperately. Eisenhower seemed to be thinking on a different level: his concern was not American overextension or Soviet instability but whether "the suggested courses of action would markedly reduce the threat of the holocaust described yesterday."[31] He continued with this theme after the New Year, concluding another NSC discussion by noting that "War had always been hitherto a contest, but it was preposterous to describe a war of missiles as a contest. . . . The concept of deterrent power has gone as far as it can. In view of this incredible situation we must have fresh thinking on how to conduct ourselves."[32]

In February it was time to rewrite basic policy for 1957. In a preliminary discussion of this task Eisenhower instructed war planners to "concentrate on what measures we should undertake in the first week of the war. It would all be over by that time." Given that fact, he continued, we might as well "put all our resources into our SAC capability and into hydrogen bombs."[33] Three weeks later, the Assistant for National Security Affairs, Robert Cutler, presented the first draft of the new strategy, NSC-5707. But the Planning Board had not heeded Eisenhower's suggestions, instead preserving Dulles's flexible strategy from the previous year and noting Eisenhower's instructions only in a footnote.

After Cutler finished presenting NSC-5707 the NSC commenced debate. Cutler stated that—given the obvious discord about the subject—the Planning Board was looking for guidance on nuclear weapons strategy. "Certain members of the Planning Board," he said, "had expressed fear that the United States would refrain from [limited war] lest the result of the involvement end up with the United States becoming involved in general nuclear war." Secretary of the Treasury Humphrey, counting himself among the discontented, complained that despite the declared policy of flexibility, the military always said that it could not win without nuclear escalation. It was time to decide once and for all whether the United States was going to use nuclear weapons in a limited war or not.[34]

Dulles complained that a footnote in NSC-5707 contained the "fallacy" of assuming that any nuclear war would develop into all-out war with the Soviet Union: "it is not true," he protested, "that we would be obliged to choose between doing nothing in the event of local Soviet aggression or else of engaging in general nuclear war." Eisenhower's reply was curt. If the Soviets were to be deterred from starting a war with the United States, he stated, "they would not be swayed by any fear that the United States would bomb airfields in Communist China. Their calculations would be based on quite other considerations."[35]

The NSC returned to work out this disagreement on April 11. But on that day Dulles was absent, and that gave Eisenhower an opportunity to push his position more easily through the council. The dissent of the past year had to stop; it was time, he said, to "write the right kind of directive in the matter of the use of atomic weapons." Cutler reminded the president that "the State Department had a certain interest in this area." Undersecretary of State Christian Herter tried to stand up for his absent boss, observing that "Secretary Dulles felt that we still needed a considerable degree of flexibility in the weaponry of our armed forces."[36] Eisenhower ended the debate by stating very clearly his opinion that we had now reached a point in time when our main reliance, though not our sole reliance, should be on nuclear weapons. Up until recently our main reliance has been on conventional forces, to which we have added here and there in various units atomic capabilities. This situation must henceforth be revised.[37]

Recognizing that the days of suggestion were over and the day of directive had arrived, Cutler returned to the White House basement to rewrite basic policy along Eisenhower's lines.

Basic national security policies written during the Eisenhower administration would first spell out the purposes of national survival.[38] The whole point of having a security policy was to preserve not only the physical survival of the United States but its "fundamental values and institutions" as well. This language remained intact throughout the Eisenhower era. The next section, entitled "Elements of National Strategy," then stated how the government would attempt to assure that survival. Listed first here of course was the military element, and it was in this subsection that one would find the basic military policy of the United States—a general outlining of different forms of international conflict and the degrees of armed force that should be brought to bear upon them.[39]

The military policy that the NSC planning board presented on May 27 for the council's approval differed in three fundamental respects from existing policy. First, the United States would now place "main, but not sole, reliance upon nuclear weapons." Instead of deploying a diverse force structure that combined nuclear weapons with atomic and conventional ones, the American military would henceforth wage thermonuclear war "when required to achieve national objectives." Second, the new policy emphasized that limited warfare, whether in conventional or nuclear form, was to be restricted to local wars, defined as "conflicts occurring in less developed areas of the world, in which limited U.S. forces participate because U.S. interests are involved." In such a war, "force will be applied in a manner and on a scale best calculated to avoid hostilities from broadening into general war." Third, and most important, the planning board simply removed Dulles's paragraph on flexible response. That passage had argued that "with the coming of nuclear parity, the ability to apply force selectively and flexibly" was crucial if the United States was to avoid finding itself in the position of having to choose in a crisis between the horrors of thermonuclear war and the humiliation of backing down. Flexibility would not only provide a sane alternative to these two unacceptable outcomes, but would also reassure allies who were skeptical of the American willingness to respond to an invasion of Luxembourg or Turkey with all-out thermonuclear war. The planning board eliminated this passage entirely, and replaced it with nothing.

This new policy can be distinguished best by its clean separation of general from limited war.[40] The old policy conceived by Dulles back in 1954 sought to blur this line, reserving to the United States the freedom to wage war flexibly and unexpectedly in different situations. The one that Eisenhower was imposing renounced this indeterminateness: general war was going to be fought with thermonuclear weapons, period. In a limited war the military might use conventional, atomic, and/or nuclear ones, but above all the goal would be to stop local aggression without courting general war.[41]

Eisenhower's new policy guidelines signified something more than just the alteration of words. By rewriting BNSP Eisenhower demonstrated that he was determined to impose his view of war upon formal decisionmaking. If a crisis broke out he wanted his advisers to have no doubt about the basic military policy he would pursue. Eisenhower may have originally believed that his statements of 1955 and 1956 would be sufficient for that purpose, but the dissent of his advisers indicated that they were not. By overhauling BNSP, and in so doing prominently tossing Dulles's doctrinal statement on flexible response into the trash, Eisenhower hoped to erase this doubt, to make his understanding of warfare the indisputable basis of American military policy.

The NSC met on May 27 to consider the new policy. Cutler reminded the council that the main differences between it and previous policies—the "major area of policy cleavage," as Cutler described it—were the paragraphs on nuclear war. The only NSC member to record his opposition to the proposed changes was John Foster Dulles. Dulles asked if he could speak generally about the "new concept" Eisenhower had put forth. He then proceeded to advance an interesting, though certainly on the face of it incongruous, argument against the new policy. Dulles admitted that one had to adjust to military technology; he was more "realistic" about the nuclear age than many of his State Department colleagues. But, the founder of massive retaliation insisted, global opinion would condemn the United States for using nuclear weapons, especially in local conflicts. If America resorted to such a war "we will, in the eyes of the world, be cast as a ruthless military power, as was Germany earlier."[42]

The problem, Dulles explained, was not that the use of nuclear weapons was immoral per se but that other nations had yet to understand how these weapons could be used in limited ways. Until the rest of world opinion came around, therefore, it would be best that the limitations on war as "set forth in NSC 5602/1 should be retained in the new basic national security policy paper."[43] But Dulles did not press his point. Indeed, after declining an offer from Cutler to establish a study group on limited nuclear war, he left the meeting early to meet with President Adenauer. Eisenhower interrupted Dulles only once, to reassure the NSC that by local war he meant a conflict specifically not involving American basic interests and hence not to be expanded into general war. Upon Dulles's departure, the NSC approved the changes as written and the meeting came to an end. A week later, the NSC completed the final version, NSC-5707/8.[44] Eisenhower's new military policy was now official.

The Strategy to Evade Nuclear War

A word to describe recent scholarship on Dwight Eisenhower and nuclear weapons might be *puzzled.* Here is a capable president, astute on many issues, masterly when it came to military policy. About his understanding of the ramifications of thermonuclear war there can be no doubt: dozens of times he warned that the only result of such a war would be misery and destruction. And the president did not issue these warnings in front of UN assemblies or Boy Scout troops—he issued them, as we have seen, in top-secret NSC and White House meetings that the public would know nothing about for decades, directing fist-pounding diatribes on the horror of thermonuclear holocaust toward hardened diplomats and military men.

Yet in 1956 and 1957 Eisenhower rearranged official American basic security policy so that a war with the Soviet Union would escalate, automatically, into general thermonuclear war. He made *a point* of eliminating strategies that could be used to moderate or prevent that escalation; he derided advisers, like his Secretary of State, who thought such moderation possible and desirable. By getting rid of NSC plans for conventional or limited nuclear warfare in the event of conflict with the Soviet Union, Eisenhower put the Cold War on a hair-trigger. In any confrontation between the two sides the United States would soon face a choice between capitulation and initiating thermonuclear war. Eisenhower regularly assured his colleagues that when that moment came he would be ready to launch the missiles.

The evidence is plain: a masterly chief executive, terrified by the specter of nuclear annihilation, pushes through with a great exertion a military policy which makes any war with the chief adversary of the United States an automatic, all-out thermonuclear war. How can this paradox be accounted for? Students of Eisenhower's military policy have advanced two explanations: that Eisenhower resisted the more expansive strategies of Dulles and the Joint Chiefs in order to save money; or that he rejected conventional strategies to persuade American's NATO allies to take greater responsibility for their own local defenses.[45]

Neither of these interpretations, however, explains Eisenhower's mysterious behavior in 1956 and 1957. If it were the president's intention to keep defense spending low, or to put pressure on NATO allies, then what possibly could be gained by dwelling on the specter of thermonuclear war? One might expect a president advocating a risky policy for economic or alliance purposes to *play down*, not call attention to, its unprecedented dangers. Yet in one NSC meeting after the next, Eisenhower interjects into an otherwise dispassionate discussion on civil defense or politics in Hungary anguished laments about the horror of modern war. These are experienced officials he is speaking to, quite well aware of what thermonuclear weapons can do. But Eisenhower keeps returning to the topic.[46]

This behavior makes sense only if one sees that the purpose behind it was not to keep spending down, or allies in line, but to avoid war with the Soviet Union. After his decision in 1955 to rush ICBM production, Eisenhower began to express with more clarity two views he had about modern war.[47] First, he revived his old Clausewitzean conviction that general war is not limitable. A war between the United States and the Soviet Union would escalate into an all-out thermonuclear exchange, for the simple reason that neither nation would give up when it still had powerful weapons at hand — and, realizing this, each would stand to gain by delivering a knockout punch at once. This was the belief that put him in opposition to Dulles and the Joint Chiefs, the one he hammered home in the February 1956 NSC meeting and in the conversation with General Taylor.

Second, Eisenhower concluded, especially after absorbing the awful reports on the effects of nuclear war in 1956, that once the Soviet Union had acquired a substantial ICBM arsenal, it would be impossible to prevent an all-out thermonuclear war from destroying the United States utterly. The destructive power of thermonuclear warheads, together with the technological and economic barriers to building a defense against them, made for a new level of warfare. In a general war not only would the United States suffer the physical destruction of the American state, but also the annihilation of national institutions and culture. World War III would kill American society.

So the logic is obvious: any war with the Soviet Union will lead to all-out war; all-out war will destroy the United States; ergo, do not get into a war with the Soviet Union. For the logician this is an easy one, but for a president of the United States during the height of the Cold War it was otherwise. He could not announce one day that the United States would no longer be willing to wage war against the Soviet Union. How, then, could he avoid such a war surreptitiously?

Here was how NSC-5707/8 could be put to use. A Hitler-like invasion was not going to happen, as long as the United States maintained a solid nuclear deterrent and the Soviet Union was not ruled by a omnicidal madman. On the other end of the spectrum, a "brushfire" war in a place vital to neither superpower would not be allowed to escalate into general war: Eisenhower had specified this clearly in basic policy. What could lead to serious hostilities was the outbreak of a political crisis in an area important to each side. It was in this kind of conflict that pressure would accumulate to push the crisis toward war.

In such a crisis the option of going to war with the Soviet Union would have to become unavailable. A way to do this was to reduce the alternatives available to American decisionmakers to compromise, or all-out thermonuclear war. And the way to do this was to persuade everyone involved in the making of decisions that (a) limited options did not exist, (b) in the event of war the president will push every button, and (c) the war that ensues would be a ghastly holocaust killing hundreds of millions and destroying American society. By contriving such a stark dichotomy, a strong leader could resist the pressure of those heretofore determined to wage war rather than conciliate.

Eisenhower determined in 1956 to make the primary objective of his presidency the avoidance of a thermonuclear war with the Soviet Union. His strategy to evade nuclear war was to make American military policy so dangerous that his advisers would find it impossible to push Eisenhower toward war and away from compromise. NSC-5707/8, in other words, was not so much a military policy stating basic American approaches to warfare as a strategy designed to allow Eisenhower to avoid war altogether.

This interpretation ascribes an unusual amount of sophistication and foresight to President Eisenhower. But it answers questions other interpretations have not. It accounts for the paradox of Eisenhower's military policy. It is in accord with two current scholarly perceptions of Eisenhower: that he was a president who knew what he was doing in the field of national security, and that he was a leader who pursued private political objectives to the exclusion of even his closest advisers.[48] And, finally, it explains Eisenhower's strange actions during the Berlin crisis of 1958–59, when his war evasion strategy became operational.

5 Fallout, April 1957–November 1958

On October 4, 1957 the Soviet Union launched the earth satellite *Sputnik*. It was a demonstration of Soviet scientific prowess that shocked the West, and it was also a noisy reminder to interested observers everywhere that the Soviet missile program was proceeding just fine.

Immediately, political adversaries of the president seized upon the specter of Soviet scientific superiority both to wage a partisan attack against him and to advance the interests of the aerospace industries.[1] These critics warned, with increasing hysteria, that the satellite indicated a decisive Russian advantage in the race to build ICBMs. Senator Stuart Symington and the syndicated columnist Joseph Alsop, working with information provided to them by not disinterested sources in the military and arms industries, predicted publicly that the Soviet Union would deploy arsenals of 1,000, 2,000, even 3,000 ICBMs by 1962 or 1963.[2] Symington, along with other Democratic colleagues in the Senate, including Lyndon Johnson and John F. Kennedy, demanded major increases in defense spending to forestall the imminent missile gap, and suggested that Eisenhower's resistance to these increases was due to his inability to appreciate the perils of Soviet ICBM superiority. Senator Henry Jackson called for a "National Week of Shame and Danger."[3] Hastily, the president agreed to increase defense spending for fiscal 1959, and he also authorized, ahead of schedule, a test of an American satellite, "Vanguard." In late November Eisenhower suffered a mild stroke. While recuperating, he got to watch Vanguard explode on its launching pad.[4]

In a strictly political sense, these events devastated Eisenhower. After his November stroke and the Vanguard debacle, the president's critics had a field day, forcing him to sign on to further defense increases and openly contrasting Soviet prowess with Republican inaction. Gravely warning of national peril, Senators Kennedy and Johnson (and others) succeeded in elevating themselves into the national spotlight, where they stayed long enough to seize the White House in 1960.[5]

The Soviet satellite's effect upon U.S. military policy, however, turned out to be slight. Eisenhower and his critics, in the recent struggle over NSC-5707/8, had been working from the expectation that Soviet ICBM capability was imminent, so the news that the Russians had put a 200-pound rock into orbit did not invalidate the assumptions underlying American defense policy.[6] After all, the internal debate over nuclear policy in 1956 and 1957 had been about what to do when, not if, the Soviets attained ICBM capability. All Sputnik did, from the strictly military point of view, was confirm vividly that day was soon to come. As we have seen, for fear of a Soviet advantage in missile capability Eisenhower had made, back in 1955, the development of American ICBMs a national objective "of the highest priority"; as far as he knew the first U.S. intercontinental missile was to become operational in 1959.[7] The United States deployed nuclear weapons in Europe which could retaliate against any Soviet ICBM attack, as could the large fleet of American bombers. What more could Eisenhower have done? "[W]e are getting close to absolutes when the ability exists to inflict 50% casualties on an enemy," the president said in November.[8]

It is true, as will be seen below, that the Soviet satellite encouraged the enemies of NSC-5707/8 to revive alternatives to Eisenhower's all-or-nothing policy. But the president would have none of it. Having recovered quickly from his November stroke, Eisenhower rebuffed his critics, rejecting their pleas that he alter the military policy he now had in place.[9] Moreover, he got a chance in the summer of 1958 to utilize his new policy, in a sort of trial run, during the second confrontation between communist and nationalist Chinese forces over the offshore island chain of Quemoy-Matsu.

The Gaither Report

The first and most conspicuous challenge to Eisenhower's new policy in the aftermath of Sputnik came in the form of yet another top-secret study on modern war. In April of 1957 the NSC had put together a commission to study American civil defenses. In early November this commission, having been emboldened by the Soviet satellite to expand its task into evaluating American nuclear defenses generally, completed their study, entitled it "Deterrence and Survival in the Nuclear Age," and presented it to the president. Because of the Sputnik controversy the study, popularly known as the "Gaither report,"[10] was leaked immediately, and it thus became a topic of public debate rather than a secret report for the disposal of American policymakers.

The Gaither report was a comprehensive criticism of Eisenhower's nuclear policies. The United States, it stated, had virtually no defense against a surprise Soviet missile attack and could be vulnerable by 1959 to a devastating defeat. The nation's retaliatory forces were inadequate, as were its military and civil defense programs and overseas missile deployments. In effect, the report stated, the Sputnik critics were right: because of poor warning systems and lagging ICBM production, the Soviet Union was on the verge of attaining decisive superiority. "The peril to the United States," the chairman of the commission himself warned, "must be measured in megatonnage in the years ahead."[11]

Eisenhower met with the commission on November 4 to discuss its top secret report, soon to be summarized in the New York Times. He responded to the report's criticisms by reiterating his new views on thermonuclear war. Both sides would soon have massive ICBM arsenals. "In these circumstances," he stated, "there is in reality no defense except to retaliate. . . . maximum massive retaliation remains the crux of our defense." Gaither's proposal for a national bomb shelter program would not solve the problem either. It "would be better to use the same funds for other things," Eisenhower said, because, shelters or not, if "50% destruction of our industries and cities occurred, [he] did not see how the nation could survive as an organized society."[12]

If the Gaither report's authors hoped to capitalize upon the Sputnik furor by persuading Eisenhower to take active steps to reduce America's vulnerability to Soviet ICBM attack, they failed. The president believed that, in the event of general war, there was no escape from mutual destruction: it would be futile, as well as expensive, to limit or defend against a war of missiles between the United States and the Soviet Union. Three days after the Gaither presentation, the NSC directed the Departments of Defense and State, the CIA, and the Budget office to take some of the report's arguments into consideration, and Eisenhower would later create a scientific advisory board and agree to spend more on civil defense. But he was not going to take more fundamental steps. In this, he received direct support from General Thomas of the Net Evaluation Committee, who predicted in November, that a Soviet attack could "kill from 1/4 to 1/2 of the U.S. population and injure many more in the process; and the military and civilian leadership of the U.S. at the Seat of Government would be virtually wiped out."[13] In January Eisenhower used this terrifying news to belittle the Gaither commission's main objective, the construction of a nationwide shelter program. The president

> noted that it had been said that fallout shelters might save 50 million people, a reduction of 35% in casualties. In talking about such figures, we were talking about the destruction of the United States. There would be no way of living in a situation of such large casualties.[14]

Dulles's Renewed Dissent

As soon as Eisenhower had pushed through NSC-5707/8 back in April and May, Dulles began to imply publicly that Eisenhower's new military policy was not what it was. The Secretary of State wanted to suggest to America's European allies that in the event of a Soviet attack NATO would have some option other than a spasmodic nuclear retaliation. Dulles feared that the Europeans would become demoralized by an all-or-nothing policy: some would push for more conciliatory approaches to the Russians, in order to avoid the immediate holocaust that war would bring; others would demand their own nuclear arsenals, skeptical that in the end the United States would really wage an intercontinental nuclear war to defend Western Europe.[15] Dulles also directed his implied disapproval of the new policies toward the president. He thought NSC-5707/8 was a disastrous mistake, and wanted to show Eisenhower the error of his ways.

Speaking at a June 1957 Defense Department secretaries' conference in Quantico, Virginia, Dulles tried out his new line. He noted that massive retaliation "has certain apparent weaknesses" in the thermonuclear age, and worried that there was "a growing question in the minds of some of our allies" as to whether the United States could be relied on to "perhaps destroy human life on the northern half of the globe" when faced with communist aggression. Fortunately, though, the United States was developing tactical nuclear weapons to deal with Soviet "nibbling operations," a plan based "on the theory that we would not, in fact, respond with the only weapon at hand because that would involve excessive cost to humanity."[16]

Going further, Dulles reiterated in the October 1957 number of *Foreign Affairs* the argument he had made at Quantico and at the NSC meeting on NSC-5707/8 back in May. The United States, he wrote, had once been forced to threaten massive retaliation against the Soviet Union, but now "it is possible to alter the character of nuclear weapons. It seems now that their use need not involve vast destruction and widespread harm to humanity.

"In the future," Dulles continued, "it may thus be feasible to place less reliance upon deterrence of vast retaliatory power." While the Soviet Union clung to its propagandistic claim that nuclear bombs were merely "horror" weapons, civlized statesmen in the West, Dulles implied, were learning otherwise. "New weapons possibilities are opening up in rapid succession. Political thinking finds it difficult to keep up with that pace."[17]

This article informed Europeans that the American Secretary of State looked down upon the policy of using "vast retaliatory power" to defend them, and this was certainly his intention. Dulles's ambiguity about American military policy might make Europeans inclined toward neutralism or nuclear independence think twice. He was also able to reassure these allies without explicitly contradicting his administration's policy—after all, he was writing about a future technological innovation, to which enlightened policymakers would naturally adapt.

However, the peculiar thesis of this article, together with the fact that Dulles had presented it pretty much verbatim back in May in his opposition to Eisenhower's new proposals, suggests that Europeans were not the only people Dulles hoped would read it.[18] The Secretary of State was genuinely disturbed by the reckless policy his president had put forth that spring. He did realize that upon the question of trying to beat back a Soviet invasion with American conventional forces, Eisenhower's mind was made. A war with the Russians would be a nuclear war; Dulles, as he put it in the May discussion, was more "realistic" about that than others in Washington. But that did not mean the possibility of limited war in Europe was gone forever: maybe the prospect of new technologies, of tactical nuclear weapons that were clearly well-suited to battlefield use, could cause the president to rethink his all-or-nothing approach. Dulles could not accept the fatalistic conclusion that to defend Europe from the communists it would be necessary to wage general thermonuclear war. There had to be an alternative. "No man," he argued in January 1958, "should arrogate the power to decide that the future of mankind would benefit by an action entailing the killing of tens of millions of people."[19] It was crucial, Dulles mistakenly believed, to persuade Eisenhower of this.

In March of 1958 the NSC returned to its annual update of basic policy, and it was during the spring months that Dulles and other administration critics—including, now, national security special assistant Robert Cutler—waged a last campaign to change Eisenhower's mind. On March 20 Cutler made his opposition to Eisenhower's military policy clear, stating that "our allies are losing their faith in our will to make use of our nuclear retaliatory capability in the event of Soviet attack."[20] Dulles, more optimistic about the Europeans, demurred, and during the next NSC meeting a week later he kept his own counsel as Eisenhower rejected Cutler's logic outright. When "we talk about a vast nuclear exchange between us and the enemy," the president said, adding a preposition, "we are in fact talking about something the results of which are almost impossible to conceive of." Shelters were too expensive to build on a nationwide basis; and in any case limited war with the Russians was impossible. All-out attack would continue as the basis of American military policy.[21]

On April 1 Dulles met with Eisenhower privately to discuss America's "national strategic concept." During this conversation he formally told Eisenhower that he opposed official policy. NSC-5707/8, he stated, "too much invoked massive nuclear attack in the event of any clash anywhere of United States with Soviet forces." This was wrong and needed to be changed. The United States must develop tactical nuclear weapons and other limited strategies, so that it could wage a war with the Soviet Union "short of wholesale obliteration." Eisenhower's current policy "did not adequately take account of the possibilities of limited war."[22] The president did not want simply to dismiss so clear a dissent from his vigorous Secretary of State. He asked Dulles to set up a study group. Eisenhower could consider its report when the NSC met to discuss the new BNSP for 1958.

The leading members of the new study group, Dulles and Cutler, took to their task seriously. Dulles, belying the optimism he had displayed in front of Eisenhower on March 20, warned during an April 7 meeting that without a change in American policy a loss of will in Europe was indeed possible. Using language similar to that which the Kennedy campaign would use in 1960, he complained that if current military policy "is simply that of general war we build weapons only for that, thus leaving us unable to take other kinds of action, and making us prisoners of a frozen concept." Cutler agreed, urging in a memorandum sent to Defense Secretary Neil McElroy that American military policy be changed to deal with limited aggression. In a study group paper, which he hoped to present to the president before the rewriting of BNSP, Cutler warned of a "growing doubt in the Free World whether the United States will use its massive nuclear capability, except in direct retaliation to direct attack on the United States or its forces."[23]

On May 1 the NSC finally met to discuss NSC-5810, the proposed BNSP for that year. The new draft, essentially a reprise of NSC-5707/8, contained no significant changes in its section on "military elements." Immediately, the critics of Eisenhower's all-or-nothing policy went on the attack. General Taylor, echoing the argument Nitze had put forth the previous fall, urged that the United States, by increasing its limited-war forces, could use massive retaliation as an "umbrella," under which smaller wars could be fought without their automatically escalating into all-out nuclear war.[24] He proposed, on behalf of the Navy and Marine Corps chiefs as well as himself, that the council adopt an alternative paragraph (one evidently drafted by the study group) to the one Eisenhower had dictated on the separation of general from limited war. Dulles seconded this proposal, saying that without a new American nuclear policy NATO would collapse in "three years or so."[25]

Eisenhower offered an interesting rebuttal of Taylor's proposal. "Actually," he argued,

the umbrella would be a lightning rod. Each small war makes global war the more likely. For example, the President said he simply could not believe that if the Soviets tried to seize Austria we could fight them in what the President called a nice, sweet, World War II type of war.

"Obviously," Eisenhower added, "the Secretary of State takes the opposite view."[26]

Indeed, Dulles stepped up the attack. The lack of significant American non-nuclear forces in Europe, he warned, would undermine NATO and lead to the collapse of the Western alliance. Without a credible conventional deterrent in Europe, NATO allies could reach the demoralizing conclusion that the only way to repel Soviet aggression would be to destroy the world. "These allies," he insisted, "must *at least have the illusion* that they have some kind of defensive capability against the Soviets other than the United States using a pushbutton to start a global nuclear war." Exasperated, Dulles

said that he would presently go to Berlin. When he got there he would repeat what he had said in Berlin four years ago—namely, that an attack on Berlin would be considered by us to be an attack on the United States. Secretary Dulles added that he did not know whether he himself quite believed this or, indeed, whether his audience would believe it. But he was going to perform this ritual act.[27]

Unruffled, Eisenhower

expressed surprise, and said that if we did not respond in this fashion to a Soviet attack on Berlin, we would first lose the city itself and, shortly after, all of Western Europe. If all of Western Europe fell into the hands of the Soviet Union . . . the United States would indeed be reduced to the character of a garrison state if it was to survive at all.[28]

Eisenhower's answer to Dulles's challenge was, for the frustrated Secretary of State, no answer at all. The president stated that a small war over something like Berlin would be a "lightning rod" sure to ignite general war; such a war would destroy American society. Yet the United States, to avoid being reduced to a "garrison state, if it was to survive at all," must regard an attack upon the peculiar Cold War outpost of West Berlin *as an attack upon the United States* justifying an all-out U.S. response. To save Berlin, in other words, it would be necessary to destroy the United States. The president had persisted in committing this fallacy. How long would he maintain such an illogical position?

After the May 1 NSC debate, opposition to retaining the language from NSC-5707/8 came to an end, and NSC-5810/1 became formal policy later that month. Dulles accepted this decision, though only after issuing a caveat that "military doctrine is in flux at the moment and that the military paragraphs which we write into Basic Policy at the moment may not remain valid very long."[29] This was doubtless how Dulles saw it, but his suggestion that with time policy would change turned out to be incorrect. As of the summer of 1958 Eisenhower was done entertaining alternatives to the stark basic national security policy he had conceived back in 1956. Criticism of this policy would continue, but he would no longer take it seriously.

The Second Quemoy-Matsu Crisis

On August 23, 1958 the Chinese communists resumed their artillery attacks upon Nationalist forces stationed on Quemoy and Matsu. American policy, which stemmed from the first crisis in 1955, stipulated coming to the aid of the Taiwanese to defend these tiny islands. Suddenly, Eisenhower had to decide whether to interpret the Chinese shelling as an attack on the islands, follow written policy, and go to war against mainland China, or to find a way to avoid war. The second Taiwan straits crisis lacked the intensity of later crises, because the United States was not as committed to the offshore islands as it was to other parts of the world, and because it was not certain that the Soviet Union would join the Chinese if the war escalated. Nevertheless, during late August and September the United States faced for the first time a crisis that could plausibly have triggered global thermonuclear exchange.

The Chinese communists began a campaign of rhetorical threats about two weeks before they actually initiated their attack, so Washington had time to prepare for hostilities. Dulles suggested to Eisenhower on August 12 "that perhaps we should consider that an attack on them [Quemoy and Matsu] constitutes an attack on Formosa." Since American policy had made Taiwan a basic Cold War stake, the Secretary of State was proposing that the United States should consider launching a war against China, and then perhaps Russia too, once the Chinese moved against the islands. Eisenhower declined to agree, even after Dulles suggested that the whole affair signified a Chinese and Soviet probe to see how the Soviet attainment of missiles would soften American resolve. The president did, however, instruct Dulles to make a general announcement that an attack on the islands would bring the United States into the conflict. Meanwhile, Cutler retrieved NSC-5723, a policy blueprint for the offshore islands, which stated that the American objective in any crisis would be to maintain the status quo. Only the president, however, could authorize actual U.S. military action to help the Nationalists.[30]

Undersecretary of State Christian Herter asked Policy Planning Staff director Gerard Smith to look more specifically into the military element of NSC-5723, the use of atomic attacks against Chinese coastal bases. Smith reported back after meeting with the Joint Chiefs that current war plans "call for the defense of Quemoy and Matsu by nuclear strikes deep into Communist China, including military targets in the Shanghai-Hangchow-Nanking and Canton complexes where population density is extremely high." In case his point was missed, Smith added that in the event of such attacks "there would be millions of non-combatant casualties." Further, Smith wrote, an NIE report had predicted that after an attack like this "Peiping and its Soviet ally would probably feel compelled to react with nuclear attacks at least on Taiwan and the [U.S.] seventh fleet. Under our present strategic concept, this would be the signal for general nuclear war between the U.S. and the U.S.S.R."[31]

After the usual NSC meeting on August 14 a small group met with Eisenhower to discuss NSC-5723. Eisenhower repeated his opinion that the islands were worth nothing from a military point of view but were important in maintaining Taiwanese morale. Referring to Smith's memorandum, Herter noted that the Joint Chiefs believed that repelling the Chinese from the islands would require attacking Chinese air bases on the mainland. JCS chairman Twining confirmed this. Eisenhower rejected the idea that defending Quemoy and Matsu justified using atomic weapons. He said that "we should not be drawn into spreading out the area of conflict, and thereby probably bringing the USSR in to render support to its principal ally, thus leading to general war." The president laid out the basic plan: the United States would preserve the status quo by helping the Chinese nationalists hold onto Quemoy and Matsu, but the help would not include bombardment of Chinese air bases—a step the Chiefs thought necessary—for fear of nuclear escalation. "We must try to define fixed limits to the action," Eisenhower concluded.[32]

Eisenhower's recommendation, of course, skirted the issue: the Chiefs were declaring that defending Quemoy and Matsu required the use of atomic weapons, and instead of rebutting this claim on its own terms the president simply stated that while the defense of the islands was necessary, nuclear weapons would expand the conflict into general war and therefore ought not to be used. On August 15 Herter met with the Joint Chiefs to make sense of Eisenhower's illogic. Twining warned that if the United States failed to support the Nationalist effort to hold onto the islands, Taiwan would eventually fall. It would be necessary, at the outset, "to use low-yield atomic bombs" to repel a Communist attack. Herter agreed that Eisenhower simply had to "make a determination that an attack on the Offshore Islands is an attack on Taiwan." Once he committed to this, Herter reasoned, then he could not reject plans to use atomic weapons, since the defense of Taiwan had long been designated as essential to U.S. security and worthy of nuclear war. It was a matter of pinning Eisenhower down.[33]

On August 23 the Chinese communists began to attack Taiwanese forces stationed on Quemoy-Matsu with artillery shelling. For the moment, they were making no obvious preparations to invade the islands, so it was up to

Washington to decide how to interpret this action. Dulles declared, via a public statement to Thomas Morgan, Chairman of the House Foreign Affairs Committee, that an actual Chinese attack would "constitute a threat to the peace of the area."[34] Eisenhower's private reaction was equally moderate. The United States, he declared in an August 25 White House meeting, would refrain from publicizing the Chinese aggression, while quietly informing the Nationalists of American contingency plans should the Chinese actually invade the islands.[35] Herter wondered whether the U.S. should not offer the Nationalist government something more solid than that. Eisenhower's reply was negative. There should be "no full commitment," he said. It was crucial to "avoid making statements from which we might later back off."[36]

Those on the scene demanded more commitment. Chiang Kai-Shek, surprised that Eisenhower had not responded more forcefully, demanded on August 24, 26, and 27 that the United States provide him with the "moral and military support" to beat back the communist attack. Chiang was not happy about enduring the bombardment passively. He had deployed an astonishing proportion of his troops on the small islands in order to confront the communists provocatively, believing that the Americans meant what they said about "liberating" the mainland. Here was a golden opportunity to begin the great liberation, but Eisenhower was instead asking him simply to absorb the communist attack. Via the sympathetic American ambassador to Taiwan, Everett Drumright, Chiang pleaded for more support.[37]

At the same time U.S. military commanders in and around the Islands demanded more discretion. General Felix Smoot, Commander of U.S. forces in Taiwan, suggested in a telegram that Eisenhower give local commanders authorization to "employ [their] own forces against artillery position. In the event that a[ir]c[ra]ft are engaged by substantial Chicom air opposition," Smoot continued, "we must be prepared, as the next step, to attack Chicom airfields immediately, preferably with nuclear weapons." The Commander of the Seventh Fleet concurred: the problem of supplying the offshore islands from the Taiwanese mainland had become "critical . . . we will have to knock out Chicom batteries if islands are to survive."[38]

Neither Chiang nor the military commanders got what they wanted. Dulles was on vacation over the last week of August, and during this crucial period Eisenhower did not waver, either in public declarations or in private meetings, from his policy of supporting the Nationalist position in general terms while specifically ruling out any action that might escalate the conflict into a wider war.[39] During the August 25 meeting the president approved a plan which, in the event of an actual communist invasion of the islands, would offer the nationalists limited American military backing. The U.S. would establish a formal convoy between Taiwan and the islands, and attack Chinese coastal bases with conventional forces only—this despite the Chiefs' opinion that a conventional attack would be ineffectual. No local commander was to move against the Chinese mainland without direct authorization from Washington, and the decision to use atomic weaponry, of any kind, was to be made only by the president himself.[40] On the 29th, the same day that Chinese Communist radio demanded that the U.S. "get the hell out of Taiwan," and urged Taiwanese to kill their American advisers and defect, Eisenhower went further. He ordered that the United States was not to use nuclear weapons in the limited war to defend Quemoy and Matsu. Nuclear weapons were only for general war, he declared, and "there would be no difficulty in identifying the type of massive attack which might require more drastic action."[41]

Publicly, Eisenhower also took a moderate stance. On August 27 the Chinese Communist government publicly asserted its determination to overrun Quemoy and Matsu and then go on to retake Taiwan as well.[42] This was a provocation to which the American administration in 1955 would have surely responded by rattling some nuclear sabers, by comparing nuclear weaponry to "a bullet," for example. Yet on two separate occasions that day Eisenhower made a point of foregoing two kinds of nuclear threats: the conspicuous demonstration of power, and the cavalier allusion to nuclear war. During a meeting with SAC representatives to discuss nuclear testing, a proposal to go through with a scheduled explosion of a "large weapon" at the Eniwetok testing area came up. Instead of seizing this opportunity to demonstrate America's will Eisenhower canceled the test. He "did not think it was a good moment to conduct a large test in the Pacific."[43] Later that afternoon, during a long press conference, Eisenhower refused on several occasions to turn a reporter's obviously leading question into a public threat. May Craig of the *Portland Press Herald* asked Eisenhower whether the United States could "be defeated in an all-out first-blow nuclear war"; Eisenhower did not answer with a gritty negative but instead assured her that any nation "foolish" enough to launch a first blow "would itself be destroyed," as if that were at issue. Chalmers Roberts of the *Washington Post* asked if Eisenhower considered the two islands "more important than ever to the defense of Formosa itself," to which Eisenhower replied with the evasive "you simply cannot make military decisions until the event reaches you." Perhaps concluding that his colleagues were insufficiently blunt, Felix Belair of the *New York Times* asked Eisenhower if local commanders had discretionary power to use tactical atomic weapons. Eisenhower answered this question literally, stating that he was unsure about any exception to his ultimate authority, thus spurning an easy chance to scare the Chinese by suggesting that American—or maybe even Nationalist Chinese—colonels could initiate nuclear war.[44]

As later events would also show, however, Eisenhower could not simply put forth a moderate, non-nuclear policy and expect all happily to accept it. Chiang Kai-Shek, for example, was shocked to learn that the United States was not determined to defend Quemoy and Matsu with atomic war. As Drumright reported it, the Generalissimo's reaction to Eisenhower's announcement was "furious," the "most violent I have seen him exhibit."[45] Chiang demanded that Eisenhower specify the American commitment to the islands. Instead, Eisenhower responded with a vague statement, noting his "firm, unwavering policy to support the security and international prestige of the Government of the Republic of China."[46] Of more concern to the president than Chiang was Dulles, back from vacation on September 1. Eisenhower invited Dulles immediately up to his vacation home on the naval base in Newport, Rhode Island, in order to coordinate crisis policy, but the Secretary of State declined, proposing instead that he first meet with representatives from the Joint Chiefs and the Pentagon. Dulles wanted to know, before meeting with the president, what American military options in the Taiwan straits really were.[47]

In a meeting the next day JCS chairman Twining gave Dulles an answer. Reiterating his earlier position, Twining rejected Eisenhower's plan to use conventional weapons only to rebuff a Chinese attack. To repel an invasion of Quemoy and Matsu, he said, "we would strike at Communist air fields and shore batteries with atomic weapons. All the studies carried out by Defense indicated that this was the only way to do the job," he added; "the use of conventional weapons would mean our involvement in another protracted Korean War-type conflict." Dulles noted that Twining's view "had important implications affecting the government's whole foreign policy," and expressed his specific fear that using nuclear weapons in the Pacific would terrify the Europeans, causing them to reject a NATO defense policy based upon nuclear warfare. Chairman Twining demurred, saying that he "could not understand the public horror at the idea of using nuclear weapons. . . . we must get used to the idea that such weapons had to be used." Here was proof for the Secretary of State of the inadequacy of NSC-5707/8. "[I]f we shrink from using nuclear weapons when military circumstances so require," Dulles concluded, "then we will have to reconsider our whole defense posture."[48]

On September 4 Dulles went to Newport to finalize policy with the president. He brought with him a memorandum he had completed after the September 2 meeting, which stated that the fall of Quemoy and Matsu would surely lead to the collapse of Taiwan. If that happened America's other allies along the Pacific rim, including Japan, would "probably fall within the Sino-Soviet orbit." To defeat a Chinese invasion of Quemoy and Matsu the United States, as Twining had asserted, would have to use nuclear weapons. And this was a terrible dilemma, because such an action, Dulles added, would create a "strong popular revulsion against the United States in most of the world."[49]

The two met at 10:30 on the morning of September 4, and Dulles immediately handed Eisenhower the memorandum. The Secretary of State was direct: referring Eisenhower to the section on nuclear weapons, he reminded him that "we have geared our defense to the use of these in case of hostilities of any size, and stating that, if we will not use them when the chips are down because of adverse world opinion, we must revise our defense setup."[50] Dulles here, as in his memorandum, was pointing out to Eisenhower the defect of current military policy. By eliminating limited war options and diminishing conventional capabilities Eisenhower had ensured that every significant crisis would be a nuclear crisis. Not only did this threaten the world with general nuclear war over some insignificant islands off the Chinese shore, it also damaged the really important alliance the United States had (in Dulles's eyes), because the Europeans were understandably terrified by the idea that World War III would go immediately nuclear, and at the same time skeptical that the Americans would really trade Boston for Bonn. The confrontation over Quemoy and Matsu gave Dulles the opportunity to show the president how misguided NSC-5707/8 was in the real world of international diplomacy and crisis.

But Dulles also understood quite well that nothing could be done about Eisenhower's military policies now. Indeed, on September 3 Dulles had received from Gerard Smith an updated version of the memorandum Smith had completed in August, reminding the Secretary that the Joint Chiefs' plan to respond to an invasion of the islands by striking Chinese coastal targets would—according to a recent National Intelligence Estimate—invite Sino-Soviet nuclear retaliation and trigger the outbreak of general war. The same estimate argued that neither China nor the Soviet Union was ready to risk war over Quemoy and Matsu.[51] As far as this immediate crisis was concerned, reason dictated finding a compromise.

Dulles and Eisenhower considered the issue at Newport. When Dulles proposed that, in the event of a direct assault on the islands, the U.S. attack Chinese bases with low-yield air-burst atomic weapons, Eisenhower replied that the "Communist retaliation with nuclear weapons might well be against Taiwan itself and beyond rather than simply directed at Quemoy." What point would there be in defending Quemoy and Matsu if in the ensuing war Taiwan, "and beyond," were destroyed with nuclear weapons?[52] According to the Goodpaster account of this conversation, Eisenhower rejected Dulles's suggestion, and then diverted the discussion by reminiscing about D-Day preparations. He spoke of the problem of night bombardment from dispersed bases in China, recollecting that the United States could be put in a similar situation to that of the Germans in 1944.[53] That afternoon Dulles issued a rather bland public statement of U.S. intentions, reiterating the U.S. determination to defend Taiwan, and his own view that the fate of the two islands were "increasingly . . . related" to that end. Then Dulles promised that "military dispositions have been made by the United States so that a Presidential determination, if made, would be followed by action both timely and effective."[54]

As this strange account suggests, something else not meant to appear in the formal record was going on in the September 4 discussion between Eisenhower and Dulles. On that day Dulles composed a memorandum of a conversation he had had with Lord Hood, the British ambassador. In this conversation Dulles broached the idea of forcing the Nationalists to demilitarize Quemoy and Matsu, in exchange for a promise from the Communists not to invade the islands.[55] Such a compromise, while bound to enrage Chiang, would prove face-saving to both sides and prevent the war that neither side, even the supposedly fanatical Chinese Communists, wanted to occur.

Events moved quickly following Dulles's suggestion to Hood. On September 6 the Chinese premier, Chou En-lai, announced a Chinese willingness to commence talks with the United States. Not slow to react, Eisenhower on that same day demanded that Dulles secure "concrete and definite acceptance of Chou En-lai's offer to negotiate." On the 7th, Dulles stated in a department memorandum his "decided interest" in demilitarizing the islands, and instructed the State Department's Bureau of Far Eastern Affairs adviser, Marshall Green, to make clear to the Joint Chiefs that there were to be no "provocative actions" in the Straits area. The next day Dulles sent a telegram to the American ambassador to Poland, Jacob Beam, authorizing him formally to pursue negotiations with his Chinese counterpart in Warsaw. Dulles also contacted Drumright in Taipei, to inform him of the new reality: the negotiators in Warsaw, and then perhaps the United Nations, were now the "arbiters" of the Offshore Islands crisis. It was Drumright's unenviable task to tell Chiang this news, and to ensure that neither the American nor Nationalist forces provoked further conflict.[56]

With only a vague promise conveyed indirectly to them by the arch-capitalist John Foster Dulles to go by, the Chinese initially refused to meet the Americans in Warsaw, and continued to shell Quemoy and Matsu. Once, such obstinance would have led Dulles immediately to cancel the offer and seriously threaten war, but now things were different. Eisenhower had ordered Dulles to secure "concrete" negotiations with the Chinese and defuse the crisis, and that was what the Secretary of State was going to do. On September 11 Dulles met with the New Zealand ambassador Sir Leslie Munro, ostensibly to discuss his prime minister's recent call for Taiwan to turn Quemoy and Matsu over to the Chinese. Rather than deporting Munro for his government's public support of the communist position in a global Cold War crisis, Dulles told him that it had been "foolish" for Chiang to commit so much to Quemoy and Matsu. Therefore, the United States was interested in finding a compromise. "If we could get some assurance that the islands would not be attacked," Dulles told Munro, "then it might be possible to demilitarize them."[57] The same day Dulles secured support for his position from the military: Secretary of Defense McElroy confirmed for Dulles that the Joint Chiefs had "reassessed" the importance of Quemoy and Matsu for the defense of Taiwan; the Chiefs would "probably conclude," McElroy stated, "that the islands were not required."[58]

On September 12 Dulles issued the *coup de grace*. He wrote a long letter to the British Prime minister Harold Macmillan, who had been communicating to Dulles his tremendous fear that a conflict over the tiny islands might lead to global thermonuclear war. In the letter Dulles reassured MacMillan, urging him to pay particular attention to Eisenhower's recent statement that the crisis "will not be a thorn in the side of peace," and restating America's determination to prevent Chiang from using the islands in a provocative way. It "could be said," Dulles continued, "that the presence of such large numbers of Nationalist forces is itself a kind of 'provocation.' " Dulles noted that the British had long advocated asking Moscow to restrain the People's Republic. "The time is propitious," he said, "for such a move."[59]

Dulles had suggested to Lord Hood back on September 4 that the U.S. might be willing to demilitarize the islands in exchange for a Chinese agreement to stop shelling them, but Peking's unwillingness to agree to commence negotiations in Warsaw indicated that this suggestion had not been sufficient. Therefore, Dulles conveyed a more explicit message to the Chinese via a New Zealand government that had recently sided with them, and then, to finish off any doubt, he told Macmillan that the United States was willing to regard Chiang's troops on Quemoy and Matsu as a provocation to be removed, and asked him to relay this position to the Soviet Union for the purposes of international compromise. Dulles fulfilled Eisenhower's order. The Beam-Chang talks in Warsaw commenced on September 15.

The onset of these talks signified the ending of the second offshore islands crisis, its "moving into a discussion stage."[60] On one level, and certainly to an observer at the time, this could not have seemed so: over the rest of September the two diplomats conducted fruitless, bitter negotiations, and the Chinese artillery shelling had not yet stopped. In his September 11 radio and TV address Eisenhower compared the Chinese action against the two islands to Hitler's late 1930s aggression and argued that similar appeasement by the West would make it likely that the United States would "have to fight a major war";[61] in a September 19 letter that Eisenhower found so objectionable that he sent it back with no reply, Khrushchev warned of a Soviet nuclear retaliation should the U.S. strike China with atomic weaponry.[62]

This belligerent rhetoric was posturing, bluster to obscure the quiet compromise. The Chinese obstinance in Warsaw, and Khrushchev's hostile correspondence simply indicated, Deputy Director of Central Intelligence General Charles Cabell noted, that they "are relying on words rather than contemplated military action." Such was true of the American side too.[63] By the end of the month the compromise became public. On September 30 Dulles announced at a press conference that if the Chinese stopped their bombardment of the offshore islands, even without formally signing a cease-fire, the United States would agree to the evacuation of American and Nationalist forces from the Quemoy-Matsu area.[64] Fulfilling their end of the deal, on October 6 the Chinese announced a week-long suspension of their attack, which they extended until October 25, at which time they recommenced their shelling only on odd days of the calendar. This last move was a fitting ending to the second Quemoy-Matsu crisis. Once all sides realized that general war was not going to happen, they began to affect poses of toughness, like dogs snarling at one another across a fence they know is secure.

Among those disturbed by the snarling of mid-September were Prime Minister Macmillan and his foreign minister Selwyn Lloyd. Satisfied with their role in defusing the straits crisis, they wondered whether the United States had really been willing to wage nuclear war had the compromise failed and the Chinese invaded the islands. This had been Macmillan's main line of questioning in his earlier letters to Dulles: was the defense of a remote stake such as the offshore islands indeed vital to the safety of the free world, and would the United States have defended them even if as a "prelude" to World War Three? From the British perspective Dulles's conciliation indicated that perhaps such was not the case—that there was a discrepancy between declared U.S. policy and the real intentions of the Eisenhower administration.[65] To learn more about the American position Lloyd came to the States on September 16.

Lloyd first met with Dulles, who informed him that the United States had indeed been willing to use small nuclear weapons to keep the offshore islands in nationalist hands.[66] Alarmed, Lloyd saw Eisenhower on September 21. Eisenhower made it clear first of all that the decision to abandon the islands had been his idea: the West had to stand up for them to preserve morale in East Asia, but it "would be nice" if Chiang could find a way to evacuate them quietly. Lloyd, introducing a position that would become the redundant British line over the next year, suggested that the two superpowers meet for a Summit meeting.

Lloyd got to the main point. The British government and people were terrified by the idea of using nuclear weapons to hold Quemoy-Matsu. There "was going to be hell to pay," he predicted, if the Americans started a nuclear war with China. Eisenhower's reply revealed a difference between him and Dulles. If "nuclear weapons were going to be used," he said, "it would have to be an all-out effort rather than a local effort." Moreover, he "did not plan to use nuclear weapons in any local situation at the present time." Lloyd told the president that he was "very relieved" to hear this.[67]

The second straits crisis revealed many things. Most interesting, perhaps, was the conciliatory diplomacy of John Foster Dulles: no brinksman was he over Quemoy and Matsu. Indeed, looked at in broad terms Dulles's actions in this crisis were, in the end, a series of retreats. In reaction to the Chinese bombardment of the islands, the United States engaged in no substantial military retaliation, took the lead in seeking negotiations, forced Chiang to accept a humiliating compromise, was the first nation to announce the deal publicly, and tolerated the Chinese resumption of alternate-day bombardment passively.

Also clear was Dulles's subordination to Eisenhower. The adversarial role that Dulles often took when debating military policy with the president was not to be found during the straits crisis, at least not after the crucial meeting at Newport on September 4. Dulles followed Eisenhower's order of September 6 to the letter, engaging in forms of conciliation that were probably unpleasant for him.

A question that still remained, the one that seemed to have prompted Lloyd's visit, was whether this conciliatory American behavior reflected a general policy, or was only particular to the crisis over Quemoy and Matsu. By refusing to commit to a concrete military plan, resisting subordinates' calls for confrontation, and quietly jumping at a chance to negotiate, Eisenhower and Dulles had evaded war in a way that might be used in the future. Dulles's and Eisenhower's different replies to Lloyd's question suggested that this matter was not yet resolved—that Quemoy-Matsu, at least from the Secretary of State's point of view, was an exception not to be repeated. This question would be answered more clearly over the next several months.

6   Berlin, November 1958–July 1959

Having observed the American alarm over Sputnik and then Eisenhower's tentativeness during the second Taiwan straits crisis, Soviet leader Nikita Khrushchev decided to test Western resolve over a much more substantial Cold War issue. After more than a decade of acquiescing in the continued Western occupation of West Berlin, Khrushchev demanded in the fall of 1958 that the occupying powers finally depart from that city. The formal refusal of the United States and its European allies to accede to this demand, even though they understood that the USSR was on the verge of acquiring intercontinental missiles, led to the first direct, bipolar crisis of the thermonuclear age. During this crisis Eisenhower put his strategy to evade war to the test.

Khrushchev's Ultimatum

On Monday, November 10 Khrushchev addressed a Polish-Soviet friendship rally at the Moscow Sports Palace, where he called for the occupation of Berlin to come finally to an end. The Soviet Union would therefore cede control of its sector to the East Germans, and recommend that the Western powers make similar arrangements. Western reaction was swift: State Department spokesman Lincoln White declared that the West was prepared to defend West Berlin with force; the United States ambassador to Moscow, Llewellyn Thompson, wired to Washington the next day that the speech was indeed a "most dangerous move on [the] part of Khrushchev." European governments sent urgent telegrams to Georgia, where Eisenhower was vacationing in his apartment above the pro shop at Augusta National.[1]

The United States had planned for a showdown over Berlin. In 1954 the NSC developed a contingency paper, NSC-5404/1, which concluded that the Western powers must regard an attack upon West Berlin as an attack against a NATO nation;[2] this paper was supplanted in late 1957 by NSC-5727, "U.S. Policy toward Germany," which contained a specific supplement on Berlin. The latter policy was unambiguous: any Soviet attempt to deny Western access to West Berlin must prompt "immediate and forceful action to counter the Soviet challenge, even though such counter-measures might lead to general war."[3] NSC-5727 even suggested, albeit obliquely, that the United States might be best served by taking the initiative:

> In addition to resisting the initial attack and to placing itself in the best possible position for immediate global war, the United States should, if circumstances permit, address an ultimatum to the Soviet Government before full implementation of emergency war plans.[4]

Thus the official American strategy on Berlin, as it was written less than a year before the outbreak of the crisis, was to treat any Soviet move to deny access to west Berlin as an attack upon the United States, and to regard that attack as a potential prelude to general war which the United States "should, if circumstances permit," launch unilaterally. The decision made by the Truman administration back in 1948, to make Berlin a basic Cold War stake, still stood.

Early U.S. reaction to the Khrushchev speech followed official policy. On the diplomatic side, Dulles urged that NATO present a united front and refuse to budge from Berlin, while at the same time admitting at a press conference that the U.S. would deal with East German officials—"minor functionaries," as he hoped to trivialize them—on logistical questions regarding access to West Berlin and border arrangements in the city.[5] This latter step was something NATO policy had hitherto prohibited, and it angered West German President Konrad Adenauer and Mayor Willy Brandt of Berlin.[6] On the military side, General Lauris Norstad, supreme commander of the European allied forces (SACEUR) and also head of the U.S. European command, urged action. A few days after the November 10 speech armed East Germans had stopped an American convoy headed eastward on the Autobahn for Berlin; Norstad argued for an immediate Western military probe to assure land access to Berlin and, if the Soviets were to turn over control over Berlin checkpoints to the East Germans, he recommended that the United States "force the issue promptly by dispatching a test convoy supported by appropriate force."[7] Dulles related Norstad's "rather extreme views" to Eisenhower on the 18th; the president, echoing his sentiments during the straits crisis, noted that "we perhaps should not have committed ourselves as deeply as we had to Berlin . . . [but] we were where we were and had to stand firm."[8] Also on that day the NSC completed document 5803, an updating of NSC-5727: it reiterated the basic American view that a Soviet attack on Berlin would mean that "general war is imminent."[9]

On November 27 Soviet Foreign Minister Andrei Gromyko handed Thompson a formal note which at the same time intensified the stakes of the crisis and diminished its immediate explosiveness.[10] The note was an ultimatum from Khrushchev: the Western powers had six months to get out of West Berlin. Only "madmen," Khrushchev warned,

> can go the length of unleashing another world war over the preservation of privileges of occupiers in West Berlin. If such madmen should really appear, there is no doubt that straitjackets could be found for them.[11]

Khrushchev's combination of dire warnings and ultimatums outraged the West. Dulles, for example, described the note as "vicious and unacceptable."[12] But the ultimatum made the crisis more predictable and, for the time being, more stable. Over the next six months Western military decision-makers would have the luxury of planning for a confrontation in which the time, place, and adversary were apparently going to be known in advance. Unfortunately for Eisenhower, the six-month deadline also meant that it was going to be particularly difficult to dodge his subordinates' increasingly insistent requests that he openly commit to an ironclad plan for "K-Day," May 27, 1959.[13]

Initial Planning

In the immediate wake of the November 27 note both sides assumed confrontational stances. For his part, Khrushchev was eager to demonstrate recklessness. On December 3 the Soviet leader launched into a virulent tirade in front of Senator Hubert Humphrey, who was visiting him in Moscow. The United States, Khrushchev warned, must not dare interfere with the transfer of control to the East Germans; in the event of war the Soviet Union was quite ready to deal a devastating blow against the West. The continued Western occupation of Berlin, Khrushchev said, was a "bone in my throat."[14] Upon Eisenhower's return from Augusta a week later several key aides met with the president to discuss Khrushchev's belligerence. Eisenhower admitted during this meeting that his main concern was the freedom of two million Berliners rather than the strategic value of West Berlin; perhaps it had been a mistake to make that outpost a Cold War bastion. But now that the die was cast the United States would not back out on its commitment. He suggested to his advisers that the United States "make it clear that we consider this no minor affair. In order to avoid beginning with the white chips and working up to the blue, we should place them on notice that our whole stack is in this play."[15] In other words, he was telling them, he would wage general thermonuclear war if that became necessary to maintain the West Berliners' freedom.

In the meantime, delegates from NATO nations began to coordinate a unified Berlin strategy. During December and January Dulles tried to persuade edgy NATO allies to accept his view that a unified and steadfast Western position on Berlin would cause the Soviets to back down.[16] During a NATO ministerial meeting on December 17 Dulles specified his position. The "Soviets will not risk war about Berlin," he wrote, and any "threat to devastate Europe if [the] West [is] firm on Berlin is an empty one which ought not to frighten anyone."[17]

Despite Dulles's assurances, however, the British again wanted to raise questions about the wisdom of seriously preparing for thermonuclear war over occupation rights in West Berlin. In their eyes this was hardly less scandalous than readying the missiles to defend Quemoy and Matsu. British ambassador to Washington Harold Caccia let the American Secretary of State know that London opposed taking a hard line on Berlin, suggesting that a heads-of-state summit could serve to soothe Khrushchev. Dulles complained about this "mushy" British position in a January 9 letter to Eisenhower, and again on the 26th. On the military side, the Joint Chiefs reminded their Western counterparts that unless the Soviets did back down there would be war. As JCS Chairman General Twining had put it, during the December 11 meeting, the West had to stop Soviet aggression somewhere. He added,

We must ignore the fear of general war. It is coming anyway. Therefore we should force the issue on a point we think is right and stand on it. Khrushchev is trying to scare people. If he succeeds, we are through.[18]

The NSC began to prepare more formally for "K-Day" in late January. On the 22nd the NSC met to review NSC 5410/1, "U.S. Objectives in the Event of General War with the Soviet Bloc." Though reconciled to Eisenhower's policy, Dulles did want to say that the idea of "victory" in a general nuclear war needed reconsideration. There was, whatever American policy said, a real difference between limited and general war. In response, Eisenhower reiterated his policy. American objectives in the event of general war were simple: to "hit the Russians as hard as we could." There was no need for strategy. The Russians "will have started the war, we will finish it. That is all the policy the President said he had."[19]

The next NSC meeting, on January 29, would deal explicitly with planning on Berlin. The Secretary of State, now seriously ill, wanted to leave his mark on this meeting.[20] In preparation for it he composed a think piece on Berlin. "I am convinced," Dulles stated, "that the striking power of the United States constitutes a genuine and effective deterrent unless the Soviets calculate that there is not the moral courage to use it when necessary." In a January 26 telegram to the American mission in NATO he repeated this sentiment, stating that it was "essential" that the Soviet Union realize that blocking Berlin would risk major war.[21] Going into the January 29 meeting Dulles was solidifying his position: the West must genuinely intend to fight a general war if it wanted to deter the Soviet Union. Bluffing and delay tactics would not suffice, because the Russians would discern the Western moral irresolution. Limited war threats would not work, because, alas, the West did not have the forces. If the Western leaders were not certain in their own minds that they were ready to risk general war over Berlin, then their position vis-à-vis the Soviets would crumble; the temptation to back down as May 27 neared would become irresistible, the Russians would press for more concessions, and all would be lost. The strategy had to be morally sound and rationally credible. This was the way Dulles regarded diplomacy.

All at the January 29 meeting agreed that the United States would not accede to Khrushchev's ultimatum and would fight to preserve a Western presence in Berlin. Dulles proposed provoking a conflict with East German authorities once they were given control over Berlin after May 27. In the meantime, he suggested a "double-barreled" approach, whereby the United States would marshal world and U.N. opinion while proceeding with a military buildup in Germany, so that when the confrontation was at hand the Soviets would be facing a united front of military might and world opinion.[22]

Dulles then noted that the Joint Chiefs had recommended that the

United States prepare for a large-scale war on May 27. Twining defended this approach by arguing that we "make up our minds now as to our sequence of action rather than attempt to address the problem only after we are stopped." Eisenhower responded that the lone American division in Germany "has insufficient capability to do an acceptable job. In the event we resort to force, we will have to conquer the entire German zone."[23] Twining replied that

> The Joint Chiefs of Staff fear that the United States will go half way and then quit. They feel that if we do not carry through with our resolution to risk general war we might as well get out of Europe. . . .
> General Twining pointed out that our policies forbid a limited war in Europe, that we cannot fight the USSR on the ground conventionally, and that if we make up our minds to go through we must be prepared to fight a general nuclear war. To this the President expressed the view that the Soviets will not interfere with direct use of force. . . . Our policy must be to force the Soviets to use military force, after which we are in a position to issue an ultimatum prior to initiation of general war.[24]

As was his style, Eisenhower concluded this meeting by summarizing his own view and expressing it in more official terms. Dulles's plan to provoke a confrontation with the East Germans after May 27, rather than simply commencing armed hostilities, was "generally the best way to start." In the meantime, the United States would explore the possibility of discussing the German question with the Soviets. Finally, "In the event that the Soviets carry through with their threats, we will utilize gradual steps to allow for the breakdown. We will withdraw our ambassador, then break relations and, if necessary, resort to major armed force."[25] Of course, Eisenhower added, all of this depended on a unified NATO front: before any military action on Berlin could begin, he reminded his advisers, it would be necessary to carry "our allies with us."

Following this meeting, the ailing Dulles left for Europe. His first priority was to organize the united Western diplomatic front which, he firmly believed, would force the Russians to back down before May 27. He also brought with him a general military contingency plan from the January 29 meeting in case they did not. Throughout the first half of February the American delegates, led by the Secretary of State, worked to persuade their

NATO allies to reject the Soviet ultimatum and prepare to fight rather than quit Berlin. The question was one of Western moral resolve: "If we in the West were united and willing to take the risk of such general war," Dulles stressed, "the Soviets will withdraw from their present position."[26] While the Secretary of State cajoled his colleagues in Europe Eisenhower reminded his colleagues at home of the consequences of war. Secret estimates over the last four years, he told Twining, "have included the Soviet capability to destroy the United States 100%. This was first based on one-way bomber missions and is now based on the ICBM."[27]

On February 16 the NATO ministers agreed to the American strategy, and proposed that the three Western powers involved in Berlin suggest to the Soviet Union the convening of a four-power Foreign ministers' meeting on Berlin. To encourage the Soviet Union to accept this proposal, Macmillan flew to Moscow on the 21st to appeal to Khrushchev personally. In a volatile speech on the 24th Khrushchev seemed to reject the proposal, stating that only a Head-of-State summit would be suitable, but on March 2 Gromyko handed Thompson a note of acceptance. Macmillan scheduled a visit to the United States around March 20 to secure Eisenhower's approval and then coordinate with him Anglo-American strategy for the proposed ministers' meeting.[28]

With this meeting imminent, Eisenhower's national security advisers thought it was time finally for him to sign on to a specific contingency plan on Berlin; without something concrete, after all, the Western delegates in Geneva would have a hard time persuading the Soviets that they were ready to fight for Berlin. All that Eisenhower's military and diplomatic aides wanted was for him to state that if the Soviets took step A the West would automatically take step B. As acting Secretary of State Christian Herter more delicately put it to Eisenhower, "the need for advance planning was evident."[29]

Herter had become acting Secretary of State because Dulles had been hospitalized. He had been battling with stomach cancer since 1957, and after the lengthy and difficult Western foreign ministers' meetings in February,[30] Dulles came home and then checked into Walter Reed Hospital for good. He would live only two more months.

His illness returned at a pivotal moment. Eisenhower was about to come under vehement attack, from virtually every one of his main foreign policy advisers, for his increasingly obvious attempts to evade "advance planning" on Berlin. Had a healthy Dulles chosen to side openly with Eisenhower's opponents in the spring of 1959 the president might well have found it impossible to continue stonewalling. Without the presence of his imposing Secretary of State, Eisenhower was able to withstand the withering criticism directed his way and continue his strategy of avoiding making any irreversible decision.

Eisenhower Stonewalls

On March 5 the NSC convened a special meeting to establish a formal Berlin contingency plan. The president cautioned that it was important "not to get hysterical." He said that it is "very difficult to work out what constitutes the critical point in the denial of access to Berlin, and what we would do next if that point had been reached." Herter, in response, minced no words: "Are we prepared," he asked, "to use all force necessary to reopen access to Berlin, even at the risk of general war[?]" Eisenhower replied that without unified allied support "he did not see how we could successfully use force in Germany to reopen access to Berlin. . . . The only other solution if our access is stopped would be to decide if we were going to put bombs on Moscow."[31] The meeting ended desultorily, with the last word coming from Allen Dulles, who perceptively noted that "Macmillan's position would be considerably dependent upon the President's position."[32]

Disgruntled participants of the March 5 meeting evidently leaked their displeasure to Congress. The next day Eisenhower, along with the ailing Dulles, who had left the hospital to attend the hearings, Secretary of Defense Neil H. McElroy, and other major advisers, met with key defense lawmakers on Capitol Hill to discuss Berlin. Senator Everett Dirksen pointedly asked Eisenhower to describe "our courses of action in the case of the worst situation." Eisenhower replied that "that this decision will not be easy and that we must see what happens." Lyndon Johnson wondered why, during this tense crisis, the United States was not sending more conventional forces to Europe. Eisenhower replied that current budget requirements forced the United States to rely on nuclear weaponry. He added that "when we reach the acute crisis period, it will be necessary to engage in our rights. . . . the question is whether we have the nerve to push our chips in the pot."[33]

Eisenhower's evasiveness was not lost on some outspoken critics. One blast came from Dean Acheson, who published a scathing article, "Wishing

Won't Hold Berlin," in the March 7 *Saturday Evening Post.* Acheson warned
that the loss of Berlin

> might open the way to the final isolation of the United States in North
> America, not daring to use its thermonuclear weapons unless attacked.
> . . . Germany and all Europe would know that Khrushchev was the
> master of Europe. And we Americans would have shown that we, too,
> knew that Khrushchev was master.[34]

To prevent this outcome Acheson recommended that the United States
mobilize a large conventional army and prepare for conventional war in
Europe. While defeat at the hands of the Soviet army would still be possible,
at least the United States would have demonstrated a willingness to defend
Berlin without initiating nuclear holocaust. For Acheson, as for Dulles, the
crux was to develop a serious plan: casually and indirectly threatening general war was insufficient, "fatally unwise," for it provided no direction for a
local crisis. Precisely what, Acheson demanded, should the United States
do if the Soviets follow through with their ultimatum and turn over control
to the East Germans? "There are those," he warned, "some in high places,
who hope and who seem to believe that somehow we will not have to answer
that question."[35]

Maxwell Taylor added his voice to the chorus of criticism in testimony
before the Senate Armed Services Committee on March 11. Unlike Acheson, Taylor was supposed to be a loyal supporter of official Presidential
policy; his testimony on that difficult day for Eisenhower bordered on political insurrection. Taylor suggested, following Dulles, that the West could
avert a war with the Soviet Union only by being unequivocally resolved to
wage general war. The allies should make "at once," a military probe in
East Germany so as to test the Soviet Union's will to escalate the war.[36] If
the Soviets responded with force then "we must be willing *now* to make up
our respective minds *now* that we will use all force necessary to secure the
lives and safety of these two and a half million Germans to whom we are
committed unalterably in language that cannot be compromised."[37]

While Taylor testified, General Twining sent Secretary McElroy a memorandum that included a Berlin contingency plan adopted by the NSC in
February. The Joint Chiefs, he told McElroy, had to have a "clear United
States position on Berlin." The attached contingency plan "does not face
up to the vital need for decision now that the safety of Berlin is worth running

the risk of general war with the USSR." Twining lamented "the absence of an unqualified assertion of determination to fight for Berlin if all other measures fail." We must, Twining wrote, "be visibly prepared for military conflict growing out of the Berlin situation."[38]

It is highly unlikely that Eisenhower was not aware of, and affected by, these pointed criticisms. That afternoon he met with the press, and was asked point-blank whether he was prepared to "use nuclear war if necessary to defend free Berlin?" He misunderstood (or chose to convolute) the reporter's terminology, but the meaning of his response is clear enough: "Well, I don't know how you could free anything with nuclear weapons."[39] Answering a follow-up question, Eisenhower elaborated in a way that epitomizes his "non-strategy" of early 1959.

> And, I must say, to use that kind of a nuclear war as a general thing looks to me a self-defeating thing for all of us. . . . I don't know what it would do to the world and particularly the Northern Hemisphere; and I don't think anyone else does. But I know it would be quite serious. Therefore, we have got to stand right ready and say, "We will do what is necessary to protect ourselves, but we are never going to back up on our rights and our responsibilities."[40]

Eisenhower thus responded to his subordinates' demands that he clarify his Berlin strategy by publicly issuing an entirely nonsensical statement on that issue, one that did not fail to allude both to the destruction of the Northern Hemisphere and the American commitment to stand "right ready" to unleash such destruction. One can only imagine how this was received by Taylor and Twining, not to mention Dulles; after March 11 the determination of those who wanted to pin Eisenhower down seemed to falter. On the morning of March 17 he met with Herter and his aides to discuss Macmillan's imminent visit. Herter, still game, could not help but bring up the issue of contingency planning for Berlin, reminding Eisenhower that he "expected that in the meeting to be held later in the day this matter would be clarified."

At the outset of the afternoon meeting Herter and McElroy handed to Eisenhower a memorandum on Berlin contingency strategy prepared by the "Berlin Contingency Planning Group," a committee of senior policymakers that the new assistant for National Security Affairs, Gordon Gray, and McElroy set up ad hoc after the March 5 meeting.[41] Their memorandum included a summary of a contingency plan developed by the NSC back in February. This plan contained four alternatives, "in the event of failure of political negotiations": a substantial effort to reopen access to West Berlin on the ground; a similar effort to reopen air access; reprisal against communist targets elsewhere; and, last, "General war measures." At "what point," Herter and McElroy ended the memorandum asking, "should we be prepared to resort to one of the four alternative uses of forces described above?" Herter's objective was to get the president to answer this question.

Eisenhower would not budge. He admitted that if he were on the Soviet side "he could see flaws in the U.S. position." He noted too that the views of Adenauer's West Germany and Macmillan's Great Britain "appear to be diametrically opposed."[42] For some reason the discussion turned to nuclear testing, and Eisenhower had this to say: "[T]he scientists will say that any nuclear war would be disastrous, at least for the Northern Hemisphere. This might point to a suspension of the use of all atomic weapons, around which we have built our forces, and require us to go back to conventional forces."[43]

Eisenhower's critics thus failed, though not for a lack of effort, to get the president to sign on to a concrete contingency plan. When the British Prime Minister arrived on March 19, the United States, and by extension NATO, had yet to decide exactly what the West would do when the Soviet Union followed through on their November 27 ultimatum. That there was no binding strategy was, of course, precisely what Eisenhower had intended. His next task was to get Khrushchev to postpone the ultimatum.

Macmillan's Visit

Prime Minister Harold Macmillan arrived in the States on March 19, checked in with the British embassy, and dined at the White House that evening. The following morning, he and his Foreign Secretary Selwyn Lloyd met with Eisenhower and Dulles in the latter's room at Walter Reed Hospital to discuss allied strategy on Berlin. The British plan was to talk the Americans out of their confrontational stance, an objective with which Eisenhower was quietly sympathetic.

In this early meeting Macmillan foresaw four outcomes of the Berlin Crisis. The Soviets would give in, the West would give in, the two sides would successfully negotiate the Berlin question, or there would be war. If the last were to occur, Macmillan noted that he would need time to "remove all the young children from the United Kingdom to Canada so as to keep their stock alive as against the total devastation of nuclear war." Taken aback, Dulles retorted that "there is not going to be the war of which the Prime Minister spoke. . . . What is the use," he added, "of our spending $40 billion a year or more to create deterrent power if whenever the Soviets threaten us . . . we have to buy peace by compromise."[44] That afternoon Eisenhower and Macmillan left Dulles at the hospital and went to Camp David. In an initial session there Macmillan proposed a summit meeting to defuse the Berlin crisis, an idea Eisenhower rejected.

Following the formal afternoon sessions Macmillan and Eisenhower went for a drive. The subject of their conversations during the drive has not been revealed.[45] But that night the two sides met again and an "exceedingly emotional" Macmillan unleashed the British view in full force. He warned that stubbornness had led to World War I — "the war which nobody wanted." He "could not take his people into war without trying the summit first." If that were to fail, Macmillan reiterated, it would be necessary to disperse Anglo-Saxon stock, for "eight bombs" could destroy most of England. "Throughout the discussion," noted the meeting's secretary, Livingston Merchant, "he kept repeating this reference to eight bombs."[46]

Eisenhower reminded Macmillan that though the United States itself would lose 67 million people in an all-out war, it was nevertheless necessary to stand firm. He would refuse to be "dragooned to a Summit meeting." But the British Prime Minister had made his point. Relenting, Eisenhower said "that if there was even slight progress" at a Foreign Ministers meeting that he would meet Khrushchev.[47] Agreed in tacit principle, Macmillan and Eisenhower concluded their talks and the British delegation left on March 23. On the 26th Thompson handed Gromyko a formal Western reply to a Soviet note of March 2, proposing an immediate four-power foreign ministers meeting and then a summit "as soon as developments" justified one. Macmillan had gotten what he came to Washington for.[48]

Eisenhower had to explain this concession to his military advisers. Following several preliminary meetings, on April 23 the NSC met to formulate yet another "final" Berlin strategy. Gordon Gray, unaware that his earnest contingency planning was no longer desired, presented the new strategy to Eisenhower: if the communists closed off West Berlin, the West would re-open air access, by force if necessary, escalate the war by launching reprisals against communists in other areas, and, if all else had failed, proceed with "General War Measures." Eisenhower brusquely replied that it would not do to develop "rigid plans of action"; any move on Berlin would "have to be played by ear." He added that he was assuming that "Khrushchev had really meant what he said when he stated that he was not going to upset the applecart once negotiations over Berlin had been started between the West and the USSR." Only three possibilities remained, Eisenhower, sounding like Macmillan, concluded. There would be "some kind of deal through negotiations . . . to maintain the status quo for three or four years"; the Soviets would back down; or there would be war, and once that began "there are really no limits that can be set to the use of force."[49]

"Terminating the Farce"

Eisenhower was telling his national security assistant that there was no longer really any reason to worry about developing a military contingency plan on Berlin.[50] Either there would be a peaceful resolution to the crisis, or there would be a total war. Eisenhower preferred the former, and by accepting Macmillan's proposal to invite a Soviet delegation to a foreign ministers' meeting he was indeed "negotiating under ultimatum." The commencement of the talks on May 11 turned this concession into a tangible diplomatic reality: the Berlin crisis seemed to be resolved. The Western powers had put aside their determination not to negotiate under ultimatum, and the Soviets had responded by allowing the deadline to pass without event. Any possibility that the Soviets might have revived the specter of May 27 was scotched by Dulles, who managed to conjure one of the better ironies of the Cold War by dying on the 24th and being buried on "K-Day." The conferees in Geneva adjourned to attend the funeral, and it would have taken more *Realpolitik* than Soviet Foreign Minister Andrei Gromyko possessed to renew talk of ultimatum and war while Dulles's body was being lowered into the ground. All that remained was for Eisenhower to acquiesce to the "inevitable"[51] summit, where the two sides could formalize a grand compromise on Berlin that would allow everyone to save face. The problem was that Eisenhower had conspicuously declared in the earlier days of the crisis his unwillingness to attend a summit if the foreign ministers had not accomplished something tangible beforehand. Moreover, since the British had been skillfully cultivating the common perception that a summit was "inevitable," nothing substantial was going to issue from Geneva. Why haggle to produce some minor accomplishment when the real business would be taken care of at the summit?

Eisenhower had painted himself into another corner, and this time the

only solution was to back down from his oft-stated principle. At first he
refused to do so. In a June 15 letter to Khrushchev, he reiterated his condition that the foreign ministers must "reach positive agreements" before
any summit. Alarmed, Macmillan immediately urged Eisenhower to con-
vene an "informal" heads-of-state meeting, and hinted that if Eisenhower
was going to stall, Macmillan himself might issue such an invitation. Eisenhower saw through this ploy and refused to go along with it; on the 17th
Khrushchev reminded Eisenhower that "it is impossible endlessly to drag
out a peaceful settlement with Germany and to preserve the occupation
regime in Berlin." If the foreign ministers could not proceed on this question, then "a Summit meeting will become even more urgently necessary."[52]
With the British and the Soviets now publicly advocating a summit, the
harried delegates in Geneva had not even a nominal reason to proceed, and
so agreed on June 19 to recess the talks until July 13.

During the recess the British and the Soviets tacitly teamed up to persuade Eisenhower to drop his condition. Macmillan, who may not be accused of inconsistency during the Berlin Crisis, once again suggested to the
president that the West offer the Russians an "interim settlement" on Berlin
whereby the duration of Western occupation could be negotiated at a later
date. Again he reminded Eisenhower that the British were averse to fighting
an "even more horrible war" than World War II "to defend the liberties of
people who have tried to destroy us twice in this century."[53]

Surprised that Eisenhower was not quickly seizing such an obvious opportunity to finesse the Berlin Crisis, Khrushchev was growing impatient
and bellicose.[54] On June 25 he told former Ambassador to the Soviet Union
Averell Harriman that "we are determined to liquidate your rights in West
Berlin. . . . If you want to perpetuate or prolong your rights, this means war."
Using rhetoric unequaled in the public record of the Cold War, Khrushchev
reminded Harriman that in a European war "we may die but the rockets
will fly automatically." Berlin would be the first to fall: "Your generals talk
of tanks and guns defending your Berlin position," Khrushchev noted. "They
would burn."[55]

Later that day Eisenhower showed Herter Khrushchev's warnings, wondering whether they were simply designed to provoke a summit, or if they
perhaps reflected Khrushchev's genuine mood. Herter reminded Eisenhower that confronting the Soviets was no longer an option, at least for the
moment, because the West had agreed not to initiate hostilities without
complete allied unity, and the British would never go along with war unless

and until the "inevitable" summit had been tried.[56] There was no alternative but for Eisenhower to agree, and in light of Khrushchev's recent rhetoric and British impatience it could not be forestalled for long.

In July Eisenhower worked it out. On the 1st he told Herter that the West should indicate to the Soviets a new willingness to negotiate an interim arrangement regarding West Berlin. The main issues of dispute—the date of Western departure and the number of Western troops to remain in Berlin afterwards—could be left, as if they were technicalities, "to fill in at a Summit conference." On July 9 Eisenhower, in a meeting with Herter, brought up the idea of staging an informal summit by inviting Khrushchev to the United States. "The key point," Herter emphasized, "is to find a way of doing it without appearing to be kowtowing or weakening." The next day Eisenhower discussed this idea with Herter, Robert Murphy, and other State Department officials, and directed Murphy to broach the informal summit proposal with Frol Kozlov, a Soviet deputy premier visiting Washington.[57] Murphy did so on July 12.

Eisenhower wanted to prevent his invitation from appearing to be what it was: another instance of his backing down from a stated conviction. Perhaps he was interested in appearing resolute to future historians; perhaps he believed that a more candid retreat would reveal his fear of nuclear war and thus endanger American security. For whichever reason, in late July he decided to take unusual, even bizarre steps to pretend that he had not abandoned his condition of achievements in Geneva before attending a summit.

On July 21 Herter sent Eisenhower a telegram from Geneva assuring the president that there was no chance for even a token accomplishment to come from the conference there. That evening Eisenhower wrote back to Herter, agreeing that the Geneva talks were obviously going nowhere and suggesting that it was time to consider "terminating the farce." He also told Herter that he had met with Soviet ambassador Menshikov and reiterated to the Russian his firm conviction there must be progress at Geneva before any summit meeting.[58]

The next day Eisenhower conducted an unusual discussion, as his own son John Eisenhower recorded it, with Vice-President Richard M. Nixon, who was leaving for an extended visit to the Soviet Union. Nixon asked about the president's plans for a summit. Eisenhower first said that his original plan had been to meet with Khrushchev in order to prod the ministers at Geneva, but "this had been discouraged by his advisors."[59] Nixon then wanted to know what would actually constitute "progress" at Geneva. Ei-

senhower said that Western "rights" must be assured, "plus the setting up
of machinery to study the overall problem." This "machinery," he explained
to a doubtless mystified Nixon, "could be amorphous in nature." Eisenhower finally admitted to his Vice President that "he would like to find soon
a reasonable excuse for a Summit Meeting."[60]

That afternoon Eisenhower met with Murphy and Undersecretary of
State Douglas Dillon. Dillon commented that Khrushchev's visit was of
course contingent upon progress at Geneva. Despite what he had told Nixon
that morning, Eisenhower replied that was an "automatic" condition because it would pave the way for a formal summit meeting; hence Khrushchev
could not come until the conditions for a summit were met.[61]

The veteran diplomat Murphy, head of the Berlin ad-hoc group and a
long-time aide and confidant of the president, then announced that he had
not understood this distinction, and had instead given Khrushchev an unqualified invitation! An "extremely disturbed" Eisenhower castigated Murphy for his presumption, complaining, Claude Rains-like, about the new
predicament in which he now found himself, but then resignedly acknowledged that "it all boiled down to the fact that in light of the unqualified
invitation that had been given, he would have to pay the penalty and hold
a meeting he despised." He then directed Murphy and Dillon to draft a new
policy statement: Khrushchev could come without any progress at Geneva.[62]

Eisenhower engaged in this theater because he was determined to give
Khrushchev the summit they both wanted without appearing to have dis-
carded his principles. Either he and Murphy had already agreed to engineer
the scene for Dillon's (and posterity's) benefit;[63] or, perhaps after Khrushchev's outburst to Harriman, Eisenhower privately decided to abandon his
condition, manipulate Murphy into issuing an unconditional invitation, and
then make a scapegoat out of his unwitting aide.

This bizarre epilogue to the Berlin crisis captures the unusual nature of
thermonuclear confrontations. When statesmen on both sides of a crisis
personally believe that the costs of war far outweigh the benefits of victory,
then the important diplomacy becomes less a matter of engaging in substantive negotiations over traditional objectives and more one of finding ways
for both sides to save face. As petty as Eisenhower's attempts to appear un-
yielding were, they were necessary for him to achieve the objective — finding
a compromise over Berlin without undergoing obvious humiliation — that
he had pursued since November. The foreign minister talks that summer
could have never existed and the history of the Berlin crisis might be sub-

stantially the same as it is. Had Eisenhower not figured out a superficially honorable and speedy way to get out of his solemn commitment, however, it is easy to envision Khrushchev growing increasingly impatient, angrily canceling his offer to visit that fall, and reactivating the ultimatum.

Berlin and Eisenhower's Strategy to Evade Nuclear War

Eisenhower's clever and resolute steering of American diplomacy toward compromise on Berlin played a decisive role in keeping that crisis peaceful. But his diplomatic skills were not employed in a vacuum. The president was able to stonewall the Berlin planners pleading with him to sign on to a contingency plan, and to latch on to the British plan to force a summit, because he had eliminated from American military policy the option of waging limited war to defend Berlin. By placing before his advisers no options other than conciliation or thermonuclear annihilation, he could belittle contingency plans as unrealistic and ill-suited, foment British anxiety over the notion of irradiating the Isles so as to defend the erstwhile capital of the Third Reich, and feasibly insist that no military action of any kind be taken without his personal approval. Had the advocates of flexible response been successful back in 1956 and 1957, the United States would have had in place a strategy for fighting limited war in Europe and, presumably, the forces there to make that strategy viable. In that event it is difficult to imagine Eisenhower successfully steering the United States away from war. Writing a contingency plan would have been simple—Eisenhower's efforts to evade signing on to it, implausible. British panic about "eight bombs" could have been met with reassurances that current planning limited war to Central Europe. The president's demands to approve of any military action would have seemed odd, since the initiation of hostilities in a limited war context would not supposedly have been so grave.

If the political scientist Richard Neustadt is correct, an American president cannot simply issue commands and expect obedience. To attain actual power in the "sphere of executive relations," Neustadt writes, a president needs to coerce people into doing what he wants them to do.[64] To avoid nuclear war, Eisenhower wanted to make a deal on Berlin. But every one of his major national security advisers opposed compromise, preferring to force the Soviets to back down by pushing the crisis toward war. To make his task more difficult, Eisenhower could not simply state what he wanted, as if the debate were on the minimum wage or a highway program; the president was not going to say openly that he wanted to back down on Berlin, so he had to pretend that he also wanted to stare down the Russians. By using basic policy as a means of giving his advisers no reasonable military options, and then by quietly attaching his Berlin diplomacy to that of the conciliatory British, Eisenhower was able to realize his objective.

7   Intermission, July 1959–January 1961

The scheduling of Khrushchev's visit to the United States of course doomed the Geneva talks, which had been persisting only in deference to Eisenhower and his now-discarded principles. On August 5 the delegates adjourned, having produced no tangible agreements at all. On that day Eisenhower announced "with anything but enthusiasm," as he later portrayed it,[1] that the talks had failed and Khrushchev would be visiting the United States. The August 5 announcement signified the official end of the 1958–59 Berlin Crisis; Nikita Khrushchev came to America in September.

The August 5 announcement also signified, as it happened, an end to the turmoil over nuclear policy that began with the Soviet thermonuclear test in 1953. For six years the question of how the United States should regard thermonuclear war had divided the Eisenhower administration: in NSC and White House discussions, in the annual making of basic national security policy, and finally during the Berlin crisis of 1958–59, Eisenhower struggled to enforce his decision, codified in NSC-5707/8, that general war against the Soviet Union would invariably mean all-out thermonuclear warfare, which in turn was unsuitable for anything other than a final, world-destroying retaliation. With the crisis now over, and with his main adversary in this struggle — John Foster Dulles — gone, Eisenhower and his stark military policy had survived its two greatest challenges.

Eisenhower's aides, in particular his new national security adviser, Gordon Gray, did try to revive the case for limited war in the summer of 1959. The president indulged Gray, perhaps to avoid the political risks of appearing too dogmatic on the volatile question of thermonuclear war as the 1960 election neared. He did not, however, alter the basic military policy he had created in 1957 and put to use during the Berlin Crisis. It was this policy that he would pass on to the incoming administration in January 1961.

Basic Policy After the Fact

While Eisenhower worked in the summer of 1959 to avoid a showdown over Berlin, his main national security aides sat down for the final time to write a basic national security policy. Critics of his policy, most notably Gray and the new Secretary of State, Christian Herter, took their mission seriously and tried once again to talk Eisenhower out of his all-or-nothing policy. In a July 2, 1959 conference with the president, Herter wondered why the initiation of "any hostilities involving the U.S. and U.S.S.R. forces would automatically be a situation of general war," and grilled Eisenhower on the sticky question of exactly how he would distinguish between limited and general warfare.[2] Herter, the Joint Chiefs, Dillon, and Gray all lobbied to have NSC 5801/1's paragraph 12-a, the text incorporating Eisenhower's demand that the United States now place "main, but not sole, reliance on nuclear weapons," replaced with one endorsing the possibility of limited war against the Russians.

Debate on this question went on throughout July. It exasperated Eisenhower. Though willing to allow his subordinates to raise this issue for the sixth straight year, he was unable to see why his colleagues did not understand that he, the maker of American security policy, was happy with it just as it was. "My guess is that paragraph 12-a represents the President's thinking," wrote Policy Planning Staff director Howard Furnas, "and was perhaps drafted by Gray under instructions." Eisenhower, according to Furnas, had told Dillon that this paragraph "was what the President intended, and that he would not want a big campaign of oppostion built up against it." Yet his advisers continued to raise objections. Eisenhower wished he could find a better way to "communicate to everyone his clear intention."[3]

Stubbornly, critics of paragraph 12-a, especially Herter, would not relent. To appease them, Eisenhower permitted Gray to add this new sentence: "Planning should contemplate situations short of general war where the use of nuclear weapons would manifestly not be military necessary nor appropriate to the accomplishment of national objectives, particularly in those areas where main Communist power will not be brought to bear."[4]

Even though the subordinate clause restates Eisenhower's position that limited war is possible only in areas away from "main Communist power," it is true that this passage moves slightly away from Eisenhower's all-or-nothing policy. This would have been important had Eisenhower, after an intense NSC debate in say 1956 or 1957, allowed Dulles to impose the new text. But it was now the summer of 1959. Eisenhower had utilized his all-or-nothing policy in the Berlin crisis, which was coming to an end. His authority on the question of when and how the United States would wage war was now unquestioned, whatever basic policy said. Any operational effects of Gray's semantic change, moreover, would occur well after Eisenhower had left office and a new administration would be doing as it chose. In case any of this was in doubt, Eisenhower made a point of inserting a footnote into the new text, which stated that he approved of paragraph 12-a only "with the understanding that it is not to be interpreted as a change in policy but rather as a clarification of existing policy with respect to the use of nuclear weapons and the requirement for maintaining balanced forces."[5]

The writing of NSC-5906/1 was an exercise in indulgence. Eisenhower allowed Gray, Herter, and the Chiefs to add the new sentence to avoid a showdown, since there was no longer any important reason not to avoid one. It seems needless to say that had another crisis broken out, the new sentence would have had no effect on Eisenhower's decisionmaking. The NSC wrote no new BNSP for 1960; the obvious reason for this was that the new adminstration would be making its own policy, but one suspects also that Eisenhower saw no reason to endure another season of his advisers' fruitless complaining.

The declaratory military policy Eisenhower had put into place by 1958, therefore, was the one that the incoming administration would be inheriting in January 1961. This policy, as we have seen, contained three elements. The first was the American nuclear deterrent. Heeding Eisenhower's 1955 directive to make the production of ballistic missiles a national priority, the Pentagon spent billions of dollars over the ensuing five years on several new programs, including the burgeoning "Minuteman" ICBM and "Polaris" submarine-launched ballistic missile (SLBM). Eisenhower approved of a Pentagon plan to combine, with these missile programs, a large deployment of long-range manned bombers loaded with thermonuclear gravity bombs. Bombers served to bolster the deterrent in its early years while the missile arsenal was still small, and they also could be recalled once sent on their way. ICBMs, SLBMs, and the manned bombers then formed the "triad" that would underpin America's nuclear deterrent force for the next three decades.[6] The second element was the signficant downgrading of America's conventional force capabilities. Non-nuclear forces would not play a serious role in any war with the Soviet Union; nuclear missiles and bombers would now be taking care of that mission. Instead, American conventional forces would serve two, lesser, purposes: to provide a "tripwire" in Europe and east Asia, and to put out "brushfire" wars in more peripheral areas before they spread. As basic policy stated, the explicit purpose of American conventional forces was to prevent limited wars from expanding into general war. By 1959 and 1960 the budgets for the Army and Navy were reduced considerably, with the money being sent to the Air Force's Strategic Air Command.[7]

The final element, the policy with which we have been dealing here, was Eisenhower's elimination of the idea that war with the Soviet Union could be limited. By far the most controversial of the three, Eisenhower's policy had by 1960 worked its way into actual military planning, most notably in the form of the Single Integrated Operational Plan (SIOP), a new command system developed by SAC and the Defense Department designed to facilitate the delivery of thermonuclear weapons to enemy targets once a president gave the order. The SIOP was in complete accord with Eisenhower's all-or-nothing approach to thermonuclear weaponry. In the event of general war, the SIOP gave the president the ability to bypass traditional layers of command and directly launch just about every nuclear warhead the United States owned. A president who executed the SIOP would have little flexibility or room for reconsideration: a blunt instrument, it was meant to be used once. That, of course, was the president's intention: anyone advocating the initiation of war with the Soviet Union, while Eisenhower's policy was still in effect, would have to make the case that it justified putting the SIOP into operation—and that it justified absorbing the inevitable, all-out Soviet retaliation. This was something Kennedy and his advisers would discover in their first year.[8]

Astutely, strategists in the Kennedy campaign were able to identify and attack each of the three elements of Eisenhower's military policy. Employing the political rhetoric that Senator Kennedy had used effectively in the wake of Sputnik, they complained that Republican inattention to the American deterrent had created a "missile gap" between U.S. and Soviet forces. If the United States did not take immediate and drastic measures, the USSR would soon be able to overcome the American deterrent and dictate terms. Kennedy strategists also accused the president of neglectfully allowing America's conventional forces to deteriorate, a decision for which General Maxwell Taylor hoped to make Eisenhower pay.

Finally, they attacked Eisenhower for his curious elimination of American limited war strategies. This latter problem received special attention from a group of scholars and other military writers[9] who supported and advised the Kennedy campaign; these strategists fashioned an alternative for Kennedy which differed in no substantial way from the policy Dulles had been recommending since 1954.

Kennedy's Critique of Eisenhower's All-or-Nothing Policy

Several critics of Eisenhower administration military policy had voiced their dissent early on, among them the retired Army General James Gavin, and civilian strategists such as Bernard Brodie, William Kaufmann, Henry Rowen, and Herman Kahn. The latter three worked for the RAND corporation, a California think-tank devoted to analyzing military problems. RAND had made Eisenhower's all-or-nothing nuclear policy the great focus of its studies in the latter part of the 1950s.[10] Probably the two most important critics of Eisenhower, however, were the Harvard political scientist Henry Kissinger and General Maxwell Taylor, who had retired from the Army in 1959. Both Kissinger and Taylor ended up working for the Kennedy administration, no doubt due in part to their trenchant critique of Eisenhower's military policy, and their advocacy of a clear alternative, "flexible response," that proved attractive in contrast.

"Does the nuclear age permit the establishment of a relationship between force and policy?"[11] This was the question Henry Kissinger meant to answer in his 1957 book *Nuclear Weapons and Foreign Policy*. In 1957 Kissinger's mission was clear. The Eisenhower administration, he believed, had shirked its obligation to implement a rational military policy by using the awesome technology of the nuclear age, together with the excuse of fiscal conservatism, to avoid dealing with the difficult task of creating a real nuclear strategy. Kissinger would propose a new strategy for the future, one that dealt with realities and could be applied to objectives, one that could "create alternatives less cataclysmic than a thermonuclear holocaust."[12]

Kissinger wanted to replace Eisenhower's massive retaliation with a new strategy of flexibility, one that would require decisionmakers to forget the taboo of nuclear weapons and become willing to think of nuclear war as an extension of policy. The problem, Kissinger wrote, was that "we have thought of war more in moral than in strategic terms."[13] Americans needed to lose their fondness for righteous wars and adopt a more dispassionate approach, using warfare here, diplomacy there, in order to achieve realistic objectives that grew out of national interests. A more flexible approach to war would harmonize the relationship between politics and armed force.

Instead of clumsily responding to communist aggressions by threatening all-out war, Kissinger continued, America needed to take an activist approach to the Cold War by invigorating its forces in Europe, designing tactical nuclear war strategies that could respond quickly to aggression, as in the case of Korea, and at the same time dangle the carrot of eased tensions as a reward for acquiescence. By using America's military forces for real objectives rather than reaction, the United States could put the Soviet Union on the defensive and eventually prevail in the Cold War rather than co-exist with a nation determined to dominate the world.

In chapter six of his book Kissinger laid out his argument for limited war. His first point was that Americans had to adjust their mentality to new technological realities. Just as automobile manufacturers had figured out not to design motorcars along the lines of the horse-drawn carriage, military decisionmakers had to modify their "design" of warfare to conform to the nuclear age. "Yet the dilemma of nuclear war is with us not by choice," Kissinger emphasized, "but because of the facts of modern technology."[14] His second point stressed that limited war, unlike the total wars of recent history, was a process, a game with tacit rules, an extension of diplomacy. During hostilities Americans had to "convey to our opponent what we understand by limited nuclear war, or at least what limitations we are willing to observe."[15] Kissinger's third point spoke to the paradox of limited war, the one which, unbeknownst to him, was driving Eisenhower's all-or-nothing military policy. The paradox grew out of this question: how would a nation surrender when it still retained powerful weapons, weapons that could obliterate its enemy instantaneously? Kissinger had an answer to this central problem. If neither side would surrender with weapons in hand, he argued, then a limited war strategy would lead either to a stalemate or to an all-out war — in other words, to the situation created by Eisenhower's NSC-5707/8 policy. But, according to Kissinger, this scenario begged the question: "A power which is prepared to unleash an all-out holocaust in order to escape defeat in a limited nuclear war," he wrote, would hardly be more restrained by an initial distinction between conventional and nuclear weapons."[16]

Kissinger was, in effect, trying to refute Eisenhower's most important argument, the one he had made with such force in the February 1956 NSC discussion and his meeting with Taylor. The president had declared that it was "fatuous" to believe that a limited war with the Soviet Union was possible, because no nation in a modern, total war would surrender with devastating weapons in hand. Kissinger replied to this logic by saying that a nation brutal enough to blow up the world rather than accept defeat in a limited nuclear war would also blow up the world if a conventional war was leading to the same kind of political defeat. Therefore it was fallacious to argue that limited nuclear war strategies would make all-out nuclear war more likely. Eisenhower, however, was one step ahead of Kissinger. He was not simply opposed to limited nuclear war: he was opposed to limited war itself. By eliminating all *conventional* means of waging war against the Soviet Union, the president had in effect already foreseen Kissinger's objection. Eisenhower, in order to avoid war with the Soviets altogether, wanted his advisers to believe that he was "prepared to unleash an all-out holocaust" to escape defeat in a conventional war, much less a limited nuclear one. But Kissinger had no way of knowing this.

One who might have had a better grasp of Eisenhower's real intentions was Maxwell Taylor. Taylor had had the tense meeting with the president back in 1956, and had given a speech in the summer of 1958 spelling out more clearly his desire to see a flexible military policy that provided a central role for conventional forces. And he had given the insubordinate testimony to Congress during the Berlin Crisis. This record of criticism suggests that Taylor had an inkling of what Eisenhower was up to, and in any case he knew quite well, as Kissinger did not, that Eisenhower's policies were directed toward the elimination of limited war itself, not limited nuclear war.

Immediately upon Taylor's departure from government he published a best-selling book, *The Uncertain Trumpet*. In this work Taylor got at the weakness of Eisenhower's policy more acutely than did Kissinger, and in calling his alternative policy "flexible response" he coined a phrase that Kennedy would adopt in the upcoming election. Taylor advanced the familiar argument that the threat of nuclear war had become incredible, except as a deterrent to an all-out attack on the United States or NATO. Thus the Soviet Union could feel free to move against lesser objectives—like West Berlin—without having to fear American retaliation. To avoid being overwhelmed by a series of such moves, the United States needed to develop a comprehensive new strategy based upon a vast expansion of conventional forces—and a much higher defense budget.

Taylor tried to deal with the argument Eisenhower had always used in his rejection of Taylor's pleas for more money. There "are still voices," he suggested, in a not-so-subtle allusion,

> who assert the impossibility of having a limited war in the NATO area. Such an assertion means that any collision of patrols over, say, Berlin would automatically result in general atomic war. It offers no alternative other than reciprocal suicide or retreat in the face of the superiority of Soviet forces.[17]

Like Kissinger, however, Taylor danced around Eisenhower's central point. He argued that the United States should use tactical nuclear weapons "where their use would be to our national interest" while avoiding general war, which would produce "no real victory." Yet he never said when the use of tactical nuclear weapons would stop being "in the national interest."[18] If that point would be, presumably, somewhere short of general war, then was the United States to surrender before general war commenced?

Flexible response had a fundamental flaw that Eisenhower had discerned long before Kissinger or Taylor put pen to paper. It presumed that American military and political decisionmakers would be able to surrender to the Soviet Union if it came to that or to escalation to a general war, and Eisenhower believed that this was not a realistic presumption. He was sure that the Soviet Union, and probably the United States as well, would be unable to resist the fierce temptation to launch its full arsenal once a war had begun, in the desperate hope that such an attack might destroy the other side's ability to counterattack. Indeed, since both sides recognized this temptation, their determination to get in the first punch would be that much more firm. This was why many of his military advisers, above all Twining, spoke so often of pre-emptive attack.

But flexible response contained an attractive feature that, on the surface, made it look so much more sensible than the Eisenhower policy — its provision of an alternative in the event of any Cold War crisis other than holocaust or humiliation. This was alluring to a presidential candidate hoping to portray himself as a vigorous leader determined to address problems rather than ignore them, and as early as 1958 Kennedy began to use the arguments put forth by the new strategists. Eisenhower's policy of mutual destruction was, in Kennedy's view, defeatist: it gave the side willing to take chances every advantage. Showing off his erudition in an August 1958 Senate speech, Kennedy said that we have developed what Henry Kissinger had called a Maginot-line mentality—a dependence upon a strategy which may collapse or may never be used, but which prevents the consideration of any alternative. When that prop is gone, the alternative seems to many to be inaction and acceptance of the inevitability of defeat. After all, once the Soviets have the power to destroy us, we have no way of absolutely preventing them from doing so. But every nation, whatever its status, needs a strategy. Some courses of action are always preferable to others; but there are alternatives to all-out war or inaction.[19]

A year later Kennedy reiterated this point, lamenting that a choice between "world devastation or submission" not only recklessly endangered American security, but also "leaves the initiative in the hands of our enemies." His argument was clear: Eisenhower's manifestly dangerous nuclear policy was a result of, above all, laziness. His new adminstration would use a vigorous strategy—one senses that exactly which kind of strategy it should be was a less important matter—to approach the Cold War.[20]

Eisenhower's Response

Eisenhower's response to Kennedy's criticisms was muted. He did deny that a missile gap existed, and he defended the condition of America's conventional forces. But on the question of whether it made sense to try to wage limited war against the Soviet Union, the dilemma that had provoked so many rancorous debates within his administration. Eisenhower was quiet. He declined to stand up for this element of his military policy, allowing the Kennedy campaign's attacks on the issue to go unanswered. It is hard to know whether his silence played a decisive part in Kennedy's victory in November; the votes of Cook County's dead may have been more important. But what one can say is that the margin of Kennedy's victory was so slim that Nixon could have used all the help he could get.

What can explain Eisenhower's silence? The nuclear danger facing the United States in 1960 was still acute. An American president could try to end it by seeking international accord, but Eisenhower, poised perhaps like no other president in the century to pursue a bold course of peace, chose to end his career anticlimactically. Why? Mundane interests do not seem to provide clues: there were no apparent economic costs in reducing tensions with the Soviet Union; one cannot imagine that Eisenhower contrived a dangerous situation at the end of his reign in the hopes that it would unravel a future Democratic administration.

The answer to this riddle seems to lie in Eisenhower's personal approach to policy, and his negative approach to politics. He had attained his objective of avoiding war with the Soviet Union by engaging in a form of personal administration. Eisenhower had contrived an atmosphere in which he, and only he, would be able to resist the demands of military men and hard-line diplomats that the United States back down no further. Only he knew what he was doing, what his real purpose was—no one could fill in for him. Officially, both the writing of nuclear policy and the decisionmaking during the 1958–59 Berlin crisis incorported the efforts of dozens of American planners, negotiators, and soldiers. Effectively, both endeavors were undertaken by the president himself, with aides from Dulles on down simply accomplices.

Eisenhower's inclination to pursue negative rather than positive objectives stemmed from his formative experience during World War II. His orders were merely to drive the Germans out of France, to restore the status quo ante, a mission to which he steadfastly held in the face of more aggressive types such as Montgomery and Patton. This experience played a major part in forming his view of political ends. His ideology, so to speak, was *defensive*.[21] Others could try to perfect society; he would work to make sure it survived for another day. This was how he had approached politics since taking command of Allied forces in Europe, and it was how he ended his last days in office.

Eisenhower's modesty during the last year of his term was certainly understandable, but with the coming of a new administration in January 1961 it was also dangerous. By eschewing improved relations with Khrushchev and leaving nuclear policy as it was, Eisenhower was putting Kennedy in an extremely difficult situation. None of the real political disputes over Berlin was actually resolved during the 1958–59 crisis, and it was obvious to many that Khrushchev would simply revive the crisis once Eisenhower was gone. Moreover, Eisenhower bequeathed to his successor a military policy that would give him no option in the event of war over Berlin other than all-out nuclear war, and a force posture—the SIOP—which conformed utterly to this policy. Thus John F. Kennedy entered office in January 1961 to find a Berlin crisis imminent, a policy to defend the city only with general war, and an operational plan that made waging a general war a simple matter of launching the entire American nuclear arsenal at once.

Yet Eisenhower was not entirely indifferent to this awful legacy, and in the records of his last year in office one can find a few glimmers of anguish. One warning came of course in his famous farewell address, a radical statement that ought to have given his most cynical critics pause.[22] Every study of Eisenhower has its own interpretation of this address, and the conventional one—that the manic fear-mongering after Sputnik prompted Eisenhower to identify a "military-industrial complex" in America, one which would quash American freedom if not stopped—remains the most persuasive. Yet Eisenhower's concerns about the power of the American military may also have stemmed from his experience during the Berlin crisis. For it was all he could do to keep his military advisers' intensive, almost inexorable demands for pushing the crisis toward war in check, and that was after having installed a military policy designed to do just that. How would a less capable leader, and one who did not command his considerable authority in military circles, have fared in his place?

On May 10, 1960, nine days after the downing of an American U-2 spy plane and a few days before the Paris Summit was to begin, Khrushchev warned that continued American flights over the Soviet Union "might lead to war." Herter presented Eisenhower with a draft statement of response, warning Khrushchev that Soviet belligerence could provoke a NATO response in Berlin. Eisenhower responded to Herter's proposal not by belittling the possibility of limited war over Berlin, or by taking the familiar, procrastinating tack of saying that it would be impossible to know what to do ahead of time. Instead, "the President read through the statement, suggesting changes and additions. In particular, he wanted to say that the use of force or threat of force would lead to such serious consequences in the Berlin situation that none of the participants should even think of it."[23]

Part 3

Aftershock

8   Berlin Looms Again, January–July 1961

John F. Kennedy took over the White House from Eisenhower on January 20, 1961. Traditional studies of his administration's ensuing military policy have tended to focus on the urgent efforts of Secretary of Defense Robert S. McNamara and several defense intellectuals on his staff to reinvigorate an American national security policy left stagnant and dangerous by their predecessors. Agreed that their task was to move away from Eisenhower's static policy of massive retaliation, these leaders devised and implemented a dynamic new policy, flexible response, which brought the concept of limited war back to White House decisionmaking and U.S. military operational planning.[1]

To their dismay, Kennedy and his advisers were unable to implement the new policy until 1962.[2] This was because the likelihood of an imminent crisis over Berlin forced them to focus on immediate planning, and on the prospect of a war in Europe to be fought with the weapons and strategies left to them by Dwight D. Eisenhower. From January to June Kennedy and his advisers engaged in a messy struggle to develop a policy on Berlin. Khrushchev's ultimatum in June, and then his decision to build a wall around West Berlin in August, however, forced them to make decisions before they were ready. From August through October, especially, Kennedy's civilian and military advisers struggled over the question of limited war with an intensity that made the battles between Dulles and Eisenhower seem mild. But the latter's strategy would prevail.

Disorganization for the Inevitable Crisis

Due to circumstances largely beyond his control, Kennedy walked into an exceedingly difficult situation on Berlin. Eisenhower's decisions to avoid military confrontation over Berlin but then to eschew further negotiations with Khrushchev had left everything up in the air. The city remained in limbo, divided into World War II occupation sectors that even Eisenhower had admitted were "abnormal."[3] Moreover, Berlin lay in the middle of a nation, East Germany, which the West had refused to recognize formally, even as informal contacts increased. And the glamour of working-class progress had begun to wear thin among many educated East Germans, many of whom were so shaken by the conflict in 1959 that they crossed into West Berlin and asked for asylum. Seeing the cream of his country flee to the West, and resenting also the demeaning task of providing Western access across East German territory into West Berlin, the East German leader Walter Ulbricht was insisting in 1961 that Khrushchev put an end to the capitalist enclave.[4]

Because Eisenhower had managed the 1959 crisis by executing war-avoiding maneuvers rather than articulating and adhering to a common Western diplomatic position, Kennedy inherited no solid consensus among the United States and its major allies. As we have seen, the British opposed taking a rigid position on Western "rights" in Berlin and were willing to risk war only in the event of a communist attack on the outpost; indeed, it is doubtful whether they would have been willing to launch major war to prevent an East German absorption of West Berlin. Adenauer's government regarded Berlin as a symbol of Western, and particularly American commitment, but by 1961 he was more concerned with the question of whether NATO would defend West Germany with nuclear weapons.[5] Naturally, Willy Brandt, the mayor of West Berlin and Adenauer's opponent in the fall elections, put forth a harder line on Berlin. The French President, Charles de Gaulle, wanted to see the Americans stick to a tough position. De Gaulle was not overly concerned with the fate of West Berliners or the propagandistic value of the capitalist island; rather, Berlin was for him a test to see if the United States was really ready to initiate world war to save Western Europe. An aggressive American position on Berlin, and especially a clear willingness to defend it with nuclear war, could allay his fears. A weak stance, on the other hand, could make de Gaulle more determined to develop an independent nuclear force for France.[6]

Eisenhower's stubborn diplomacy during the last year of his presidency had alienated Nikita Khrushchev, and this was another problem Kennedy had to face. The Soviet leader had been heartened by Eisenhower's forbearance during the Berlin crisis and the friendly summit in September 1959, which was why Khrushchev decided in early 1960 to press for further accords with the West.[7] Détente could free up resources for nonmilitary production and aid to third-world leftists, and it would lessen the possibility of nuclear war. Tolerating a Western outpost in Berlin was reasonable payment for these objectives, and that was the deal Khrushchev thought he arranged and was ready to formalize at the Paris Summit in May, 1960.

Khrushchev regarded the U-2 flight on the eve of the Summit to be an abrogation of this deal, not so much because he was outraged by the flight per se but because it made him appear—as Eisenhower must have known it would—a fool in the eyes of Soviet militarists opposed to détente with the Americans.[8] His retribution would be to destroy the Paris Summit and revive the Berlin Crisis after Eisenhower had left office. This was no shock to the new administration: Llewellyn Thompson, whom Kennedy chose to keep on as ambassador to Moscow, was one of several advisers to note that a Soviet ultimatum on Berlin was nigh; Georgi Bolshakov, a KGB agent and representative of Khrushchev in Washington, had been warning the administration consistently that his boss considered the Berlin situation unacceptable.[9]

Further, Kennedy had little time to gain control over his policymaking bureaucracy. By the time of the first Berlin crisis in 1958, all efforts to change Eisenhower's mind about limited war had failed, and there was no longer any question, especially after Dulles's illness, that any American decision about war in Berlin would reflect the president's will only. Thus the story of American decisionmaking during that crisis can be told by concentrating primarily on Eisenhower. The circumstances could not have differed more for Kennedy. Between his inauguration and the outset of the second crisis in June, several people vied for control over American policy on Berlin, creating a disorganized decisionmaking process that Kennedy was wholly unable to master. Advisers, consultants and Cabinet officials deluged Kennedy with position papers, contingency plans, and formal recommendations, often written in an admonitory tone unimaginable in the previous administration.[10] A single U.S. stance on Berlin did not really exist before June, though some key advisers had begun to stake out their own positions. It would take Khrushchev's ultimatum and then the Wall to force a clarification in Kennedy administration policy.

But the most difficult problem Eisenhower had bequeathed to Kennedy was a rigid military policy, a nuclear strategy, and a force structure that conformed to the dictates of NSC-5707/8. As a consequence of Eisenhower's decision to reduce U.S. non-nuclear forces in Europe, the Western armies around Berlin were completely outnumbered by those of the Warsaw Pact. NATO's military posture, moreover, consisted not only of forces on the ground but also strategies in the minds of its commanders. After eight years of Eisenhower, military planners in Europe, above all General Lauris Norstad, the Supreme Commander of American forces in Europe and NATO commander as well, were determined to carry out the official policy of nuclear retaliation following any significant military setback in Europe. Norstad believed that without the nuclear option his NATO forces were doomed to defeat; he therefore opposed any suggestion that the West refrain from using such weapons in a war over Berlin. Articulating a policy of flexible response in campaign speeches and position papers was one thing; implementing it on the ground in the space of months was quite another.

In January and February Kennedy relied on Ambassador Thompson and Secretary of State Dean Rusk for advice on Berlin. Both were sure that Khrushchev would revive the Berlin Crisis, and both recommended that Kennedy remain publicly quiet about the issue, avoid provoking Khrushchev, and plan for the inevitable Soviet ultimatum.[11] In late February, Rusk sent a memorandum to McNamara urging him to reduce American and NATO reliance upon the threat of nuclear war. Rusk went as far to argue that the West should refrain from nuclear retaliation even if the Soviet Union launched a massive conventional attack against Western Europe. To make this tenable, the United States and NATO would have to increase their conventional capabilities dramatically.[12]

Despite Rusk's initial involvement, Kennedy decided in March to ask Dean Acheson to advise him on Berlin and Germany.[13] With the help of Assistant Secretary of State Foy Kohler and Paul Nitze, whom Kennedy appointed to head the Defense Department's Office of International Security Affairs, Acheson set out to dominate Kennedy's national security policy. On March 29 he sent Kennedy a lengthy memorandum on NATO, urging him to establish better civilian control over the military command structure, and making this remarkable recommendation:

> . . . it seems essential that an outstanding American civilian figure
> (1) assume a NATO office with an explicit charter to take a primary
> role in developing military policy and (2) receive a large delegation of

power from the U.S. and, in particular, a delegation from the Secretary of Defense. . . . he would be in the direct chain of command from the President through the Secretary of Defense for the release of nuclear weapons to NATO during central war or during more limited action.[14]

Whether Acheson envisioned himself in this new position was not clear: what this recommendation did show was that Acheson so distrusted the current nuclear hierarchy that he was willing to suggest to Kennedy that he appoint a nuclear czar with unprecedented (and perhaps unconstitutional) power and authority. Given that Acheson considered Kennedy to be weak and indecisive,[15] this was quite a suggestion indeed.

In early April Prime Minister Macmillan and his major advisers came to Washington to visit the new president and gauge his views on Europe. On the 5th the two sides met to discuss Berlin. Acheson dominated the conversation, reiterating the argument he had made in his 1959 article, and had recently repeated in an April 3 memorandum to Kennedy.[16] The Soviets were likely to move against Berlin soon. Abandoning that city, Acheson went on, would lead to the loss of all Germany and then perhaps the rest of Western Europe. The West must therefore respond to any Soviet or East German provocation in West Berlin with sustained, *conventional* military action. A threat to launch nuclear war over Berlin, he declared, was "reckless and would not be believed." Not surprisingly, Macmillan described Acheson's plan as "a tremendous advance in the U.S. position."[17]

Acheson's was not, yet, the "U.S. position." Perhaps a bit distressed by Acheson's March 29 letter, and by his imperious domination of the talks with the British, Kennedy issued National Security Action Memorandum (NSAM)[18] number 41, an early official Berlin directive. According to NSAM 41, Acheson would continue to work on Berlin, but McNamara would be in charge of military contingency planning.[19]

Seizing this opportunity, McNamara responded on May 5 to Kennedy's "action memorandum" with his own "Military Planning for a Possible Berlin Crisis." The "national policy guidance" on this subject was not satisfactory, McNamara reported: the existing plan was still NSC-5803, a three-year-old strategy that "does not reflect new developments in U.S. strategic thinking. Specifically," McNamara went on,

NSC 5803 implies the U.S. "will be prepared to go immediately to general war after using only limited military force to attempt to reopen access to Berlin." This is inconsistent with current thinking which proposes the use of substantial conventional force before considering resort to nuclear weapons and other general war measures. An early restatement of our national policy with regard to Berlin Contingency Planning is desirable.[20]

For the time being, McNamara stated, the United States and NATO could reopen ground access to Berlin without resorting to nuclear weapons, but to reopen air access would require "an expansion of the conflict." It was "mandatory" for the West to improve its conventional capabilities so that, at least, Soviet forces would be obliged to join the East German army in an effort to keep NATO forces from retaking West Berlin. This would force Khrushchev to think twice about the risks of expanding the war.[21]

On May 20 the Joint Chiefs conveyed McNamara's intentions to Norstad. At present, the Chiefs noted, U.S. and NATO forces around Berlin could be defeated by East German forces alone. The Secretary of Defense, they instructed Norstad, "considers it mandatory that, in any operation larger than a probe, we have force level required to defeat any solely satellite force, without employing our nuclear weapons." Norstad was to report back with the force levels he needed to achieve such a capability.[22]

By the end of May, then, the Kennedy administration's preparation for Berlin remained embryonic. Acheson was declaring that NATO must stand pat on Western rights there, and be ready to fight a conventional war the moment the Soviets tried to abrogate those rights. Even though Acheson was only an adviser to Kennedy, no one else in the administration, least of all Kennedy himself, was ready to offer an alternative to his approach. McNamara had expressed his interest in working to develop American military forces capable of fulfilling Acheson's demand, but actual deployment of such forces was a long way off. The Secretary of State, Rusk, was out of the loop. With no imminent crisis at hand, the new administration avoided making a final policy on Berlin.

The Vienna Summit and the Berlin Ultimatum

Back in February Kennedy had suggested that he and Khrushchev meet for an informal summit. After a long wait—more specifically, after the American embarrassment at the Bay of Pigs[23]—Khrushchev assented, and the two sides agreed to meet in Vienna in early June.

En route to Vienna, the American entourage arrived in Paris on May 31. Of course Kennedy and his wife Jacqueline were warmly welcomed by the Parisians, one of whom, President de Gaulle, was also eager to instruct the young president in the ways of French national interest. De Gaulle, like Macmillan, had maintained a consistent position on Berlin.[24] No nation, he told Kennedy, would run any serious risk of nuclear war to achieve some territorial gain. Therefore Kennedy's proposal to augment conventional forces in Europe and remove the strategy of massive retaliation was wrong, for, in reducing the possibility of general nuclear war, it increased, not diminished, the likelihood that Khrushchev would move against the old German capital. Kennedy responded by suggesting that conventional forces could protect Berlin as well as nuclear weapons. De Gaulle corrected the mistaken American. ". . . there is no possibility of a military victory for us in the area of Berlin," he replied. "What we must make clear is that if there is any fighting around Berlin, this means general war."[25]

The French president was thus refuting the nascent positions of Acheson and McNamara: not only were NATO's conventional forces far too weak to fight for Berlin, but it was futile to believe that this situation could be changed in the future. Better to state that a Soviet move against West Berlin would trigger all-out nuclear war and be done with it. Kennedy seemed to be persuaded by his French counterpart, asserting in an afternoon session that "Khrushchev be made to understand that we are decided, if necessary, to wage nuclear warfare."[26]

De Gaulle's suasions may have actually changed Kennedy's mind, or perhaps he was voicing agreement to avoid a pre-summit skirmish, or perhaps Kennedy did not really know what his own views were regarding the defense of West Berlin. But the legendary Frenchman had informed him that limited military action around Berlin was pointless. If nothing else this must have deflated in Kennedy's eyes the confident strategy Acheson had been advocating. It was all well to stand tough on Berlin, but backing that toughness up—then, in the spring of 1961, not in the abstract—was a token military contingent that could be wiped out by the East Germans themselves and then a NATO strategy based on the early use of nuclear weapons. De Gaulle had suggested to the American president, as his entourage left for Vienna on June 2, this troublesome alternative: if the Russians revived their Berlin ultimatum, Kennedy either had to convince himself that Berlin's defense warranted nuclear war, or he had to be ready to out-bluff Nikita Khrushchev.

The summit in Vienna focused mostly on Berlin. On the first day, June 3, the two heads-of-state discussed a test-ban treaty, the situation in Laos, the debacle in Cuba, and met for a formal dinner that evening. Khrushchev brought up the main issue, Berlin, the next morning during meetings at the Soviet embassy. Repeating the argument he made in 1958, the Soviet leader declared, in the course of a lengthy tirade, that he was going to sign a peace treaty with the East Germans. It was time to recognize the existence of two separate German states; Berlin could be turned into a "free city," he suggested, with the Soviets providing guarantees to ensure special status for the Western sector.[27]

Kennedy responded to Khrushchev's demands by stressing that American prestige hinged upon the maintenance of occupation rights in West Berlin. "If we were to leave West Berlin," Kennedy stated, "Europe would be abandoned as well." Khrushchev replied to this reasoning by stating that the Soviet Union was going to sign the peace treaty, there was nothing the United States could do about that, but it would be possible to work out an "interim arrangement" in Berlin that would preserve American prestige. The two Germanies could try to work out a plan for reunification: if after, say, six months no agreement was reached, then the Soviet Union would feel free to sign the peace treaty with, and turn over control of Berlin to, the East German regime.[28]

At the end of the morning discussion Khrushchev informed Kennedy that his aides had already prepared an aide-memoire explaining its intentions regarding Berlin—his morning tirade, apparently, had been premeditated.[29] The two leaders met again in the afternoon—this time only with interpreters—and Kennedy more forcefully accused Khrushchev of risking major war. Khrushchev answered that his "decision to sign a peace treaty is firm and irrevocable" and that it would happen in December. Kennedy replied by predicting a "cold winter," and that was the end of the Vienna Summit.[30]

Khrushchev crushed Kennedy at Vienna. The American president had gone there hoping to get Khrushchev to agree to a compromise in Laos, establish an arms-control agenda, and, most important, accept the American position on Berlin, which was to leave it the way it was. Instead Kennedy left Vienna with a formal Soviet ultimatum on Berlin in his pocket.

Many factors may have contributed to the rout, including the Soviet leader's rhetorical skills, his need to reassure the anxious East Germans, Kennedy's inexperience, and even the heavy medication Kennedy took to ease his chronic back pain.[31] But the real source of Kennedy's problems in

Vienna was his lack of resolve over Berlin. He was not sure why the West insisted on retaining occupation rights in West Berlin; this was why he concentrated on the matter of American "prestige" in his talks with Khrushchev, rather than on the merits of the Western case itself. Kennedy continually warned Khrushchev that Soviet action against West Berlin would discredit the United States and drive it off the European continent, as if he expected the Soviet premier to regard such an outcome with dread. Without coupling his talk about American prestige with persuasive, gritty threats of nuclear war—something he did not do in Vienna—Kennedy was only entreating his Soviet counterpart, appealing to Khrushchev's goodwill, and at the height of the Cold War that was a curious stance indeed. Of course, the veteran Soviet leader easily discerned Kennedy's irresolution, and bluffed him off the table. "Politics is a merciless business," Khrushchev wrote of that day in his memoirs.[32]

Kennedy returned home from Vienna by way of London, where he had the pleasure of hearing the British describe the Soviet aide-memoire as "fairly reasonable." Back in Washington, on June 6, he met with congressional leaders and informed them of the Soviet ultimatum, but in an address to the public that evening Kennedy said that there had been "no threats or ultimatums by either side."[33]

By issuing the deadline at Vienna Khrushchev rekindled a direct superpower confrontation that had been smoldering for two years. The Kennedy administration now had to face directly the questions it had danced around for the first half of the year. What, exactly, was the U.S. interest in Berlin? What, exactly, would the United States do should that interest be threatened by force?

The Minimal Approach

Kennedy may have hoped that by avoiding, and even publicly denying the existence of, the Soviet ultimatum, Berlin might go away.[34] On June 10, that wish was destroyed. Perhaps sensing Kennedy's inertia, his national security adviser, McGeorge Bundy, sent him a stern memorandum urging him—almost ordering him—to decide what to do about Berlin. The State Department, Bundy wrote, was working on a formal reply to the Soviet aide-memoire; Acheson was developing his own Berlin recommendation; McNamara was responsible for military contingency planning. But Kennedy, Bundy insisted, needed to take "immediate, personal, and continuous command." On that day as well *Pravda* reprinted the Soviet aide-memoire, thus exposing the American President's lie to the world.[35]

Over the next week things did not much improve. On June 12 Bundy asked McNamara whether the U.S. could deploy "more substantial non-nuclear force" by October; on June 14 McNamara replied that existing conventional forces in Europe were inadequate for any sustained defense of West Berlin.[36] The next day Senator Mike Mansfield, the majority leader, called for the West to accept a "free city" solution to the crisis,[37] while in Moscow Khrushchev reiterated his determination to sign the peace treaty at the end of the year. Certainly Kennedy did not distinguish himself by opening an NSC meeting on the 13th by asking "who was responsible for planning and coordination on Berlin contingencies." (Rusk answered that he was.)[38]

Despite Rusk's embarrassed reply, Kennedy's question seemed to be more clearly answered three days later at the first meeting of the Interdepartmental Coordinating Group on Berlin Contingency Planning (ICG). ICG chairman Kohler introduced Acheson as having been "requested by the President to study contingency planning," and Acheson went on to present a detailed, hard-line proposal. Dominating the meeting, Acheson argued for

> training exercises in Europe and redeployment of troops to battle stations as if in preparation for an action toward Berlin. The crash programs for Polaris and other missiles and submarines should continue. There should be a resumption of nuclear testing. There should be proclamations of limited and unlimited national emergencies, supporting resolutions in the Congress, and substantial increases in the military budget. There should be a movement of troops to Europe and a general alert of SAC.[39]

If these steps failed to dissuade the Soviets from carrying out their plan, the United States should commence an airlift, to be followed if necessary by the use of tactical or strategic nuclear weapons. By allowing for this final step Acheson was conceding that for the near future, at least, conventional forces would not be sufficient in a European war. This was a departure from his previous judgment that it would be better to fight with conventional weapons and lose than not to fight at all or to defend Berlin with nuclear weapons. But for Acheson the problem was really more one of commitment and perception than of detailed contingency planning. Echoing Dulles, he declared that "if the US were genuinely ready to fight for Berlin the Soviets would relent and war would be unnecessary." The issue was "essentially one of US will."[40]

As there seemed to be no other proposal, Acheson's confrontational approach served to define the policy toward Berlin in the immediate wake of Vienna. What would happen if this hard-line stance led to conflict? On June 26 the Joint Chiefs, responding to McNamara's May 5 demand, issued a grim answer to that question. The position of the Chiefs was clear: it would be impossible to win a conventional war over Berlin. Yes, the chiefs argued, *after a mobilization period of four months* the United States could maintain access to Berlin with conventional arms if it were opposed only by East Germany. If the Soviets joined the battle, this new force would survive for five days, fifteen if other NATO forces took part. But what were the chances that the United States could commence full mobilization, like the kind that went on during World War II, over its rights in West Berlin? Would the French, contemptuous of conventional war, or the British, hardly dedicated to West Berlin, really contribute substantial forces to such a war? The Chiefs concluded that "it would not be feasible for the European Allies or the United States to engage in non-nuclear war for any extended period with the Soviet Bloc forces which could be brought into the area by 31 October 1961."[41]

The Chiefs' reply staggered Kennedy and his advisers, because it made Acheson's belligerence seem like a recipe for nuclear war. Initially, Kennedy seemed to stick with the Acheson line: on June 29 he issued NSAM 58, which ordered McNamara to prepare military plans for a possible airlift, regional naval blockade, and nonnuclear ground action with Berlin.[42]

In early July, however, Bundy, together with White House aides Arthur Schlesinger, Jr., Abram Chayes, and an outside consultant named Henry Kissinger, began to develop an alternative position. On the 6th Bundy reminded Kennedy that a new steering group, headed by Rusk, was now in charge of Berlin planning.[43] The next day, just before Kennedy left for Hyannis Port for the weekend, Schlesinger got to the president a lengthy and detailed attack on the Acheson plan, which went as far as to list Acheson's allies and antagonists and urge the president to recommence Berlin planning with the participation of "non-Achesonians." Schlesinger warned Kennedy in a cover letter that current policy had created a "dangerously rigid" situation that "may leave you very little choice as to how you face the moment of thermonuclear truth."[44]

Kennedy brought McNamara, Rusk, and his newly appointed "military representative" General Maxwell Taylor with him to Massachusetts to discuss the Acheson plan. Accounts of this weekend vary[45] but it is clear that Kennedy decided to follow the recommendation of Schlesinger, Chayes and Kissinger, that he set up alternative planning, and push Acheson aside. On July 13 Bundy delivered a lengthy memorandum to the president that reflected this change. The United States, he said, should

> Avoid any significant military build-up at this time, on the ground that the crisis is one of political unity and firmness of will, and on the further ground that substantial military preparations at this stage would divide the alliance, stiffen the Russians, frighten our own people, and operate against an effective stand in Berlin under the fundamental shield of nuclear deterrence.[46]

This was a curious set of recommendations. It was not self-evident that a military build-up around Berlin would "divide the alliance, stiffen the Russians, and frighten our own people"; Acheson had been arguing exactly the opposite for months. Nor was it obvious that a conventional build-up might serve to *undermine*, not strengthen, the U.S. position in Berlin, since Kennedy and his colleagues had been saying otherwise for years.

The purpose of Bundy's memorandum was to rationalize a change in American policy regarding Berlin. On the same day that Bundy completed it, Kennedy announced a new U.S. policy. "There are two things that matter," he declared during a NSC discussion: "our presence in Berlin, and our access to Berlin."[47] This statement departed from the longstanding American position that Berlin was a defeated city in which the four victorious powers enjoyed the legal rights of occupier. Once-major issues like East German border regulation, the importance of American lip-service toward German reunification, and particularly the maintenance of World War Two rights of occupation were to be de-emphasized in favor of the more general demands that Western forces have open passage to Berlin and security once they were there.

A first order of business in implementing this new policy was to inform Dean Acheson of his new status. On July 17 Kennedy met with key Cabinet members to discuss Berlin. Not invited were Vice President Johnson and the three main figures in the ICG: Nitze, Kohler, and Acheson. At the meeting Rusk went over allied opinion, while McNamara described his plan to achieve a moderate conventional buildup by the beginning of 1962. Kennedy announced that organization on Berlin planning was going to change: from now on, he reiterated, the ICG would conduct day-to-day planning at the "lower level," while a new Berlin Steering Group would have "fundamental responsibility" for official United States policy. This steering group would be chaired by Rusk and composed of other Cabinet members, Bundy, and Chairman of the JCS Lyman Lemnitzer. Acheson was not on the list.[48]

The next day Kennedy and McNamara met with the Joint Chiefs. Kennedy informed the chiefs that he planned to supplement the Pentagon budget immediately. Chairman Lemnitzer confirmed that with this budget supplement, the United States would be ready to wage conventional war in Europe by January 1962. He said that the new force, while not capable of actually defeating its serious Warsaw Pact counterpart, would indeed "provide some additional time for negotiation before resorting to nuclear warfare."[49] This was a clear acknowledgement on the part of the Chairman that it would indeed be impossible to wage a serious conventional campaign to defend West Berlin before 1962. That meant that Acheson's plan was dead.

To get Kennedy to accept and confirm this reality, Bundy sent him a memorandum on the morning of the 19th, hours before the weekly NSC meeting. He warned the president that the "hard wing" of the ICG, "led by Acheson and Nitze," would press for an American declaration of national emergency. The national security adviser recommended that Kennedy instead state that neither an East German-Soviet peace treaty nor Berlin border-regulation by East German soldiers was a "fighting matter," and suggest that the United States "extend serious feelers" to the Soviets about negotiating on Berlin.[50]

At three that afternoon the Berlin Steering Group met. All agreed with McNamara's plan to build up conventional forces by the end of 1961, raise taxes to pay for that build-up, and shelve the idea of declaring a national emergency. At four the rest of the NSC, including Acheson, was let into the Cabinet room. Quickly the meeting centered upon "a very important exchange" between Acheson and McNamara. Their argument existed on two levels. Literally, they disagreed about the national emergency declaration and the question of calling up major reserve forces. McNamara, of course, supported Kennedy's decision to put these actions off until a later date, to avoid exacerbating the crisis. But their debate was also a struggle for power in front of the entire National Security Council, to see whose military policy on Berlin would prevail. Bundy concluded his account of this exchange by reporting "general agreement that the plans as presented by Secretary McNamara were satisfactory. Mr. Acheson," Bundy added, "specifically indicated his own approval."[51]

A second step in the implementation of the new policy was to get the United States position in writing, pass it on to European allies, and declare it officially. This job fell to Rusk, whose patient tolerance of Acheson's usurpations was now paying off. Working from a paper he had prepared on July 17,[52] Rusk developed an official American position on Berlin, and delivered it to the British, French, and West German ambassadors on July 21. The nub of the new strategy, Rusk explained, was to make access to and the security of West Berlin "vital interests" worthy of military action. Less important were the issues of reunification and East German recognition. The United States would go on record as supporting self-determination for all Germans but would not go to war for it.[53]

Kennedy himself sent versions of this new policy to Adenauer, de Gaulle, and Macmillan on July 20, and on the 25th outlined it in a public address to the nation, and, by extension, to the Soviet leadership.[54] Much of the president's speech reiterated in familiar terms the American commitment to the West Berliners; he also announced the increase in conventional forces and defense spending, while stressing his desire to resume talks with Khrushchev. But the most significant aspect of Kennedy's speech was his conspicuous use of the term *West* Berlin.[55] He was telling his audience that the United States no longer considered the division of the city to be a temporary remnant of World War II, but rather a fact of the Cold War. West Berlin mattered; East Berlin was beyond American purview.

With the general American position now public, it was time to hammer out a more specific policy with the Europeans—particularly the French, who were not likely to be pleased with the new turn of events. This was the kind of thing Dean Rusk was good at. On July 27 the Secretary of State sent a "groundwork" team, led by Kohler, Nitze, and Chayes to Paris to work on an accord with the French, British, and West Germans.[56] On August 5 Rusk arrived, to engage in formal ministerial consultations.

The Secretary of State presented the new American policy in detail to his colleagues. On the diplomatic front, the United States would support commencing negotiations with the Soviet Union sometime well before the December deadline. In the event of diplomatic failure—i.e., if the communists forcibly moved against West Berlin—Rusk suggested that the West first react with various nonmilitary initiatives, including an economic embargo, another airlift into the Western sector, and a "roaring debate" in the United Nations. Only after these measures failed should NATO respond with military action, and the United States would insist that "significant Allied conventional forces" be used to make Khrushchev aware of allied determination and give him time to back off before nuclear war began. The United States would not support a rapid and public mobilization of Western forces, nor would it advocate taking a hard line on the general question of recognizing East German authority.[57]

The British of course supported the American plan wholeheartedly, although Foreign Secretary Alec Home wondered why, if the West were going to offer negotiations, it could not be done sooner rather than later.[58] The French, and to a lesser extent the West Germans, opposed offering the Soviets negotiations under the threat of ultimatum; the French also rejected the new American timidity on nuclear war—Rusk was invited to meet with de Gaulle personally on the 8th to be informed of this[59]—and the talks concluded on August 9 without concrete agreement. But Rusk had made it clear that the United States would look for ways to avoid war, and particularly nuclear war, during a confrontation in Berlin and would emphasize the security and accessibility of West Berlin, not the lesser issue of whether East Germans or Russians patrolled its borders. Assuming Soviet infiltration of these talks, this news would have gotten back to Khrushchev by August 10 or so.

The June ultimatum, then, had forced the Kennedy administration to come up with a solid diplomatic position on Berlin. Afraid that Acheson's confrontational stance might provoke a war that could not remain conventional, Kennedy signed on to a more conciliatory policy, a plain declaration that the West was determined to preserve its position in West Berlin, but West Berlin only. This indicated clearly to Khrushchev that the United States would not oppose a termination of its occupation status in East Berlin, whatever its sixteen-year old rights were.

The Kennedy administration had not, yet, resolved at all the question of how it would respond to a challenge to its position in Berlin. McNamara had begun to rewrite American military policy, but in early August the chances of actually keeping a war over Berlin non-nuclear were remote. Bundy reminded Kennedy of this on the 21st: the Joint Chiefs, he stated, "say that they can't study a substantial non-nuclear ground action in Europe until Basic National Security Policy has been revised, since present (Eisenhower) NSC policy prevents such action."[60]

But the revision of American policy had made war over Berlin seem much less imminent. And if Khrushchev maintained his ultimatum, it was not to expire until the end of the year, so McNamara would have several months to deploy the new forces and persuade the Chiefs and Norstad to sign on to the new program. He and Nitze left for Europe in late July to meet with Norstad and begin that difficult task.

9 The Wall and the Prospect of War, August–October 1961

In the early hours of August 13, 1961, East German soldiers, "Vopos," they were called, began to set up barriers blocking traffic from East into West Berlin. By morning they had set up barbed-wire blockades around the entire western sector of the city. East Berliners heading west for work were turned back; West Berliners crowded around the new fortifications to boo the hapless Vopos as they pounded fence posts into the ancient Berlin cobblestones. Over the next few days the Vopos began to replace these temporary barriers with an immense wall that would eventually encircle all of West Berlin.[1]

Khrushchev approved this action, despite its dismal testimony to the appeal of communism, because it expediently solved two pressing problems. The wall obstructed the flow of resources, labor, and, especially, talented East German refugees into West Berlin. Capable people were fleeing East Germany by the tens of thousands, and that nation's leader, Walter Ulbricht, was incessantly demanding that Khrushchev allow him to close the border before the DDR was reduced to a hollow shell. At the same time, the wall allowed Khrushchev to defuse the Berlin Crisis unilaterally, well before the deadline of his ultimatum in December, when he would have had to face risking war or once again backing down.[2]

In the days immediately following the "border closing" not one official in the Kennedy administration recommended military response. On the evening of August 14 Rusk emphasized that exploiting the wall's propaganda value was "the most important" item on the West's agenda. In a memorandum to Kennedy, Bundy argued against any reprisal at all. As George

Kennan and the columnist Joseph Alsop had already pointed out, Bundy noted, the Soviets were bound to have taken such a step sooner or later — better that it happened now, well before the deadline, than in reaction to a Western move in the "cold winter" of 1961–62. Kennedy sent to Rusk a memorandum asking him to list "what steps will we take this week to exploit politically propagandawise" the wall.[3]

The Berlin steering group met the next day to formalize this policy. Rusk offered the State Department view that "while the border closing was a most serious matter, the probability was that in realistic terms it would make a Berlin settlement easier." McNamara emphasized his opposition to the "gesture" of sending a reinforcement to West Berlin. Bundy summarized the group's conclusion: because "the closing of the border was not a shooting issue, the problem was essentially one of propaganda." Therefore, Washington would reject "temporary and incommensurate reprisals." Rusk met with the French, British, and German ambassadors that evening to inform them of the American position. The West would issue protests, but not take any military action against the wall; the United States would send military reinforcements (against McNamara's recommendation) in order to restore West Berliners' morale.[4]

With hindsight, one can see that the official United States decision not to act put an end to the Berlin crisis.[5] Once the Americans concluded that the "border closing" was not worth war, both superpowers had effectively signaled each other that accepting the artificial division of Berlin was an expedient solution to a lingering Cold War problem. Seen in this light, the skirmishes after August appear as aftershocks, not central to the international crisis.

In some respects, this was how Kennedy and his advisers saw it too. The Wall indisputably reduced their fears of all-out war, making their immediate task one of reassuring the isolated people of West Berlin that they would not be abandoned. However, they could not be sure that the Wall signified not a Soviet decision to end the crisis but rather an opening move to drive the West out. Therefore, the administration continued to prepare for war. And by sending Lucius Clay to soothe the West Berliners, they almost succeeded in starting one.

Preparing for War

There was no reason to suppose that the West Berliners would gladly welcome the encasement of their city with armed guards, barbed wire, snarling dogs, and a ten-foot-high concrete wall, even as the price for easing Cold War tensions. West Berlin Mayor Willy Brandt sent an urgent and not entirely politic letter to Kennedy on the 16th, demanding that the West take immediate political action against the "accomplished extortion." Brandt realized quite well that the Wall might be seen as an acceptable device for avoiding a nuclear war. He wanted to disabuse Kennedy of this feeling. The continuing tragedy of Berlin, Brandt warned, meant that the West "will not be spared [the] risks of ultimate decision."[6]

Kennedy wanted to be spared the risks of ultimate decision, and in late August he began to renew his search for alternatives to all-out nuclear war. On the 18th he approved Maxwell Taylor's proposal to send a U.S. battle group down the Autobahn to Berlin, to demonstrate American willingness to deploy conventional forces on the Berlin scene.[7] Three days later Kennedy issued NSAM 78, which demanded from McNamara an update on contingency planning. McNamara replied on August 25 that Norstad was preparing plans based on the assumption that the U.S. would have to act unilaterally— that its NATO allies would refuse to go along with a conventional war to maintain access to West Berlin. "We do not yet have the additional forces needed to expand our military options," McNamara told Kennedy, "nor do we have Allied agreement that non-nuclear options are necessary and possible."[8] To remedy this, the next day McNamara decided to move up the date for deploying conventional reinforcements from January 1 to November 15, while Rusk instructed Norstad that in the event of war the United States did not intend to use nuclear weapons, but rather would try to settle "the problem of Berlin while progressively making the Soviets aware of the danger of general war."[9]

Perhaps Kennedy, McNamara, and Rusk still believed that American conventional forces could adequately defend Berlin; General Norstad did not. In an August 28 telegram Norstad belittled the new ideas coming out of the White House. How, he asked, was the United States supposed to "settle the problem of Berlin" without using nuclear weapons? "What are the new options? Are they based on real probability or thin probability? Would we be in a position to exercise them in any event by 1 January 1962? By 1 July 1962?"[10] The European commander was telling his superiors, once again, that war over Berlin was going to be a nuclear war—or an immediate and ignominious defeat. Conventional forces were not going to be adequate in any foreseeable future. It was time, he urged, for Washington to accept this reality.

The Berlin steering group met again on September 7. Acheson was invited this time, and he argued for a serious military attempt to defend that city. This meant getting rid of both token conventional deployments and a suicidal nuclear strategy. McNamara demurred, claiming that a moderate increase in conventional forces, while not providing the U.S. with the capability to win a war, would convince Khrushchev of the American will to use nuclear weapons. In the meantime he proposed to call up the national guard, suspend the movements of dependents to Europe, and transfer 37,000 Army personnel there. Acheson replied that these "gestures" would not deter Khrushchev from "doing as he pleases" and called for all-out mobilization as "the only chance of making [nuclear] war unnecessary."[11]

Bundy noted that Acheson's plan could lead to the "reverse," by which he meant, following both de Gaulle's reasoning before Vienna and Bundy's own July 13 memorandum, that a conventional build-up might indicate to Khrushchev that the West was afraid to use nuclear weapons to defend Berlin, hence tempting the Soviet leader to invade.[12] This distinction interested Kennedy, who issued another action memorandum, in which he asked McNamara this question: "Will an increase of our conventional forces in Europe convince Khrushchev of our readiness to fight to a finish for West Berlin or will it have the opposite effect?"[13]

Kennedy, in other words, was asking McNamara whether flexible response was still valid. Initially McNamara stuck to his guns, arguing that a conventional build-up would assure allies that the United States was committed to their defense; in the end "it is probably a more convincing course for the allies actively to prepare to engage in substantial non-nuclear conflict in Europe—a conflict which inevitably would carry a substantial risk of nuclear war—than to threaten, unconvincingly, the certainty of a nuclear response to a political aggression."[14] But a week later McNamara retreated from this position. "Inevitably it must be quite uncertain what would convince Khrushchev of our willingness to fight to a finish over Berlin," he wrote. "While a conventional build-up alone would be unlikely to convince him, the absence of a build-up would probably increase his doubt of our determination. To continue efforts focused mostly on nuclear forces and nuclear threats," McNamara concluded, "would carry less conviction than building up *both* non-nuclear and nuclear forces."[15]

McNamara was shifting his views because he could not get around Norstad. Whatever his own long-term strategic preferences, McNamara, like Dulles in September 1958, realized that for the time being the United States was not going to be able to wage a conventional war to defend Berlin. The

Secretary of Defense bolstered his new position by attaching a memorandum written by Norstad to his reply. In it Norstad pressed his point home: a conventional, nuclear war-fearing policy, the SACEUR wrote, could destroy American credibility. "It is absolutely essential," Norstad argued, "that the Soviets be forced to act and move at all times in full awareness that if they use force they risk general war with nuclear weapons." A build up even of 30 divisions (McNamara was contemplating seven) could not provide assured defense against a massive Soviet conventional attack. As Norstad concluded, "in these times no operation regardless how limited, can have real credibility except in the context of a nuclear threat, direct or implied."[16]

As was constantly the case in the Kennedy White House, however, just because McNamara had decided to side with Norstad over immediate Berlin contingency planning did not mean the issue had been put to rest. Norstad would be returning home in early October to coordinate planning with the Joint Chiefs and the White House, and Paul Nitze saw this as an opportunity to turn Kennedy against the McNamara/Norstad position and revive the more activist, flexible approach that he and Acheson supported. In a preparatory memorandum for this planning, Nitze analyzed Norstad's position—as if the American General were an adversary at the negotiating table—for McNamara and Rusk. Norstad, he wrote, believed that the United States and NATO "must succeed" in any European war. In the event of hostilities over Berlin Norstad would see his options simply as either surrender or the initiation of "actions rapidly with the forces he has available." Norstad himself, meeting on the same day with the Joint Chiefs, confirmed Nitze's suspicions. An "ordered" escalation in Berlin was a doubtful proposition; it could be more like a chemical reaction, "so rapid that it is uncontrollable." NATO will be "involved from the first shot," Norstad declared, every day sounding more like Eisenhower, and it was necessary to convince NATO as well as the Soviets of "our determination to use as many nuclear weapons as soon as required to insure success of our actions."[17]

Kennedy's aides coached him for his meeting with Norstad. Bundy, stating the obvious, described Norstad as a "nuclear war man, and all his preferences move accordingly." Taylor, also eager to preserve flexible response, told Kennedy that it was crucial that Norstad realize who was in charge: "Norstad must know your mind clearly," Taylor told Kennedy, especially since McNamara was wavering on the question of conventional war. This was unacceptable. "You need to make him know who is boss," Taylor said.[18]

Kennedy sat down with Norstad on the afternoon of the 3rd and asked him about his views on limited war. Norstad was all for balanced NATO forces, but once "major forces were engaged, the United States must be in a position to use whatever forces were necessary." Terms like *graduation* and *escalation* were "unrealistic," he added: "in normal war escalation is apt to be explosive." It was crucial that the Soviets and the NATO allies understand that: recent talk about conventional build-up had "cast doubt on the importance of nuclear warfare."[19]

Kennedy asked Norstad to envision a scenario in Berlin. Norstad replied that if the Soviets blocked access to the city, he could send a small platoon probe. If that were repelled, he could send a battalion probe. If that were repelled, "there would have to be a prompt and larger reaction." Kennedy grasped Norstad's meaning. "As soon as someone gets killed," the president observed, "the danger of major involvement is very great." That was disturbing news indeed. "We must privately clarify our own decisions on contingency planning," Kennedy concluded.[20]

Norstad's message to the White House had been unwavering. It would be quite impossible to win a limited war over West Berlin. American forces there were ridiculously outnumbered by their East German, not to mention Russian, counterparts. Because this had long been the case, the United States and NATO had together developed a strategy to defend the German city with nuclear war. Soldiers in Europe from Norstad on down assumed that this would be their primary mission. With the possible exception of the British, America's NATO allies were content with this strategy and could not be relied upon to join an American attempt to fight for Berlin with conventional forces. Every military and diplomatic factor weighed against trying to use flexible response to defend Berlin. By early October, Bundy and McNamara seemed reconciled to this reality.

But the lack of a strong center in White House planning, together with the fact that war seemed remote, encouraged Nitze to press his case. Working from a paper written by his aide Admiral John Lee, Nitze developed a four-stage plan and presented it at an October 10 meeting.[21]

Nitze argued in this meeting that following an unsuccessful local bid to reopen Western access to West Berlin, comprehensive conventional military action should precede nonmilitary steps (like Rusk's embargo or United Nations protests). McNamara and Rusk "strongly recommended" that these stages be reversed, a recommendation with which Kennedy agreed. The participants then turned to "Paragraph IV," of Nitze's plan, the section dealing with nuclear war. Kennedy worried that the limited nuclear strikes outlined in that section would quickly lead to the subject of Paragraph IV, section C: "General Nuclear War."[22] In concluding his minutes of this meeting Bundy noted that "the division of opinion over Paragraph IV was not flatly resolved."[23] But apparently Kennedy had been persuaded: he asked McNamara to prepare a set of official instructions for Norstad based on Nitze's original paper.[24]

On October 10, therefore, the administration adopted a contingency plan based upon fighting for Berlin in a flexible, escalatory manner. This was so even though, as Bundy said, the administration remained undecided about whether the defense of Berlin justified general nuclear war, and even though no one had yet to refute Norstad's statement that American conventional capabilities were entirely inadequate to fight seriously over Berlin, a conclusion with which both Bundy and McNamara concurred. Such muddle was hardly new in the Kennedy White House, as we have seen. It was certainly exacerbated by the quiet assumptions of Kennedy, McNamara, and others that the Wall had made war over Berlin unlikely. When that assumption proved untrue, the Nitze strategy would fall out of favor.

Lucius Clay's Accomplished Fact

A major objective of Kennedy administration policy after the construction of the Wall was to restore the morale of the West Berliners. If they began to struggle against their confinement in this peculiar walled outpost, demanding perhaps emigration to the West or reunification with the rest of the city, the West would be faced with the old, dim choice of abandoning Berlin or fighting World War III.

Immediately after the Wall went up Kennedy decided to send the well-remembered hero of the airlift, Lucius Clay, to the besieged city. Accompanying Clay would be Vice President Lyndon Johnson. Kennedy sent along with them his reply to Brandt, in which he told the Berliner that the Wall "represents a basic Soviet decision which only war could reverse. Neither you nor we," Kennedy noted, "nor any of our Allies, have ever supposed that we should go to war on this point." Johnson and Clay visited Berlin on August 19 and 20, and Clay proved to be so popular that Kennedy proposed making him the military commander there. McNamara opposed that idea, and on August 30 Kennedy instead made Clay his "Special Representative in Berlin," a title that conferred upon the retired general the rank and power of Ambassador.[25] As Kennedy's letter to Brandt stated—and as White House inaction following August 12 indicated—the United States rejected any idea of going to war over the Wall. Clay's mission was therefore therapeutic, not military: his job was to soothe the West Berliners, to get them to accept their plight.

In September Clay immediately set about undermining this objective.[26] He openly declared that his own preference would have been to demolish the Wall, and conspicuously set up an exercise in a West Berlin forest that consisted of American soldiers repeatedly knocking down a large wall.[27] He encouraged the hopes of West Berliners that the United States would come to the rescue, tweaked East German authorities at every opportunity, and regularly sought approval from Washington to initiate more substantive action. Patiently, Rusk or Kennedy would deny Clay's requests and ask that the General please refrain from unilateral action.[28]

This continued for some time. On September 28 Clay complained to Rusk that "timid" authorities, by which he meant Norstad, had rejected his plan to send helicopters to rescue refugees from Steinstuchen, a section of West Berlin surrounded by the eastern sector. There "is no longer time," Clay stated, "for either caution or timidity when our basic rights are threatened." The next day Clay recommended that if the East Germans moved to close the Friedrichstrasse crossing (one of the last points of entry into East Berlin), the United States should "physically destroy the barrier with a tank or heavy equipment. . . ."[29] An alarmed Rusk replied on October 4, reminding Clay that access to East Berlin was not a "vital interest for which we would fight, as we have defined such interests." He told him that the president had specifically ordered that no force be used to remove any barrier the East Germans might put up at Friedrichstrasse.

Persistently, Clay demanded again on October 5 that Washington approve his plan to send "a small number of tanks, say three" through a Friedrichstrasse barrier. "If we are not prepared to go this far," Clay wrote, "we should do nothing."[30] On the 8th Kennedy himself followed up on Rusk's letter. He suggested to the General that force "may in fact not be in our own interest." Gingerly, Kennedy assured Clay that his views would be considered at the highest levels and were respected by all concerned.[31]

Not gingerly, Clay replied to the president on October 18. Suggesting that "even as able a commander as Norstad" had been hamstrung by NATO leadership, Clay demanded to be given "authority in emergency to act immediately" without having to wait for Norstad's approval. He went on to recommend a complete contingency plan, which encompassed scenarios ranging all the way from a skirmish at the Wall to the "ultimate decision." Reviving his 1948 strategy of *fait accompli*, he informed his superiors that the United States must protect "our right to cross at Friedrich Strasse as we have built it up in the minds of the West Berliners . . ." What is more, Clay went on to threaten Kennedy, in oblique but unmistakable language, that "here in West Berlin any failure to act positively and determinedly with me here in this capacity will be assumed to have your direct approval."[32]

Backing down, Kennedy issued NSAM 107, which approved a modified version of Clay's plan to demolish an obstruction at Friedrichstrasse.[33] Despite his stated opposition to making the Wall *casus belli*, by the third week of October Kennedy had given Clay the opportunity to provoke the Soviets over the question of the Berlin Wall by destroying part of it. Nitze's contingency strategy, which called for provocation and quick escalation to major conventional fighting, was at this moment the official American plan.

From Muddle to Evasion

By declining to make the hard military decisions regarding the defense of Berlin, and then allowing Clay to make the prospect of war there suddenly imminent, Kennedy had made for himself an exceedingly dangerous situation. It was time to back off, and to do so the president and his advisors began to adopt a strategy of evading war.

On October 17, Nikita Khrushchev declared in a speech to the 22nd Party Congress that he was withdrawing the ultimatum to sign a peace treaty with the East Germans and turn Berlin over to their control.[34] From a historical perspective Khrushchev's actions seem perfunctory, since his construction of the Wall was the real indication that he would allow the West to stay in West Berlin. But because the Americans could not have been sure of this, his announcement was indeed reassuring, as it signified to Kennedy administration officials that their fears of the Wall being a prelude to further Soviet aggression were exaggerated. Suddenly, Kennedy's decision to let Clay act belligerently in Berlin, and to allow Nitze and Lee's escalatory plan to dictate his military options, seemed insane. Khrushchev was giving the West what it wanted in Berlin; there was absolutely no point in considering war.

A first step in evading war was to put Nitze's escalatory strategy aside. Typically this was done in a cumbersome manner. The White House scheduled a major meeting on Berlin for the morning of October 20, to review

Nitze's paper, and to approve a letter to Norstad (which had been drafted by McNamara), telling him what to do in the event of war. Bundy, as was his habit, wrote a preparatory memorandum for the president. Both the paper and the letter, he wrote, "fudge" the issue of whether limited war would lead inevitably to general war. McNamara, Bundy added, had *deliberately* avoided making up his mind on that central matter in his letter to Norstad. Everything listed on the meeting's agenda were "essentially subordinate clauses in the main question . . . Are there a variety of steps between blocked access and general war, or not."[35]

During that morning's meeting the participants debated the main question, with the immediate purpose of drafting a final letter to Norstad. Bundy, again, suggested that Norstad's position may have reflected the view that conventional build-up diminished the nuclear deterrent. Acheson, who strongly supported the Nitze plan, demanded that the United States move quickly, rather than waiting for congressional and allied approval. A "serious military movement," Acheson stated, "by the United States is 'an ominous thing' which would clearly convey the serious purpose of the American government."[36]

Kennedy endorsed Acheson's position, but "subject to the modifying advice from the Secretary of Defense." That advice turned out to be decisive. McNamara had declared early in the meeting that the size of the American conventional build-up in Berlin was no longer important: Khrushchev's announcement meant that the "matter need not be decided now, since troops will not be ready for shipment until the middle of November. . . . the issue will be re-examined and presented to the President at that time."[37] This was a clear rebuff to the Nitze/Acheson position, which depended upon a quick and substantial conventional deployment to Europe. McNamara then presented the letter he had written to Norstad. It carefully explained that he was not to use any nuclear weapons without authorization from Washington; he demanded that Norstad spell out "with particularity" command and control procedures regarding nuclear weapons so as to ensure no miscommunications on this matter. He stressed that in case of a conflict in Berlin the West—once it had adequate forces in place—was to engage in conventional war, especially air operations. "Should it appear that Soviet forces sufficient to defeat these actions are being brought into play," McNamara wrote, "the response, on which you would receive specific directions, will be one or more of those contained in paragraph IV."[38] "At this juncture," he continued, "I place as much importance on developing our capacity and readiness to fight with significant non-nuclear forces as on measures designed primarily to make our nuclear deterrent more credible."[39]

McNamara was telling Norstad that NATO was to rely upon "our capacity and readiness to fight with significant non-nuclear forces," which, he emphasized, were being developed not just for immediate purposes but to make the nuclear retaliatory forces more credible. In other words, McNamara was saying that with the Soviet retreat it was time now to return to the longer-term task of building a limited war strategy in Europe that he and Taylor had introduced in the beginning of his term.

But McNamara was not sending a policy paper to Rusk or Kennedy outlining his hopes for a future capability in Europe: he was sending instructions to be followed in case of war to the military commander Norstad. He was telling the SACEUR, who had made his determination to go nuclear vividly clear, to rely on conventional forces in a war over Berlin, until he was given specific approval otherwise, *even though those forces did not yet exist.* McNamara was saying that if war occurred tomorrow Norstad was not to use nuclear weapons unless he received direct approval from Washington, and instead to use conventional forces which—as McNamara's letter also clearly stated—Norstad conspicuously did not have.

The following evening, McNamara's deputy Roswell Gilpatric announced to the world, via a speech to the Business Council in Hot Springs, Virginia, that the missile gap of which Kennedy had spoken during the campaign never existed. Indeed, Gilpatric said, it was the United States that held an advantage in nuclear missiles; American "destructive power" could destroy the Soviet Union even after a Soviet first strike. An enemy's move that triggered an American nuclear retaliation "would be an act of self-destruction on his part."[40]

Gilpatric referred ominously to Berlin. "If forceful interference with our rights and obligations should lead to violent conflict," he warned, "as it well might, the United States does not intend to be defeated." In such a conflict, Gilpatric continued, the United States would "join free men in standing up to their responsibilities."[41]

Something odd, even for the Kennedy administration, was going on. On the 20th, McNamara, having defeated the hard-liners Nitze and Acheson, ordered Norstad not to use nuclear weapons in a war over Berlin; the next day, he had his deputy announce to the world, in a speech that ranks among the toughest given by an American during the Cold War, that the United States was quite prepared to do so.

Subtly, and perhaps without being entirely aware of it, Kennedy and his advisers were replacing their muddled position on Berlin with a strategy to evade war that bore a nice resemblance to the one Eisenhower had used in the late 1950s. The strategy which McNamara sent to Norstad removed, as had Eisenhower's, all intermediate military options: Norstad was either to fight with conventional forces he did not possess, or wait for the administration to authorize any use of nuclear weapons. On this last point McNamara, like Eisenhower, was quite clear: Norstad was not to go nuclear until he had direct and explicit approval from Washington. At the same time, Gilpatric's speech highlighted—not only to the Soviets, but to Americans and Europeans as well[42]—that a war in Berlin would trigger a devastating nuclear war, one in which America's NATO allies had better be involved ("standing up to their responsibilities") from the beginning. By raising a public specter of thermonuclear war, while at the same time secretly adjusting military policy to make such a war unlikely, McNamara was utilizing the Eisenhower strategy well.

On the evening of October 22, deputy chief of the U.S. mission in Berlin Allan Lightner and his wife decided to attend a Czechoslovak theater performance in East Berlin. Despite the Wall American troops and officials, still formal occupiers of the defeated Nazi capital, were regularly crossing through the Friedrichstrasse opening into the eastern sector. But on that night East German Vopos stopped the American diplomat and demanded official identification. Lightner refused, citing his right as an American official to pass freely throughout Berlin. The Vopos insisted that unidentified civilians could no longer enter East Berlin without military escort. Lightner, forgetting about the play, demanded to speak to a Soviet official and summoned American MPs, who arrived and escorted him through the checkpoint, whereupon they returned to the western sector and then repeated their steps. A Soviet officer meanwhile arrived at the gate and apologized for the mistaken detainment; that ended the evening's events at Friedrichstrasse. But the confrontation confirmed for the East Germans their suspicion that the Americans still saw themselves as occupiers of all Berlin. The next day East German authorities announced that nonuniformed Western officials would have to show passports when entering East Berlin.[43]

The East German decision would have been a classic example of "salami slicing"—the strategy of demanding concession after concession, aware that each was in itself too minor likely to provoke armed response—had it occurred *before* the Wall went up. But two months of Western inaction regarding the Wall signified, as the East Germans knew, as Kennedy had implied in his speech, as Rusk constantly explained, and as Khrushchev's ultimatum withdrawal indicated, that the West had extended *de facto* recognition of East German sovereignty over East Berlin. For the Americans to incite a conflict over access at Friedrichstrasse after accepting the Wall would have been like the Soviet Union suddenly demanding that the United States leave Guantanamo Bay after the Cuban missile crisis.

But Clay did not see events from this perspective. He was eager to stand up to the East German action and push events toward war, which in October 1961 meant either immediate defeat or nuclear holocaust, over an issue which the administration had thoroughly defined as unworthy of further action.[44] Clay, therefore, had to be stopped. On October 24 he telephoned Kennedy directly to insist that he be allowed to challenge the East German barrier at Friedrichstrasse. Kennedy allowed Clay to send civilian cars through Checkpoint "Charlie," the American border control on the west end of Friedrichstrasse, into East Berlin. When, as assumed, they were ordered by Vopos to turn back, Clay had armed Jeeps escort the cars through, while he deployed personnel carriers and ten American tanks in the rear.

The next day, Clay urged Rusk to allow him to provoke the Soviets into confronting American forces by sending his troops through the checkpoint, then tearing down a section of the Wall as they returned to the American sector. Clay's objective was to force the Soviets to demonstrate that it was they, not the East Germans, who were really responsible for the Wall: this could only be verified, as he saw it, by forcing a confrontation.[45] On that day Clay deployed ten tanks near the checkpoint.

Here, finally, was a moment when a further move by either side could have led to real hostilities. It "appears," as Norstad wrote to Lemnitzer, "that we may be faced with a showdown."[46] The Soviets replied to Clay's deployment by sending seven tanks to the border — the next move was the Americans'. Clay demanded on the 26th that Washington respond to his previous day's proposal to conduct a raid through the checkpoint: "request reply soonest," he added. Rusk did reply, telling Clay that "entry into East Berlin is not a vital interest."[47] On October 27, two months after the Wall went up, the Berlin Crisis reached its most tense moment. Late in the afternoon three more Soviet tanks appeared on the eastern side of the Friedrichstrasse. American tank crews went on full alert, ready to move against their Soviet counterparts should they try to intercept the American civilian cars that continued to zip back and forth across the border.

At 11:55 a.m., Washington time, Clay called Kennedy, who told the General to stop the civilian probes. Clay complied.[48] The Soviet and American forces faced off against each other across the broad thoroughfare for the entire day, while (on the western side) journalists fought each other for available telephones and an enterprising vendor sold pretzels.[49] That afternoon Kennedy called Clay. The General argued that the Soviets were unlikely to make any move. Kennedy congratulated Clay for keeping his nerve during the standoff, to which Clay replied, "Mr. President, we're not worried about our nerves. We're worried about those of you people in Washington."[50]

It is unknown how Kennedy himself reacted to this last slap, but it is now known that the president had authorized his brother, Robert, to work out a back-channel deal with Khrushchev to defuse the Friedrichstrasse crisis. The Soviets would withdraw their tanks, and the Americans would follow.[51] At 10 o'clock that evening Rusk sent Clay a telegram informing him, in proper diplomatic passive voice, of official planning. Instructions, Rusk wrote, "have been issued to defer any further civilian probes with armed escorts into Berlin." In addition, uniforms would be worn by all American military personnel entering East Berlin, and civilian officials would refrain from attempting to enter East Berlin—except for one such attempt per day.[52] (Like the Chinese in 1958, the United States would back down, but perform a little ritual defiance to show that it was not beaten.) Clay stopped the American probes, and on the morning of the 28th the Soviet tanks began to withdraw from their position. The American forces followed suit. Other than some desultory skirmishes over air access in February, that was the end of direct Cold War conflict in Berlin.

Flexible Response versus Evasion of War

President Kennedy and his main advisers had taken office in 1961 determined to invigorate American military policy—to replace Eisenhower's one-dimensional fixation upon thermonuclear retaliation and his incoherent security policies with flexible strategies designed to give the president interesting options in a crisis rather than the old choice between conciliation or general nuclear war. Throughout 1961 they worked to devise a Cold War strategy of flexible response, and they would continue to so until late October 1962.[53]

When the administration faced a vivid possibility of war with the Soviet Union, however—most notably between May and August, and then during the Friedrichstrasse showdown in October—key administration officials, especially Bundy, McNamara, and Kennedy himself, found themselves backing away from flexible response. The prospect of any kind of war with the Soviet Union suddenly seemed terrifying, and instead of confidently considering what kind of war would best suit American interests, these officials began to worry much more about finding ways to avoid war. Unconsciously (except perhaps in the case of Bundy), they grabbed hold of the war-evasion strategy that Eisenhower had left for them. Indeed, the Kennedy administration's behavior in October—McNamara's creation of a nonstrategy, Gilpatric's announcement of American nuclear determination, and then the White House surreptitious defusing of the tank showdown—owed quite a bit to Eisenhower.

Conversely, when the threat of war receded—in the early months before Vienna, between the Wall and Friedrichstrasse, and then for another year—the administration began to reconsider flexible response. Hardliners like Nitze and Acheson began to rise in bureaucratic power. Those who were unsure of their stance, like Kennedy, fell in stature. A strategy that offered alternatives to "holocaust or humiliation" became appealing again to an administration filled with men bent upon finding new and innovative solutions to tough political problems.

This pattern demonstrates how Eisenhower's strategy of evading war extended into the Kennedy era. Eisenhower had left for the new administration a military policy which stipulated nothing but massive nuclear retaliation should the United States go to war with the Soviet Union. When such a war became a vivid possibility, the prospect of all-out thermonuclear destruction flew up in the faces of Kennedy and his advisers, literally forcing them to back away from conflict and pursue war evasion tactics quite reminiscent of the old master.

What happens when the likelihood of war becomes more remote? When Eisenhower was president, he personally made sure that flexible response did not become attractive by defeating its advocates in the all-important struggle to define basic American security policy. There was, however, no comparable figure in the Kennedy administration. As a consequence, the administration drifted away from Eisenhower's strategy after the Friedrichstrasse crisis. It would take Khrushchev's decision to deploy missiles in Cuba to bring it back.

Epilogue:
McNamara's Dialectic

The Kennedy administration might well have decided after Berlin simply to adopt Eisenhower's strategy of evading war and be done with it. Whether he realized it or not, the strategy had worked well for Kennedy during the fall of 1961, by making the plausible option of war unavailable when the East Germans erected the Wall and when Clay instigated the Friedrichstrasse standoff. Moreover, staying with the all-or-nothing policy was the course of least resistance, always a major factor in Kennedy's decisionmaking. To adopt an alternative policy would mean having to get more money from Congress, alarming NATO allies, provoking Khrushchev, confronting Norstad, and disrupting a stable element of Cold War rivalry. Certainly it would be easier to let things remain as they were.

The man primarily responsible for fighting this potential inertia and maintaining the cause of flexible response was Secretary of Defense McNamara. For McNamara, the Berlin crisis had demonstrated above all else why the United States needed to obtain a flexible military policy as soon as possible. The administration had been handcuffed by Eisenhower's policy—forced to tremble during the summer of 1961, accept the Wall passively in August, and then face the prospect of spasmodic thermonuclear war over Clay's game at Friedrichstrasse. To be sure, McNamara had done well to evade war in October, but like Dulles during the Quemoy-Matsu crisis he did this only because for the moment he had no other choice. Like Dulles, McNamara viewed that experience not as an example of what to do in future crises, but as a regrettable necessity not to be permitted again.

With no one else in the administration determined or powerful enough to stop him, McNamara succeeded during late 1961 and early 1962 in making limited war against the communist bloc a genuine option of American military policy for the first time since 1955. This heralded a triumph for the idea that a major war, and particularly a nuclear war against the Soviet Union, could be limited and won—an idea promoted by people like Taylor, Kissinger, and now above all the brilliant theorist Thomas Schelling. But McNamara's triumph was short-lived, killed in its infancy by the events in Cuba during October 1962.

Schelling's Thesis

As we have seen, during the late 1950s strategists in think tanks and universities across America had been working intensively to develop an alternative to Eisenhower's all-or-nothing strategy. Kissinger, Taylor, and many others besides had argued in favor of a strategy that would dictate reacting to Soviet aggression with a limited form of retaliation: by developing flexible military strategies, the United States could keep a general war with the Soviet Union from progressing all the way to thermonuclear annihilation.

There were two problems with these original strategies of flexible response. First, as has been pointed out already, they danced around the central deficiency of all limited nuclear war strategies: the question of how a nation stops fighting when it still has immensely destructive weapons at its disposal. Eisenhower had foreseen this problem from the beginning, and had made it the conceptual basis of his all-or-nothing military policy. A second problem, and one perhaps of greater interest to McNamara and his colleagues, was these strategies' rather bleak message. Both Taylor and Kissinger argued that a general war with the Soviet Union could be limited, and won, at a level somewhere below all-out thermonuclear destruction. But how attractive really was a strategy that promised fifty million dead rather than 100 million, ten years of national recovery rather than thirty? Was there not something better than that? The brilliant theorist and economist Thomas Schelling of Harvard believed that there was.[1]

In 1960 Schelling published *Strategy of Conflict*, a pioneering study that applied game theory to human conflict, especially warfare.[2] In a chapter devoted particularly to the question of nuclear war, entitled "The Threat That Leaves Something to Chance," Schelling unveiled an argument that departed substantially from the early ideas of flexible response—both from the published strategies of intellectuals like Kissinger and from the policy recommendations of John Foster Dulles. Schelling believed that the United States could use nuclear weapons in an aggressive manner to intimidate the Soviet Union, raise the specter of all-out war, and *prevail* in a Cold War crisis. Such a result would be better than Eisenhower's choice of conciliation or all-out-war; it would also be superior to the limited wars of Kissinger and Taylor.

The threat of nuclear retaliation, Schelling argued, rests upon the ability of one side to persuade the other that in the event of a given transgression punishment *will*, not *may*, happen. The adversary must fear that if it makes a false move retaliation, and maybe holocaust, will follow. Eisenhower's all-or-nothing strategy, by placing before the Soviet Union the unreal threat of blowing up the world over incremental forms of aggression, lacked this credibility.

A more credible nuclear policy, Schelling continued, should seek to convey the message to the other side that things will get out of hand, should aggression occur, even if the deterrer would rather avoid it.[3] By provoking a crisis or starting a local war the aggressor would be playing with fire, pushing the deterrer toward a reaction that would *inadvertently* spiral into spasmodic war. It is to the deterrer's advantage to cultivate this fear, to demonstrate by action that even modest aggression is going to lead to uncontrollable escalation. While Eisenhower's strategy could not be faulted for failing to emphasize the specter of uncontrollable war, it lacked the mechanism to "demonstrate by action" to the Soviets what was soon to follow.

An effective way to show the Soviet Union that holocaust was to follow would be to "introduce new weapons" during the early stages of a conflict[4] somewhere on enemy territory. The purpose of doing this is not to attain a tactical end, like blowing up a railway or a tank division, but to illustrate vividly what will happen unless the aggressor backs away at once. This escalation signifies that armageddon is nigh. That neither side wants this to happen is obvious; the terror exists for everyone. But the only way it can be stopped is for the aggressor to retreat. By doing so, it saves not only itself, but civilization as well.[5]

A new fact, Schelling wrote, exists in international politics: the world's great powers were all terrified by the idea of general war. The United States could exploit this new fact by deliberately, actively, raising the specter of general war in order to force the Soviet Union to back down or unleash armageddon. Schelling called this kind of activism *compellence*.[6] One does not wait, terrified, for something to happen: one takes the initiative. During times of crisis it is better to administer "punishment *until* the other acts, rather than *if* he acts."[7] To prevail in conflict, one must neither shy away from facts, nor throw up one's hands and say that nothing can be done, but use them boldly to obtain advantage.[8] Instead of giving in to nuclear fear, *use it.*

Immediately following the publication of *Strategy of Conflict* Schelling elaborated upon his argument on nuclear war, both in a public scholarly article and in a private memorandum delivered to the president. In these two writings, Schelling made his ideas known to a wider audience and applied them more specifically to potential international crises.

In a 1962 article (written in 1961) published in the influential journal *World Politics*, Schelling made his recommended course of action for conflicts like the one happening in Berlin very clear. Eisenhower's military policy was wholly unsuited to crises like these, because neither local resistance nor all-out retaliation were acceptable options in a war over an intermediate Cold War stake. In between these two extremes, Schelling wrote, "there is the strategy of risky behavior, of deliberately creating a risk that is credible precisely because its consequences are not entirely within our own and the Soviets' control."[9]

What kind of risky behavior should this be? It is worth recalling Norstad's statement in the fall of 1961 that if the communists shut off access to West Berlin the United States could respond at the probe level; once a battalion was defeated, the U.S. would have to choose between nuclear war and defeat. This was America's military option in 1961. In this light, Schelling's elaboration deserves to be quoted at length:

> If we wish to convey that the war is getting out of hand, that it will shortly become locally very destructive in spite of efforts to confine it to military targets, we should pick military targets that cause destruction commensurate with the notion we want to convey. . . . In a nuclear exchange, even if it nominally involves only "tactical" weapons against tactically important targets, there will be a conscious negotiating process between two very threatening enemies who are worried that the war will get out of hand. . . .
>
> In the desperate circumstances in which we were about to lose Western Europe, if there were no prospect of militarily winning an all-out war against the Soviet Union, and if there were little reason to

suppose that the Soviets could expect to win militarily an all-out war against us, some kind of limited punitive warfare would almost certainly suggest itself.[10]

Here was an argument that clearly (despite the obfuscative passive voice at the end) made the case for an activist, aggressive policy of nuclear intimidation in crises like Berlin. The next time the United States gets into a showdown with the Soviet Union, Schelling was saying, it should "deliberately" create a risk designed to warn the Soviet Union that major war was about to erupt if it did not back off. Should the Soviets not surrender at this point, Schelling's next step is clear (is it not?): the United States should "pick military targets" with the aim of persuading the Soviets that the war is about to become locally very destructive; tactical nuclear weapons, he writes, are well suited for this purpose. If at that point the Soviets did not give in, it would be time for pre-emptive nuclear war. Such a strategy would make everyone's fear of nuclear war an advantage for the United States, for only a Soviet leadership made of stone would not back down.

At the same time he was composing this article, Schelling was invited by the Kennedy administration to comment on the Berlin Crisis. His paper, "Nuclear Strategy in the Berlin Crisis," was included in Kennedy's reading packet for the trip to Hyannis Port in July. Once again, Schelling's laid out his strategy of compellence clearly:[11]

> The important thing in limited nuclear war is to impress the Soviet leadership with the risk of general war—a war that may occur whether we or they intend it or not. If nuclear weapons are introduced the main consequence will not be on the battlefield; the main consequence will be the increased likelihood and expectation of general war.
>
> . . . Limited and localized nuclear war is not, therefore, a "tactical" war. However few the nuclears used, and however selectively they are used, their purpose should not be "tactical" because their consequences will not be tactical. With nuclears, it has become a war of nuclear risks and threats at the highest strategic level. It is a war of nuclear bargaining.
>
> This is the way nuclears should be used if they must be used;[12] this is therefore the way our plans should be drawn. And our *requirements* for nuclear weapons in Europe—numbers of weapons, their location, state of readiness, and means of delivery—should be derived from this concept of their use.[13]

Following upon the logic of his *World Politics* article, Schelling was recommending, in a paper directed to the President of the United States, that the administration use nuclear weapons after the outbreak of local war around Berlin to compel the Soviet Union to back down. As we have seen, and as Schelling's last comment implies, this recommendation was moot for the moment for the simple reason that the hardware in Europe did not exist. Schelling's awareness of this fact suggests, however, that he was hoping in his paper not so much to affect the way that Kennedy dealt with Berlin, as to use the crisis as a means of persuading the administration to prepare for future crises his way.

McNamara's "No-Cities" Doctrine

As we have seen, McNamara was one of the administration's original proponents of flexible response.[14] Though he had backed away from it out of necessity during the Berlin crisis, he had not stopped believing that it was necessary to continue the fight to eliminate Eisenhower's all-or-nothing military policy and develop a serious strategy of limited nuclear warfare. A tremendous bureaucratic fighter, by early 1962 McNamara had developed and was beginning to implement a new American military policy, which he called the "no-cities" doctrine. This new policy stipulated that the United States, for the first time since 1956, would officially seek to limit and control a war with the Soviet Union.[15]

In February, McNamara introduced this strategy at a speech in Chicago, in which he argued specifically that the gradual escalation incorporated in his new strategy was not meant so much to limit destruction per se as to threaten further war as a means of getting the Soviets to back down. "We may seek to terminate a war on favorable terms by using our forces as a bargaining weapon—by threatening further attack," McNamara argued in February. "Our new policy gives us the flexibility to choose among several operational plans." He then formally proposed the new strategy at a secret NATO meeting in early May. "[B]asic military strategy in general nuclear war," McNamara stated, "should be approached in much the same way that more conventional military operations have been regarded in the past." Berlin, he told his European colleagues, had revealed the bankruptcy of previous NATO all-or-nothing doctrine: Eisenhower's strategy "has serious limitations for the purpose of deterrence and for the conduct of general nuclear war."

To avoid the immediate holocaust that that previous strategy insured, the

United States would urge that its allies accept a new nuclear strategy which provided NATO decision-makers with a "variety of strategic choices," and the ability to wage a "controlled and flexible nuclear response." A possible element of this strategy, McNamara added, would be a "small, demonstrative use of nuclear weapons."[16]

McNamara announced the policy publicly in his famous commencement address at the University of Michigan in June 1962. "The very strength and nature of the Alliance make it possible to retain, even in the face of a massive surprise attack," McNamara said, "sufficient reserve striking power to destroy an enemy society if driven to it." McNamara elaborated this point in a part of the speech not commonly quoted:

> We are convinced that a general nuclear war target system is indivisible, and if, despite all our efforts, nuclear war should occur, our best hope lies in conducting a centrally controlled campaign against all of the enemy's vital nuclear capabilities, while retaining reserve forces, all centrally controlled.[17]
>
> We know that the same forces which are targeted on ourselves are also targeted on our allies. Our own strategic retaliatory forces are prepared to respond against these forces, wherever they are and whatever their targets. This mission is assigned not only in fulfillment of our treaty commitments but also because *the character of nuclear war compels it.*[18]

A basic national security policy draft, submitted to the NSC just after McNamara's speech, reiterated this kind of thinking: in the event of general war, the draft's authors argued, the United States should seek to reduce Soviet offensive capability, retain strategic forces for "possible selective use," and facilitate "the conduct of negotiations designed to bring the war to an end on terms which are consistent with U.S. interests. . . ."[19]

As Lawrence Freedman has noted, there were some differences between Schelling's strategy of compellence and McNamara's no-cities doctrine.[20] Most signficant of these was McNamara's argument that the limited warfare NATO would wage, to defeat the enemy locally and remind it of possible destruction to come, should mix conventional and nuclear forces. This departed from Schelling's contention that only nuclear weapons would raise the specter of war and create the climate of fear needed to compel the communists to back down.

In the bigger picture this was really a minor distinction. Since 1957 (longer than that, unofficially) it had been the policy of the United States that in a confrontation with the Soviet Union and its allies over major Cold War stakes, the West would wage general nuclear war once the conflict moved beyond minor military hostilities. A general nuclear war, moreover, would be an inherently unlimitable and uncontrollable phenomenon, something that America and its European allies would unleash only in a retaliatory, spasmodic way to begin and end World War III. Almost single-handedly, and in the space of only a few months, McNamara had discontinued this policy. In its place he had put forth a doctrine based upon the idea that the United States could win a limited war with the communist bloc by using selective military attacks to escalate the war on American terms and to remind the Russians of the destruction to follow if they did not retreat.[21] McNamara was imposing upon the military policy of the West Schelling's thesis that a direct war with the Soviet Union, even a nuclear war, could be controlled, restrained, manipulated, and eventually won. This was the aspect of the no-cities doctrine that mattered most.

The Cuban Missile Crisis: Eisenhower Wins

As Desmond Ball argues, McNamara gave up on the no-cities strategy by late 1962 for several reasons: unfavorable American reaction to the idea of a first nuclear strike; the prospect of a diversifying Soviet nuclear capability; the uniform rejection of it by NATO allies; and the exploitation of it by the services to secure unnecessary hardware.[22]

But McNamara did not simply give up on the no-cities strategy; he abandoned the entire notion of winnable nuclear war. And this abandonment manifested itself not just in a subsequent revision of American nuclear strategy but in the rest of McNamara's public life. While his reasons for shelving the no-cities doctrine itself may have been due to traditional strategic and bureaucratic reasons, his sudden rejection of Schelling's essential thesis came from a more visceral experience he underwent in late October 1962.

During the last two weeks of October 1962 the United States and the Soviet Union confronted each other over nuclear missiles that Khrushchev had deployed in Cuba.[23] The Cuban Missile Crisis was the last, most dramatic, and probably most dangerous episode of the entire 1958–1962 crisis period. Nothing remotely like it has happened since.

In the early stages of the crisis Kennedy seriously considered the option

of launching a conventional air strike against the missiles. According to the
Schelling vision of strategy, this would have been a proper move, and after
the Soviet response the U.S. would commence its "war of nuclear bargaining
and demonstration." The objective: humiliation and defeat of the Soviet
Union, and the liberation of Cuba. Here was a textbook opportunity to take
advantage of the new doctrine. The weapons were now available, the military
ready to go.

What instead happened? In exchange for a Soviet promise to remove the
missiles, simply to restore the *status quo ante*, Kennedy agreed publicly that
the United States would not invade Cuba. Through back channels, Kennedy
agreed as well to remove medium-range nuclear missiles from Turkey. Had
the back channels failed to appease Khrushchev the American administration was ready to ask the Secretary-General of the United Nations to call for
a Soviet-American agreement to remove the missiles from Turkey and
Cuba.[24] Kennedy apparently had decided as well that if the Soviet Union
had attacked the missiles in Turkey that *the United States would not respond.*

Where was McNamara in all of this? Firmly in the camp of appeasement.
McNamara argued against the proposed air strikes, encouraged compromise,
and endorsed the plan to remove the missiles from Turkey.[25] During a meeting early in the crisis, McNamara expressed a willingness to go considerably
further:

President Kennedy then said that he thought at some point Khrushchev would say that if we made a move against Cuba, he would take
Berlin. McNamara surmised perhaps that was the price we must pay
and perhaps we'd lose Berlin anyway.[26]

McNamara had worked diligently in late 1961 and early 1962 to overhaul
the basic military policy of the West. His objective was to put the United
States and its allies into a position to act confidently during a Cold War
crisis, using its new limited weaponry and strategies to raise the specter of
imminent nuclear war and compel the Soviets to back down. "Our new
policy," as he said earlier in 1962, "gives us the flexibility to choose among
several operational plans." But in confronting the possibility of war with the
Soviet Union over the missiles in Cuba, a crisis that one might have thought
to be tailor-made for the new policy, McNamara seems not to have been
particularly interested in deciding which of his "several operational plans"
he might want to use. His primary concern was to find some way to avoid
war. He feared that any military conflict with the Russians could conceivably

lead to all-out nuclear war, a prospect he found so unacceptable that he was ready to abandon Berlin to prevent it. In the heat of the Cuban crisis the idea of escalating the conflict in a virile way, of using, for example, a demonstrative nuclear attack to force the Soviets to think about all-out war, must have struck McNamara as obscene. When the tangible prospect of nuclear war materialized, McNamara shrank away from the Schelling strategy as if it were a deadly snake. Instead, he embraced Eisenhower's strategy of evading nuclear war in its pure form.

Indeed, after October 1962 McNamara himself embarked upon his own campaign of evading nuclear war. He and Kennedy got rid of the no-cities doctrine and replaced it with a policy of assured destruction that was simply a new version of NSC-5707/8. During the Vietnam War McNamara refused to consider using nuclear weapons, preferring instead to preside over a horrible and losing conventional war that destroyed his career and perhaps his life. Since the 1960s McNamara has publicly and resolutely advocated the policy of minimum deterrence, writing at length in a 1982 *Foreign Affairs* article (co-written with McGeorge Bundy, George Kennan, and Gerard Smith) and in a book that nothing good whatsoever can come from a nuclear war.[27] He renounced the Schelling strategy in as thorough a manner as it is possible to do.[28]

There is more to McNamara's repudiation of the Schelling thesis than his conciliatory role in the Cuban Missile Crisis, or his reversion to an all-or-nothing American military policy. By rejecting Schelling McNamara was changing sides in a struggle between two basic ideas about war and politics, a struggle that had been going on well before Hiroshima and the ICBM.

On one side in this long contest of ideas was an understanding of warfare and human relations deriving from the Enlightenment. According to this view, the dilemma of the thermonuclear age could be solved, as could all human dilemmas, by reason, seriousness of purpose, scientific mastery. Of course the new weapons were immensely destructive: an all-out war would be a catastrophe of unprecedented proportions. But this fact made it only more important to stress that these were still only weapons, inanimate objects, tools in the hands of their human masters, and there was therefore no essential reason why capable leaders could not wage a war with them in a rational way. To deny this was to let the specter of war win, to admit that the human race had reached its limits of mastery and control. Not only was this an admission of human limitations: it was also a recipe for all-out thermonuclear destruction when the day came that the Soviet Union and the United States finally went to war.

On the other side of this struggle stands a more pessimistic school of thought. It takes from the sorry history of modern politics and warfare the conclusion that fear and panic routinely overtake reason and equanimity during times of violent crisis. At the outset of a war between nations possessing many thermonuclear weapons, this sort of fear would rise to unimaginable levels, driving from every decisionmaker all conceivable courses of action other than the course of all-out, spasmodic attack. Tremendous, overwhelming—and probably accurate—fears that the other side would not respect any limits to the war and was about to launch everything it had would create a climate of frenzy and terror, even bloodlust. In such circumstances a lone call for a limited strike, or a nuclear "demonstration" would appear ridiculous, pathetic, entirely outside the pale. This climate of fear and panic had dictated how major wars had been started and waged in the past: the stakes of thermonuclear war would only intensify it.

The struggle between these two ideas is not a new one. Clausewitz identified it after the Napoleonic wars, and it has informed the works of theorists, historians, strategists, and poets trying to understand the ferocious and inhuman nature of modern war.[29]

The difference, of course, between the debate over the nature of thermonuclear war and previous such debates is that it remains *hypothetical*. And unless we want to bet everything on the optimists, that is what it will always be. For if we lost this bet, and the pessimists turned out to be right, a thermonuclear war will have destroyed the human race, and along with it things like discourse and memory. The debate would remain forever unresolved, because those pessimists proven right, along with those optimists proven wrong, would all be dead.

Eisenhower's genius was in recognizing that his position was indeed unverifiable. To prevent a thermonuclear war he would never be able to point to one and demonstrate its absolute nature to everyone's satisfaction. Instead, he would have to portray it as such with historical comparisons and imagery, in the hope of persuading his advisers, allies, and the wider Cold War world to accept his vision of what a war between the United States and the Soviet Union would really entail. He accomplished this by forcing his negative views about human nature and war onto United States security policy, quashing with bureaucratic and rhetorical mastery more optimistic beliefs and strategies about the waging of thermonuclear war. The irony, of course, was that his reason for doing this in the first place was not based upon a negative view of humanity at all.

Notes

Preface

1. See, for example, Joshua Muravchik, "How the Cold War Really Ended," *Commentary* 98 (November 1994), p. 10, and The Committee on the Present Danger, *What Is the Soviet Union Up To?* (Washington: The Committee, 1977).
2. See, for example, C. Wright Mills, *The Causes of World War Three* (New York: Simon and Schuster, 1958).
3. For an uncharacteristically passive comment on nuclear peace, see Bruce Cumings, "The End of the 70-years Crisis: Trilateralism and the New World Order," *World Policy Journal* 8 (Spring 1991), p. 205.

Introduction

1. August 20, 1948 paper, "Comments on the General Trend of U.S. Foreign Policy," from the George F. Kennan papers, Princeton University, Box 23. On this paper, see John Lewis Gaddis, *Strategies of Containment* (New York: Oxford University Press, 1982), p. 27.
2. The classic articulation of this point is C. Vann Woodward, "The Age of Reinterpretation," *American Historical Review* 66 (October, 1960). Also see Russell Weigley, *The American Way of War* (New York: Macmillan, 1973), pp. xix.
3. My reading of the dominant role played by American economic and cultural expansionists in U.S. foreign policy before 1945 has been influenced especially by Thomas Hietala, *Manifest Design: Anxious Aggrandizement in Late Jacksonian America* (Ithaca: Cornell University Press, 1985); and Emily Rosenberg, *Spreading the American Dream: American Economic and Cultural Expansion, 1890–1945* (New York: Hill and Wang, 1982).

4. On this point see above all Hans Morgenthau, *Politics Among Nations* (New York: Knopf, 1948). Also see John Lewis Gaddis, *We Now Know: Rethinking Cold War History* (New York: Oxford University Press, 1997), p. 7.

5. Not a ridiculous hypothesis, I think: one would begin with a French decision in the 1930s to extend the Maginot Line through Belgium.

6. The end of the Cold War has prompted some students of U.S. foreign policy who emphasize economic causation to acknowledge the exceptional nature of the Cold War; breaking from the thesis presented in William A. Williams's *The Tragedy of American Diplomacy*, they now regard the Cold War more as an aberration from the larger trend toward a world system dominated by capitalism than as its epitome. For two examples, see Bruce Cumings, "The End of the 70-years' Crisis:" 195–222; and Immanuel Wallerstein, *Geopolitics and Geoculture* (Cambridge: Cambridge University Press, 1992) pp. 2, 6–7, 14.

7. The standard account of Kennan's strategy is Gaddis, *Strategies of Containment*, pp. 25–53. Also see Anders Stephanson, *Kennan and the Art of Foreign Policy* (Cambridge: Harvard University Press, 1989), chapters 2–4, and Melvyn Leffler, *A Preponderance of Power* (Palo Alto: Stanford University Press, 1992), pp. 108–9.

8. Kennan's "Long Telegram" is reprinted in his *Memoirs, 1925–1950* (Boston: Little, Brown, 1967), pp. 547–59.

9. March 28, 1947 Kennan Lecture, "Comments on the National Security Problem," in Giles D. Harlow and George C. Maerz, eds., *Measures Short of War: the George F. Kennan Lectures at the National War College, 1946–47* (Washington: National Defense University Press, 1990), p. 165.

10. Ibid., pp. 167–68.

11. June 18, 1947 Kennan lecture, "Planning of Foreign Policy," *Measures Short of War*, p. 213.

12. "Comments on the National Security Problem," ibid., p. 168.

13. In his more recent writings Kennan has become more critical of American society, and it would probably not be going too far to say that he fears that America won the Cold War battle but lost the war. See his *Around the Cragged Hill: A Personal and Political Philosophy* (New York: Norton, 1993).

14. Kennan introduced one of his first policy planning documents, PPS 13, with this warning: "The danger of war is vastly exaggerated in many quarters." Policy Planning Staff (PPS) document 13, in the U.S. Department of State, *Foreign Relations of the United States, 1947*, vol. 1, "General: The United Nations." Hereafter in this form: FRUS 1 (1947): 770.

15. On Truman's emphasis upon military over moral strength, see Leffler, *A Preponderance of Power*, passim; Frank Ninkovich, *Modernity and Power: A History of the Domino Theory in the Twentieth Century* (Chicago: University of Chicago

Press, 1994), pp. 166–75; Alonzo Hamby, *Man of the People: A Life of Harry S. Truman* (New York: Oxford University Press, 1995), p. 345; and Gregg Herken, *The Winning Weapon: The Atomic Bomb in the Cold War, 1945–1950* (New York: Knopf, 1980), p. 79.

16. Hamby, *Man of the People*, pp. 348–55; Leffler, *Preponderance of Power*, pp. 130–34.

17. See Gaddis, *Strategies of Containment*, pp. 55–65.

18. March 17, 1948 speech by Truman to a joint session of Congress, reprinted in *Public Papers of the President 1948* (Washington, 1964), p. 183.

19. NSC 7, issued on March 30, 1948, FRUS 1 (1948): 546–49.

1. Casus Belli *in Berlin, 1948*

1. On Eisenhower's momentous decision not to advance toward Berlin see Stephen Ambrose, *Eisenhower and Berlin, 1945: The Decision to Halt at the Elbe* (New York: Norton, 1967). Also see Russell Weigley, *Eisenhower's Lieutenants: The Campaign of France and Germany 1944–1945* (Bloomington: Indiana University Press, 1981), pp. 684–87; and Richard Betts, *Soldiers, Statesmen and Cold War Crises* (Cambridge: Harvard University Press, 1977), pp. 77–78.

2. For a summary of Berlin politics before the blockade, see Ann and John Tusa, *The Berlin Airlift* (New York: Atheneum, 1988), chapters 1–4; W. Phillips Davison, *The Berlin Blockade: A Study in Cold War Politics* (New York: Arno Press, 1980), chapter 2; and Avi Shlaim, *The United States and the Berlin Blockade, 1948–1949* (Berkeley: University of California Press, 1983), chapter 2. The first work concentrates on activities in Berlin itself, while the latter two deal primarily with United States and Allied decisionmaking.

3. February 1, 1948 telegram from Murphy to Marshall, FRUS 2 (1948): 2, "Germany and Austria," p. 873.

4. This chapter will not deal with the politics of this conference at any length; briefly, France wanted to avoid antagonizing the Soviet Union by splitting Germany so obviously, while Britain and the United States favored the harder line. A record of the conference's proceedings can be found in FRUS 2 (1948): 1–374. Later, the British would come to take a softer line on Germany, while France would become much more hawkish.

5. This communique can be found in ibid., pp. 141–43.

6. On Operation Bird Dog, see Robert Murphy, *Diplomat Among Warriors* (Garden City, NY: Doubleday, 1964), p. 349; and Jean Edward Smith, *Lucius D. Clay* (New York: Holt, 1990), pp. 483–93. Also see Ann and John Tusa, *The Berlin Airlift*, p. 132.

7. Murphy related Sokolovsky's protest in a March 20, 1948 telegram to Marshall, FRUS 2 (1948): 883–84.

8. Marshall listed his legal reasonings in a formal letter to the Soviet Ambassador in July. See July 6, 1948 letter from Marshall to Panyushkin, ibid., pp. 950–53.

9. The task of justifying a Western presence in Berlin would continue to perplex American policymakers, most notably President Kennedy during the 1961 Vienna Summit. See chapter 8.

10. March 31, 1948 teleconference among Generals Lucius D. Clay and Omar Bradley, and Lieutenant General Albert Wedemeyer, from Jean Edward Smith, ed., *The Papers of General Lucius D. Clay* volume 2 (Bloomington: Indiana University Press, 1974), p. 605.

11. April 2, 1948 teleconference with Bradley and Secretary of the Army Kenneth Royall, ibid., p. 614; April 1, 1948 telegram from Murphy to Marshall, FRUS 2 (1948): 886.

12. April 10, 1948 teleconference with Bradley, *Papers of General Lucius D. Clay*, p. 623.

13. April 22, 1948 telegram from Lovett to U.S. Ambassador to Great Britain Lewis Douglas, FRUS 2 (1948): 896–97.

14. On Marshall and Truman's order, see Kennan, *Memoirs 1925–1950*, p. 246, and Walter Millis, ed., *The Forrestal Diaries* (New York: Viking Press, 1951), p. 424. On Bradley's order, see Shlaim, *The United States and the Berlin Blockade*, p. 138.

15. Editorial Note, in FRUS 2 (1948): 909–10; Shlaim, *The United States and the Berlin Blockade*, pp. 150–59.

16. On the events of June 24 and 25 see U.S. Department of State, *Germany 1947–49, The Story in Documents* (Washington, 1950), pp. 203–4.

17. Shlaim, *The United States and the Berlin Blockade*, p. 196; June 25, 1948 teleconference with Royall and General J. Lawton Collins, *Papers of General Lucius D. Clay*, p. 703.

18. Shlaim, *The United States and the Berlin Blockade*, p. 206.

19. June 26, 1948 telegram from Murphy to Marshall, FRUS 2 (1948): 919–20.

20. Harry S Truman, *Memoirs of Harry S. Truman: Volume 2, Years of Trial and Hope* (Garden City, NY: Doubleday, 1956), p. 123.

21. June 28, 1948 Marshall telegram to Clay, FRUS 2 (1948): 930; also see *Forrestal Diaries*, p. 454.

22. This is the July 6, 1948 Marshall letter to Panyushkin, mentioned above in note 8.

23. July 14, 1948 telegram from Douglass to Lovett, FRUS 2 (1948): 968.

24. Richard Betts, *Soldiers, Statesmen and Cold War Crises* (Cambridge: Harvard University Press, 1977), p. 93. On Clay's regular use of the *fait accompli* to force Washington's hand, also see Shlaim, *The United States and the Berlin Blockade*, p. 206.

25. A record of the Malik-Jessup talks can be found in FRUS 3 (1949): "Council of Foreign Ministers; Germany and Austria," pp. 694–750.

26. This is the conclusion of Robert Murphy, who believed that the United States ought to have challenged the blockade directly and with military force. Murphy writes in his *Diplomat Among Warriors* (p. 354) that he "should have resigned in protest against Washington's policy."

27. For recent examples, see Leffler, *A Preponderance of Power*, chapter 6; and Samuel R. Williamson Jr., and Steven L. Rearden, *The Origins of U.S. Nuclear Strategy, 1945–1953* (New York: St. Martin's Press, 1993), pp. 93–95.

28. Richard Betts argues that the Truman administration paid "astonishingly little attention" to the atomic bomb before the Berlin crisis. Betts, *Nuclear Blackmail and Nuclear Balance* (Washington: Brookings Institute, 1987).

29. May 19, 1948 memorandum from Royall to the NSC, FRUS 1 (1948): 572–73. On the direct relationship between the Berlin blockade and the demand by the American military to specify American atomic policy, also see Scott Sagan, *Moving Targets: Nuclear Strategy and National Security* (Princeton: Princeton University Press), pp. 15–16.

30. Memorandum of May 21, 1948 NSC discussion, Declassified Document Collection, 1996 series, document number 3474 (hereafter in this form: *DDC 1996*, number 3474), p. 7.

31. Williamson and Rearden, *The Origins of U.S. Nuclear Strategy*, pp. 87–88.

32. "You have no idea," Kennan said in a 1946 National War College lecture, "how much it contributes to the general politeness and pleasantness of diplomacy when you have a little quiet armed force in the background." (Quoted in Gaddis, *Strategies of Containment*, p. 39.)

33. Though evidence from the Soviet side is not yet clear, some historians argue that the B-29 deployment did in fact intimidate the Soviets and contribute to their decision to accept the Western presence in Berlin and eventually back off from their blockade in 1949. See Gregg Herken, *The Winning Weapon: The Atomic Bomb in the Cold War, 1945–1950* (New York: Knopf, 1981), p. 260; and Gaddis, *The Long Peace: Inquiries into the History of the Cold War* (New York: Oxford University Press, 1987), pp. 109–10.

34. See Shlaim, *The United States and the Berlin Blockade*, p. 245, and Herken, *The Winning Weapon*, p. 287.

35. To prove this latter point Clay characteristically offered to sit on the Berlin airfields throughout the crisis. His bravado, admirable here, would have different effects in the 1961 crisis. The only source for this crucial meeting that I have been able to find is Truman's memoirs. See *Years of Trial and Hope*, pp. 131–33.

36. July 28, 1948 letter from Forrestal to Marshall, FRUS 2 (1948): 994.

37. Truman, *Years of Trial and Hope*, pp. 125–26; *Forrestal Diaries*, pp. 460–62; Leffler, *A Preponderance of Power*, p. 225.

38. NSC-30 is reprinted in FRUS 1 (1948): "General: The United Nations," part 1, pp. 624–28.

39. Ibid., p. 626.

40. On this point also see David Alan Rosenberg, "The Origins of Overkill: Nuclear Weapons and American Strategy, 1945–60," *International Security* 7 (Spring 1983): 13.

41. On this point see The Journals of David E. Lilienthal: *The Atomic Energy Years, 1945–1950* (New York: Harper and Row, 1964), p. 474. Hamby, *Man of the People*, p. 552; and McGeorge Bundy, *Danger and Survival: Choices About the Bomb in the First Fifty Years* (New York: Random House, 1988), pp. 199–200.

42. Truman quoted in *Forrestal Diaries*, p. 487.

43. Also making this point are Williamson and Rearden, *The Origins of U.S. Nuclear Strategy*, p. 78.

2. General War Becomes Thermonuclear War, 1948–1952

1. On the interservice struggles see Williamson and Rearden, *The Origins of U.S. Nuclear Strategy*, pp. 92–96; Leffler, *Preponderance of Power*, chapter 7; Herken, *The Winning Weapon*, chapter 14.

2. Some of the Harmon Report is reprinted in Thomas Etzold and John Lewis Gaddis, eds., *Containment: Documents on American Policy and Strategy* (New York: Columbia University Press, 1978), pp. 360–64. Also see Williamson and Rearden, *The Origins of U.S. Nuclear Strategy*, pp. 104–5; Herken, *The Winning Weapon*, pp. 293–98; and David Alan Rosenberg, "American Atomic Strategy and the Hydrogen Bomb Decision," *Journal of American History* 66 (June, 1979): 77–78.

3. On the Soviet test and American reaction to it, see Richard Rhodes, *Dark Sun* (New York: Simon and Schuster, 1995), chapter 19.

4. See Richard Hewlett and Francis Duncan, *Atomic Shield: A History of the U.S. Atomic Energy Commission* vol. 2, 1947–1952 (University Park, PA: Penn State University Press, 1969), p. 369; Herken, *The Winning Weapon*, p. 303; and Lewis Strauss, *Men and Decisions* (Garden City, NY: Doubleday, 1962), pp. 205–6. Apparently Truman was apprehensive about acknowledging the Soviet test also because of the effect this news could have had on the world financial markets, which were at that moment undergoing a major crisis.

5. See Leffler, *A Preponderance of Power*, p. 327; Herken, *The Winning Weapon*, pp. 304–5; and Hewlett and Duncan, *Atomic Shield*, pp. 370–71.

6. Herbert York, *The Advisors: Oppenheimer, Teller, and the Superbomb* (San Francisco: W. H. Freeman, 1976), pp. 44–45; Williamson and Rearden, *The Origins of U.S. Nuclear Strategy*, p. 114.

7. Hewlett and Duncan, *Atomic Shield*, p. 374. Also see Williamson and Rearden, *The Origins of U.S. Nuclear Strategy*, pp. 123–24.

8. See *The Lilienthal Journals*, pp. 580–83. Two members of the GAC, Enrico Fermi and I.I. Rabi, dissented from the main conclusion, arguing that American

renunciation of the superbomb had to be contingent on some kind of Soviet conciliation.

9. FRUS 1 (1949): "National Security Affairs; Foreign Economic Policy," Statement Appended to the Report of the General Advisory Committee, p. 571. Also see York, *The Advisors*, pp. 52–53.

10. York, *The Advisors*, p. 53.

11. The following citations are a few examples only. The one exception was Dean Acheson, Truman's new Secretary of State, who—though he ultimately did not oppose the decision in January to go ahead with the bomb—wrote a long memorandum on atomic weaponry on December 20 in which he never expressed an opinion as to whether the United States should build it or not. Memorandum by the Secretary of State, FRUS 1 (1949): 612–17. Leffler, in *A Preponderance of Power* (p. 330) calls Acheson's memorandum "the most significant memorandum dealing with the hydrogen bomb"—a conclusion that I cannot see how Professor Leffler reached. On this matter also see Bundy, *Danger and Survival*, pp. 212–13.

12. Memorandum by the Joint Chiefs of Staff to the Secretary of Defense, FRUS 1 (1949): 595.

13. December 19, 1949 Nitze memorandum, ibid., p. 611; November 25, 1949 letter from Strauss to Truman, ibid., pp. 597–98.

14. Undated memorandum circulated by the Defense Members of the Working Group of the Special Committee of the National Security Council, ibid., p. 606. According to Rearden and Williamson the meeting that produced this memorandum took place on December 16. See *The Origins of U.S. Nuclear Strategy*, p. 119.

15. November 21, 1949 letter from McMahon to Truman, FRUS 1 (1949): 588.

16. Indeed, the entire controversy surrounding the GAC report had an air of unreality about it, as the main makers of national security policy in the Truman administration, including the president himself, acted as if the GAC recommendation might somehow become American policy against all of their wishes. Stanislaw Ulam, a mathematician working on the superbomb, described this as "the weird and unnatural things going on in Washington." Quoted in Hewlett and Duncan, *Atomic Shield*, p. 392.

17. Lilienthal's efforts to persuade Truman to wait on the superbomb are related in his *Journals*, pp. 587–634. In the interest of secrecy Lilienthal referred to the hydrogen bomb as "Campbell" ("super" = soup). Passages like "I asked him if the Commission should try to elicit the views on 'Campbell' of State and Defense . . ." or "Have just come from handing our memo on 'Campbell' to the President . . ." were rather disconcerting to this author.

18. Truman quoted by R. Gordon Arneson, "The H-Bomb Decision," *Foreign Service Journal* 46 (May 1969): 27.

19. On this point also see Rhodes, *Dark Sun*, pp. 401–2.
20. McMahon is quoted in Edward Teller with Allen Brown, *After Hiroshima* (Garden City, NY : Doubleday, 1962), p. 44. In his letter to Truman on November 21 McMahon iterates this point. "Here is a fundamental inconsistency," he stated, referring to the GAC objections. " If the super would accomplish no more than weapons already in our arsenal, why single it out for special objection? If, on the other hand, the super represents a wholly new order of destructive magnitude—as I think it obviously does—than its military role would seem to be decisive." Memorandum from McMahon to Truman, cited in note 15, pp. 588–89.
21. On this point also see Herken, *The Winning Weapon*, pp. 316–17; Williamson and Rearden, *The Origins of U.S. Nuclear Strategy*, pp. 111, 116; and Leffler, *Preponderance of Power*, p. 332, who writes that "it is essential to emphasize that U.S. officials were not worried about purposeful Soviet military aggression. They were worried about the diplomatic shadows cast by strategic power."
22. November 18, 1949 draft memorandum from Kennan to Acheson, FRUS 1 (1949): 586.
23. An excerpt from this paper is printed in FRUS 1 (1950): 22–44. Kennan noted in an attached memorandum that "since Paul [Nitze] and the others were not entirely in agreement with the substance and since I was afraid that this report might be an embarrassing one to have on record as a formal staff report, I have re-done this as a personal paper." (p. 22n) Kennan discusses this paper in his *Memoirs*, pp. 471–76. On Kennan's valedictory also see Gaddis, *Strategies of Containment*, pp. 79–83.
24. FRUS 1 (1950) p. 39.
25. February 17, 1950 draft memorandum from Kennan to Acheson, ibid., p. 164.
26. January 31, 1950 message from Truman to Acheson, FRUS 1 (1950): 141–42. This directive was adapted from a recommendation given to Truman by the Acheson/Lilienthal/Johnson special committee.
27. A standard argument regarding NSC-68 (Gaddis, *Strategies of Containment*, pp. 91–109) holds that Nitze expanded containment qualitatively beyond the basic realist formula provided by Kennan in 1946 and 1947. Other historians—for example, Walter Hixson, *George F. Kennan: Cold War Iconoclast* (New York: Columbia University Press, 1989), p. 303; and Leffler, *A Preponderance of Power*, pp. 355–56—contend that NSC-68 followed logically from Kennan's realism. A new way to address this debate might be to see how each of them approached nuclear policy with that realist formula in the 1950s.
28. April 7, 1950 Report to the President Pursuant to the President's Directive of January 31, 1950 (NSC-68), FRUS 1 (1950): 245.
29. Ibid., pp. 238–39.
30. Williamson and Rearden, in *The Origins of U.S. Nuclear Strategy*, pp. 131–38,

also do not mention this omission, doubly odd given the topic of their book. Also see Bundy, *Danger and Survival*, p. 229.

31. NSC-68, FRUS 1 (1950): 267–68.
32. Ibid., p. 268.
33. Ibid., pp. 264, 283.
34. Ibid., p. 282.
35. Also clearly implied in this passage is an endorsement of pre-emptive thermonuclear war: Nitze argues in this carefully worded sentence that the United States must defeat not only Soviet, but also "Soviet-directed" aggression of "a limited or total character." In 1961 Nitze reintroduced this idea during the second Berlin crisis.
36. Gaddis, *Strategies of Containment*, chapter 4.
37. See Hewlett and Duncan, *Atomic Shield*, p. 472.
38. Ibid., p. 525.
39. Ibid., pp. 541–46.
40. See Rosenberg, "American Atomic Strategy," pp. 20–26; and Williamson and Rearden, *The Origins of U.S. Nuclear Strategy*, chapter seven.
41. Hewlett and Duncan, *Atomic Shield*, p. 557.
42. Ibid., p. 581.
43. See July 3, 1952 letter from LeBaron to Dean, DDC 1996, number 511.
44. Truman's anxiety about detonating a thermonuclear device in early November is related in a October 9, 1952 memorandum by R. Gordon Arneson, FRUS 2 (1952–54), part 2, pp. 1032–33.
45. Richard Rhodes offers a wonderful, microsecond-by-microsecond account of *Mike's* explosion in *Dark Sun*, pp. 505–10.
46. The official announcement of the successful detonation came on November 16: it explained that the test program at Eniwetok "included experiments contributing to thermonuclear weapons research. . . . Scientific executives have expressed satisfaction with the results." November 16, 1952 press release, FRUS 2 (1952–54), part 2, pp. 1042.

3. *The Rise and Fall of Massive Retaliation, January 1953–July 1955*

1. Dulles, "The Christian Citizen in a Changing World," (originally published in August 1948) and "Principle vs. Expedience in Foreign Policy" (originally published in September 1952), both in Henry P. Van Dusen, ed., *The Spiritual Legacy of John Foster Dulles* (Philadelphia: Westminster Press, 1960), pp. 159–74, 121–32.
2. Dulles, "The Spiritual Foundations of World Order," in ibid., p. 124.
3. Dulles, *War or Peace* (New York: Macmillan, 1950), p. 253.
4. Dulles, "A Policy of Boldness," *Life* 32 (May 19, 1952): 146.

5. Ibid., pp. 149–50.

6. See Stephen E. Ambrose, *Eisenhower*, volume 1 (New York: Simon and Schuster, 1983), p. 146.

7. As George Marshall stated, in a letter of commendation to Eisenhower at the end of the war: "You have met and successfully disposed of every conceivable difficulty incident to varied national interests and international political problems of unprecedented complications." Quoted by Forrest Pogue, "The Genesis of *The Supreme Command*: Personal Impressions of Eisenhower the General," in Gunter Bischof and Stephen Ambrose, eds., *Eisenhower: A Centenary Assessment* (Baton Rouge: Louisiana State University Press, 1995), p. 39.

8. While the influence of specific ideas upon policymakers can be (and often is) vastly overrated, the effect of Clausewitz's main ideas upon Eisenhower is certain. Indeed, Eisenhower, not normally wont to drop philosophers' names during security meetings, brought him up on several occasions. During an NSC discussion on South Korean militarism, for example, Eisenhower out of the blue reminded his colleagues that it "was high time to remember the words of wisdom of people like Clausewitz." See memorandum of September 20, 1956 NSC discussion, *DDC 1994*, number 2248, p. 9. Also see Peter J. Roman, *Eisenhower and the Missile Gap* (Ithaca: Cornell University Press, 1995), p. 83.

9. On Eisenhower's attention to Clausewitz, also see Marc Trachtenberg, *History and Strategy*, (Princeton: Princeton University Press, 1991) p. 138; Ambrose, *Eisenhower*, p. 76; Gaddis, *Strategies of Containment*, p. 135; and Saki Dockrill, *Eisenhower's New Look National Security Policy, 1953–61* (New York: St. Martin's Press, 1996), p. 4.

10. On this point see Gaddis, *Strategies of Containment*, pp. 132–136, and Richard Immerman, "Confessions of an Eisenhower Revisionist," *Diplomatic History* 14 (Summer, 1990): 327–28.

11. Cf. Immerman, "Confessions," p. 331, and Gaddis, *The Long Peace*, pp. 123–26.

12. A summary of operation Solarium is reprinted in FRUS 2 (1952–54): "National Security Affairs," part 1, pp. 399–434. Solarium is discussed in Gaddis, *Strategies*, pp. 146–48; H. W. Brands, "The Age of Vulnerability: Eisenhower and the National Insecurity State," *American Historical Review* 94 (October 1989): 966–68; Immerman, "Confessions," pp. 336–37; and Trachtenberg, *History and Strategy*, pp. 136–37. Robert Cutler, Eisenhower's special assistant for national security affairs, incorrectly argued that Dulles was actually the one who set up the exercise. See Cutler, *No Time to Rest* (Boston: Little, Brown, 1965), pp. 307–10. Oddly, Bundy does not mention Solarium at all.

13. New documentation on Solarium has just been released, showing that task force C recommended that the United States "reduce Soviet capability for war before the U.S.S.R. reaches the stage of atomic plenty." See *DDC 1996*, number 78, p. 1.

14. On the transition from Solarium to NSC-162/2, see Trachtenberg, *History and Strategy*, pp. 136–41; Brands, "The Age of Vulnerability," pp. 968–72; Gaddis, *The Long Peace*, p. 172n; Immerman, "Confessions," p. 338; and Rosenberg, "The Origins of Overkill," p. 28.

15. Memoranda of July 30, 1953 and August 27, 1953 NSC discussions, FRUS 2 (1952–54): 435–440, 443–55. Also see Brands, "The Age of Vulnerability," pp. 968–72.

16. Rosenberg, "The Origins of Overkill," pp. 28–32.

17. September 6, 1953 Dulles memorandum, FRUS 2 (1952–54): 457, 459.

18. September 8, 1953 Eisenhower memorandum to Dulles, ibid., p. 461; compare Immerman, "Confessions," p. 337.

19. On this exchange also see Trachtenberg, *History and Strategy*, pp. 139–40.

20. Memorandum of October 7, 1953 of NSC discussion, FRUS 2 (1952–54): 532–33.

21. Eisenhower memorandum of December 5, 1953 dinner with Dulles, Churchill, and Eden, *DDC 1994*, number 2934.

22. Dulles, "The Evolution of Foreign Policy," speech given to the Council of Foreign Relations on January 12, 1954, reprinted in *Department of State Bulletin* 30 (January 25, 1954). Dulles elaborated his point in an article, "Policy for Security and Peace," *Foreign Affairs* 32 (April 1954): 353–64.

23. See Gaddis, *Strategies*, p. 147.

24. On Eisenhower's "atomic diplomacy" from 1953 through 1955, see Bundy, *Danger and Survival*, pp. 255–79.

25. Memorandum of March 25, 1954 NSC discussion, FRUS 2 (1952–54): 641.

26. On the formation of NSC 5422/2, also see Brands, "The Age of Vulnerability," pp. 977–80.

27. NSC 5422/2, reprinted in FRUS 2 (1952–54): 716–18.

28. Dulles, November 15, 1954 Department of State Paper, "Basic National Security Policy (Suggestions of the Secretary of State)," ibid., pp. 773–75.

29. To avoid confusion I will refer to Allen Dulles by his full name.

30. November 18, 1954 paper prepared by Allen Dulles, p. 777; November 19, 1954 paper prepared by Flemming, p. 783; November 22, 1954 memorandum from Wilson to Executive Secretary of the NSC Arthur Lay, pp. 785–86, all ibid.

31. Memorandum of November 24, 1954 NSC discussion, ibid., pp. 789–91.

32. Apparently Eisenhower considered this line of argument—to deny that there was really any disagreement—an effective tactic. In this meeting alone he used it several times, at one point asserting that "everyone really seemed to be in fundamental agreement . . . no policy change was required"; later he expressed his "inability to detect basic policy differences . . . " and declared toward the end of the meeting that "national security policies [are] now well stated." He would use this tactic again during the Berlin crisis in 1959.

33. Ibid., pp. 799–800.
34. On this point see Brands, "Age of Vulnerability," p. 980.
35. NSC 5440, reprinted in FRUS 2 (1952–54): 814–15.
36. Memorandum of January 5, 1955 NSC discussion, *DDC 1994*, no. 2259.
37. Both Dulles's and Eisenhower's statements are reprinted in "Editorial note," FRUS 19 (1955–57), "National Security Policy," p. 61.
38. For a broader discussion of Eisenhower's diplomacy during this crisis, see Gordon H. Chang, "To the Nuclear War Brink: Eisenhower, Dulles, and the Quemoy-Matsu Crisis," *International Security* 12 (Winter 1988).

4. Eisenhower Takes Over, July 1955–April 1957

1. February 14, 1955 report by the Technological Capabilities Panel of the Science Advisory Committee, "Meeting the Threat of Surprise Attack," FRUS 19 (1955–57), pp. 43–44; National Intelligence Estimate number 100-5-55, "Implications of growing nuclear capabilities for the communist bloc and the free world," ibid., p. 86.
2. Memorandum of December 1, 1955 NSC discussion, ibid., pp. 168–69.
3. Roman, *Eisenhower and the Missile Gap*, pp. 86–87.
4. On December 1 Eisenhower did approve an NSC plan to direct the defense department to acquire *intermediate*-range ballistic missiles (IRBMs) with the same urgency as intercontinental ones. The U.S. effort to build missiles with a range of 1,500 miles was, in late 1955, more promising than the ICBM program, and the NSC plan Eisenhower approved was meant to ensure that even if the Soviets did indeed get the ICBM first the United States could deter them temporarily with IRBMs deployed in Europe. See memorandum of September 8, 1955 NSC discussion, FRUS 19 (1955–57): 119–20, and memorandum of December 1, 1955 NSC discussion, ibid., pp. 168–70. For an interesting treatment of Eisenhower's illness, see Clarence G. Lasby, *Eisenhower's Heart Attack: How Ike Beat Heart Disease and Held on to the Presidency* (Lawrence: University Press of Kansas, 1997).
5. Memorandum of January 12, 1956 NSC discussion, *DDC 1987*, number 427, pp. 3, 6, 8, 18.
6. Memorandum of January 23, 1956 meeting with Eisenhower, FRUS 19 (1955–57): 189; Diary Entry, ibid.
7. Memorandum of February 7, 1956 NSC discussion, from the Dwight D. Eisenhower Library (hereafter DDEL), Ann Whitman Files, NSC Series, Box 7, p. 5.
8. February 13, 1956 memorandum by the NSC Planning Board (NSC-5602), FRUS 19 (1955–57): 195.
9. Memorandum of February 27, 1956 NSC discussion, ibid., pp. 202–04.

10. Ibid., p. 204.
11. Ibid., pp. 205–06.
12. Ibid., pp. 206–07.
13. Ibid., pp. 210–11, emphasis added.
14. Ibid., p. 211.
15. See memorandum of March 1, 1956 NSC discussion, ibid., p. 230n.
16. NSC-5602/1, ibid., p. 247.
17. Memorandum of March 30, 1956 conference, in ibid., p. 280. Radford here is using the term "atomic" generically, as did other policymakers on occasion. The context normally makes it apparent whether they mean nuclear weapons generally or fission bombs specifically.
18. Ibid., p. 281.
19. Memorandum of May 10, 1956 NSC discussion, from DDEL, Ann Whitman Files, NSC series, Box 7, p. 12.
20. Memorandum of May 14, 1956 White House conference, FRUS 19 (1955–57): 302.
21. Memorandum of May 24, 1956 White House conference, ibid., p. 312.
22. Taylor left the government in 1959, and immediately wrote a book, *The Uncertain Trumpet*, that attacked Eisenhower's nuclear policy for its immorality and inflexibility. I suspect this meeting launched Taylor's literary career. See chapter 7, below.
23. July 18, 1956 letter from Eden to Eisenhower, FRUS 4 (1955–57), "Western Security and Integration," pp. 90–92, and footnote 7, pp. 92–93.
24. October 1, 1956 memorandum from Dulles to Eisenhower, ibid., p. 97.
25. October 2, 1956 memorandum of conference with Eisenhower, ibid., p. 101.
26. December 11, 1956 telegram from Dulles to Department of State, ibid., p. 115; memorandum of December 11, 1956 conversation between U.S. and British delegates, ibid., pp. 125–26.
27. December 11, 1956 Dulles memorandum, ibid., p. 115; Dulles report from December 14, 1956 NATO Ministerial Meeting, ibid., p. 154.
28. On Eisenhower's reaction to the "Human Effects" report also see Brands, "The Age of Vulnerability," p. 987; and Wm. F. Vandercook, "Making the Very Best of the Very Worst,"*International Security* 11 (Summer 1986): 190–91.
29. Memorandum of December 20, 1956 NSC discussion, FRUS 19 (1955–57): 380.
30. Ibid., p. 381.
31. Memorandum of December 21, 1956 NSC discussion, ibid., p. 390.
32. Memorandum of January 11, 1957 NSC discussion, ibid., p. 409.
33. Memorandum of February 7, 1957 NSC discussion, ibid., pp. 414–16.
34. Memorandum of February 28, 1957 NSC discussion, ibid., pp. 427–28.
35. Ibid., 430–31.

36. Memorandum of April 11, 1957 NSC discussion, ibid., pp. 471–73.
37. Ibid., p. 473.
38. There is a growing literature on the formal NSC process during the Eisenhower administration, of which the writing of BNSP was the annual pinnacle. For a recent review, see Anna Kasten Nelson, "The Importance of Foreign Policy Process: Eisenhower and the National Security Council," in Bischof and Ambrose, eds., *Eisenhower: A Centenary Assessment*, pp. 111–125.
39. The way Eisenhower defines basic national security policy, and then its section on "military elements," resembles quite closely the way Barry Posen defines *grand strategy* ("the identification of likely threats to a nation's security, and devising of political, economic, and military remedies for these threats") and *military doctrine* (the component of grand strategy "that deals explicitly with military means"). See Barry Posen, *The Sources of Military Doctrine* (Ithaca: Cornell University Press, 1984).
40. On this point also see Dockrill, *Eisenhower's New Look*, pp. 198–200.
41. Eisenhower was, I think, unsure about whether he supported using nuclear weapons in limited wars or not. Certainly this policy endorsed that option, and Eisenhower did approve the development of new tactical nuclear weapons. Yet he worried on more than one occasion about the public revulsion to waging nuclear war, and was particularly squeamish about the idea of using nuclear weapons against Asian peoples after Hiroshima. To *threaten* their use was a different matter entirely, as Eisenhower had demonstrated between 1953 and 1955. As will be seen in the next chapter, however, when another opportunity to wage atomic diplomacy arose in 1958, during the second Taiwan straits crisis, Eisenhower was the model of caution.
42. Memorandum of May 27, 1957 NSC discussion, FRUS 19 (1955–57): 500–501.
43. Ibid. Dulles repeated this strange argument in a *Foreign Affairs* article that was published later in 1957; I will examine it more closely in the next chapter.
44. NSC-5707/8 is reprinted in ibid., pp. 509–24. A copy of the original document, still in its orange folder, can be found in the White House Office Files, Office of the Special Assistant for National Security Affairs, NSC series, Policy Papers Subseries, Box 20, at the Eisenhower Library in Abilene.
45. See, respectively, Gaddis, *Strategies of Containment* pp. 165–75, and Ambrose, *Eisenhower*, p. 435; Robert A. Wampler, "Eisenhower, NATO, and Nuclear Weapons: The Strategy and Political Economy of Alliance Security," in Bischof and Ambrose, eds., *Eisenhower: A Centennial Assessment*. My argument follows that of Richard Immerman, who in his article "Confessions of an Eisenhower Revisionist," advances a similar thesis — though in speculative form — to the one put forth here. Also see Gaddis, *We Now Know*, p. 232.
46. Another oddity of NSC meetings is that Eisenhower's is the *only* voice, after

1954 or so, speaking out on nuclear war in this way. I have a mental picture of NSC members uneasily looking down at the table as the president once again declaims on the subject.

47. These conclusions comprised his "most basic strategic insight," writes Stephen Ambrose, in *Eisenhower: A Centenary Assessment*, p. 250.

48. The classic expression of this argument is Fred Greenstein, *The Hidden-Hand Presidency* (New York: Basic Books, 1982).

5. Fallout, April 1957–November 1958

1. For a general, comprehensive account of the enormous political reaction to the Soviet satellite, see Robert Divine, *The Sputnik Challenge* (New York: Oxford University Press, 1993).

2. On the influence of Air Force and aviation industry figures on Democrats in Washington, see John Prados, *The Soviet Estimate: U.S. Intelligence and Russian Military Strength* (New York: Dial Press, 1982), p. 58.

3. Quoted in John Newhouse, *War and Peace in the Nuclear Age* (New York: Knopf, 1989), p. 117.

4. Divine, *The Sputnik Challenge* pp. 68–83; memorandum of October 10, 1957 White House conference, FRUS 19 (1955–57): 599–600.

5. On *Sputnik* and the 1960 elections, see Herbert Parmet, *Richard Nixon and his America* (Boston: Little, Brown, 1990), pp. 433–34.

6. Roman, in chapter 3 of *Eisenhower and the Missile Gap* argues that Eisenhower and his main advisers, including John Foster Dulles, did not worry seriously about altering the policy of massive retaliation before the fall of 1957. It was only the Soviet satellite that caused Eisenhower and Dulles to rewrite nuclear policy, which they did, he asserts, in 1958 and 1959. To contend that American nuclear policy did not substantially change before 1958, Roman must disregard a mountain of contrary documentary evidence (to take only an obvious example: NSC-5707/8) as well as the work of several prominent historians (such as McGeorge Bundy, *Danger and Survival*, chapters 6 and 7, Marc Trachtenberg, *History and Strategy*, chapters 3 and 4, John Lewis Gaddis, "The Unexpected John Foster Dulles,"chapter 5 of *The United States and the End of the Cold War* (New York: Oxford University Press, 1997), and Richard Immerman, "Confessions of an Eisenhower Revisionist"). I am at a loss as to why Professor Roman, in making this argument, does not try to refute this evidence or scholarship.

7. Eisenhower received this information from E. V. Murphree of the Defense Department in a January 11, 1957 NSC discussion. See FRUS 19 (1955–57): 402, and DDC 1996, number 1039.

8. Memorandum of November 4, 1957 White House conference, FRUS 19 (1955–57): 621.
9. As Dockrill writes: "Despite, or because of, the *Sputnik* shock, the New Look remained the kernel of Eisenhower's national security policy." *Eisenhower's New Look*, p. 208.
10. The commission's chairman was H. Rowan Gaither of the Ford Foundation.
11. Memorandum of November 4, 1957 conference with Eisenhower, FRUS 19 (1955–57): 620.
12. Ibid., pp. 621–22; also see Gaddis, *Strategies*, p. 185, and Rosenberg, "The Origins of Overkill," pp. 46–48.
13. Memorandum of November 12, 1957 NSC meeting, FRUS 19 (1955–57): 674–75.
14. Memorandum of January 16, 1958 NSC meeting, FRUS 3 (1958–60), "National Security Affairs; Arms Control," p. 16.
15. This fundamental problem of course led eventually to the development of independent nuclear forces in Europe and the French departure from NATO command. On the emergence of this problem during the Eisenhower administration, see especially Wampler, "Eisenhower, NATO, and Nuclear Weapons, esp. pp. 175–78; and Trachtenberg, *History and Strategy*, chapter 4.
16. Dulles speech recorded in editorial note, FRUS 19 (1955–57): 526.
17. Dulles, "Challenge and Response in United States Policy," *Foreign Affairs* 36 (October 1957): 31, 33.
18. Dulles seemed quite well aware that this argument was in conflict with Eisenhower's policy. On August 21 he sent a draft of the article to the president, together with a note predicting that it "would prove rather easy reading except perhaps for the portion dealing with nuclear weapons." August 21, 1957 letter from Dulles to Eisenhower, Ann Whitman File, Dulles-Herter series, Box 9, DDEL.
19. Memorandum of January 3, 1958 conversation with Dulles, FRUS 3 (1958–60), p. 3.
20. Memorandum of March 20, 1958 NSC discussion, ibid., pp. 51–56.
21. Memorandum of March 27, 1958 NSC discussion, *DDC 1990*, number 311, pp. 6–7.
22. Dulles memorandum of April 1, 1958 conversation with Eisenhower, *DDC 1989*, number 3430, pp. 1–2. Dulles did not relate Eisenhower's response in this memorandum.
23. Memorandum of April 7, 1958 study group meeting, FRUS 3 (1958–60): 63; April 7, 1957 memorandum from Cutler to McElroy, ibid., pp. 65–68; paper presented by the Special Assistant on National Security Affairs [Cutler], ibid., p. 78.
24. An idea that closely resembled, it is interesting to note, an argument Henry

Kissinger made in his 1957 book *Nuclear Weapons and Foreign Policy* (New York: Harper, 1957). See chapter 7, below.

25. Memorandum of May 1, 1958 NSC meeting, FRUS 3 (1958–60): 82–85.
26. Ibid., pp. 85–88. Another record of this meeting can be found in the National Security Archives, Berlin Crisis collection, document 115, (hereafter in this form: NSA, number 115) p. 10. On the May 1 meeting also see Rosenberg, "The Origins of Overkill," p. 54.
27. May 1, 1958 NSC discussion, NSA number 115, p. 12.
28. Ibid., p. 12.
29. Memorandum of July 24, 1958 NSC meeting, FRUS 3 (1958–60): 129. The day before this meeting Dulles had written a personal letter to Eisenhower, once again demanding that "we need to apply ourselves urgently to finding an alternative strategic concept." DDC 1988, number 2219. Having once again failed to budge the president, Dulles used the excuse of describing policy as "in flux" to avoid formally disagreeing with Eisenhower. Indeed, in the July 23 letter Dulles noted that he did not "want to air my misgivings on this sensitive subject before the council."
30. Memorandum of August 12, 1958 conference with Eisenhower, Ann Whitman Files, DDE Diary Series, Box 35, DDEL, pp. 1–2; August 13, 1958 NSC memorandum, NSC-5723, DDC 1990, number 348.
31. August 13, 1958 memorandum from Smith to Herter, FRUS 19 (1958–60), microfiche supplement (hereafter in this form: FRUS 19 (1958–60), *supplement*), pp. 1–2.
32. Memorandum of August 14, 1958 NSC discussion, Ann Whitman Files, DDE Diary series, Box 35, pp. 1–2.
33. Memorandum of August 15, 1958 meeting between Department of State and the Joint Chiefs of Staff, FRUS 19 (1958–60), *supplement*, pp. 1–2.
34. Dulles statement reprinted in August 23, 1958 telegram from Dulles to Drumright, ibid., p. 2.
35. Memorandum of August 25, 1958 White House meeting, FRUS 19 (1958–60), "China," p. 74.
36. Memorandum of August 25, 1958 conference with Eisenhower, FRUS 19 (1958–60), *supplement*, pp. 1–3.
37. August 24, 1958 telegram from Drumright to Department of State, FRUS 19 (1958–60): 72; August 27, 1958 telegram from Drumright to Department of State, ibid., pp. 83–86.
38. August 28, 1958 Naval Message from U.S. Command in Taiwan to CINCPAC (Commander-in-Chief of the Pacific, Admiral Harry D. Felt), FRUS 19 (1958–60), *supplement*, p. 2; August 29, 1958 Naval Message from Seventh Fleet commander, ibid.
39. Dulles's absence during this week makes it hard to see how Appu K. Soman

could argue that Dulles "played the key role in the administration's handling of the crisis." See " 'Who's Daddy' in the Taiwan Strait? The Offshore Islands Crisis of 1958," *Journal of American-East Asian Relations* 3 (Winter 1994): 374.

40. August 31, 1958 letter from Parsons to Dulles, FRUS 19 (1958–60), *supplement*, p. 3.

41. August 25, 1958 White House meeting, p. 74; August 26, 1958 telegram from JCS to Commander-in-Chief Pacific Admiral Harry D. Felt, pp. 75–6; and August 29, 1958 White House meeting, p. 97, FRUS 19 (1958–60). On the Chinese threat, see Parsons to Dulles, cited directly above in note 40. Eisenhower's statement during the meeting on the 29th is the most obvious refutation of Soman's claim that Eisenhower was ready to wage nuclear war to defend Quemoy-Matsu. See " 'Who's Daddy' in the Taiwan Strait?" pp. 383–86, 395.

42. The Chinese warning is reprinted in Eisenhower, *Waging Peace*, (Garden City, New York: Doubleday, 1965) appendix P, p. 694.

43. Memorandum of August 27, 1958 conference with Eisenhower, *DDC 1993*, number 3541, p. 2.

44. August 27, 1958 Press Conference, reprinted in *Public Papers of the President 1958* (Washington, 1959), pp. 640–42.

45. August 31, 1958 telegram from Drumright to Department of State, FRUS 19 (1958–60): 107.

46. September 1, 1958 telegram from Eisenhower to Chiang, FRUS 19 (1958–60), *supplement*.

47. September 1, 1958 telephone conversation between Dulles and Eisenhower, FRUS 19 (1958–60): 113.

48. Memorandum of September 2, 1958 meeting, ibid., pp. 118–121.

49. Undated Dulles memorandum, ibid., p. 133.

50. Memorandum of September 4, 1958 conference with Eisenhower, Ann Whitman Files, DDE Diary series, box 36, p. 1. Dulles's somewhat different account of this conference, Memorandum of September 4, 1958 conversation with Eisenhower, is in FRUS 19 (1958–60), *supplement*.

51. See the special National Intelligence Estimate, completed August 26, 1958, in FRUS 19 (1958–60): 81–82; September 3, 1958 memorandum from Smith to Dulles, ibid., p. 124.

52. Memorandum of September 4, 1958 Dulles conversation, cited in note 50 above.

53. Ibid.

54. "Authorized Statement by the Secretary of State," September 4, 1958, *Public Papers of the President*, p. 688; Memorandum of September 4, 1958 conference, cited in note 50 above. General Goodpaster's account of this conversation at Newport, and especially the arrangement between Dulles and Eisenhower on issuing the public announcement, is uncharacteristically murky. Interestingly, the most detailed account of the Newport conversations available is in Eisen-

hower's memoirs. The president wrote at length about this meeting, going as far as to include an excerpt of Dulles's memorandum in an appendix (pp. 691–93). In his account Eisenhower falsely portrays himself as determined to stand up to the Chinese with nuclear war.

55. Dulles memorandum of September 4, 1958 conversation with Lord Hood, FRUS 19 (1958–60), *supplement*. By protesting far too much that this proposal was planned at all, Dulles makes it obvious that it was indeed planned quite deliberately. "I said that this was just an offhand idea which had not been studied or staffed. The foregoing was said in the course of a very casual conversation. (I would not have attached importance to it had it not been that Lord Hood had reported it to Macmillan and the idea features largely in Macmillan's reply.)" I believe that Dulles and Eisenhower secretly agreed to take this compromising approach in Newport.

56. September 6, 1958 memorandum of conference with Eisenhower, FRUS 19 (1958–60), *supplement*; Marshall Green memorandum of September 7, 1958 telephone conversation with Dulles, ibid.; Dulles September 8, 1958 telegram to Beam, ibid.; Dulles September 8, 1958 telegram to Drumright, ibid., pp. 1–2.

57. Memorandum of September 11, 1958 conversation with Dulles and Sir Leslie Munro, FRUS 19 (1958–60) *supplement*, p. 2.

58. Memorandum of September 11, 1958 conversation between McElroy and Dulles, ibid., p. 1.

59. September 12, 1958 letter from Dulles to Macmillan, *DDC 1997*, number 755, pp. 2–3.

60. This is how Smith described it, in a September 10, 1958 memorandum to Dulles, FRUS 19 (1958–60), *supplement*.

61. *Public Papers*, pp. 695–97.

62. Khrushchev's letter, a reply to Eisenhower's of September 12, is reprinted in FRUS 19 (1958–60): 231–38. For Eisenhower's decision to reject Khrushchev's note, see Editorial Note, ibid., pp. 247–48.

63. Memorandum of September 20, 1958 conversation, ibid., p. 243. On September 11, the same day he publicly compared Quemoy and Matsu to the Sudetenland, Eisenhower said privately to his Secretary of Defense that he "was trying to find a way in which a strong country can conciliate. It is not adequate simply to say that we will stand on Quemoy and Matsu. We must move beyond that." See editorial note of September 11, 1958 conference between Secretary of Defense McElroy and Eisenhower, ibid., p. 161.

64. Dulles's announcement was recorded in *Department of State Bulletin* 39 (October 20, 1958), pp. 597–604. The Secretary of State also said that a Nationalist return to the mainland was not an immediate American objective but instead a "highly hypothetical matter."

65. Undated letter from Macmillan to Dulles, *DDC 1992*, number 220.

66. Qiang Zhai, *The Dragon, the Lion, and the Eagle: Chinese/British/American Relations, 1949–58* (Kent, Ohio: Kent State University Press, 1992), p. 194.
67. Memorandum of September 21, 1958 conversation with the president, *DDC 1991*, number 845, pp. 1, 5–6. This conversation is also recorded in FRUS 19 (1958–60): 249–52. For an account of this meeting from Lloyd's perspective, see Zhai, *The Dragon, the Lion, and the Eagle*, p. 194.

6. Berlin, November 1958–July 1959

1. Editorial Note, "Western Reaction to Khrushchev's November 10 Speech," FRUS 1958–1960: 8, "The Berlin Crisis," p. 46; November 11, 1958 Telegram from the Embassy in the Soviet Union (Thompson) to the Department of State, p. 47, ibid. Also see John Eisenhower, *Strictly Personal*, (Garden City, NY: Doubleday, 1974), pp. 211–13.
2. See NSC 5404/1, "Progress Report on U.S. Policy Toward Berlin," *DDC 1993*, number 2877.
3. "Statement of Policy on U.S. Policy on Berlin," supplement I to NSC-5727, "U.S. Policy Toward Germany," December 13, 1957, *DDC 1993*, number 2878, pp. 1–2.
4. Ibid., p. 6.
5. *Department of State Bulletin* 39 (December 15, 1958), p. 947. On this press conference also see William Burr, "Avoiding the Slippery Slope: the Eisenhower Administration and the Berlin Crisis, November 1958–January 1959," *Diplomatic History* 18 (Spring, 1994): 185–86.
6. November 17, 1958 telegram from Dulles to U.S. Embassy in West Germany, FRUS 8 (1958–60): 82–83. For an excellent treatment of U.S. relations with its European allies during the early stages of the crisis, see Burr, "Avoiding the Slippery Slope," especially pp. 185–87.
7. November 23, 1958 telegram from Norstad to Twining, FRUS 8 (1958–60): 116–17.
8. Dulles memorandum of November 18, 1958 conversation between Eisenhower and Dulles, ibid., pp. 84–85.
9. Supplement I to NSC-5803, "U.S. Policy on Berlin," *DDC 1993*, number 3127.
10. On this point also see Burr, "Avoiding the Slippery Slope," p. 196.
11. Reprint of Soviet November 27, 1958 note in *Department of State Bulletin* 40 (January 19, 1959), p. 88.
12. November 28, 1958 memorandum of conversation among Dulles and French officials, FRUS 8 (1958–60): 137–38.
13. As it was called by the "Berlin Contingency Group," no doubt to kindle memories of Normandy in Eisenhower. See undated (sometime in December or January) Defense Department contingency plan, *DDC 1995*, number 2425. In

this plan the authors set out steps the U.S. should implement in the months preceding "K-Day," designating them as K−120, K−60, etc. Also see memorandum of March 12, 1959 discussion of the second meeting of the Berlin Contingency Group, FRUS 8 (1958–1960): 471.

14. December 3, 1958 telegram from Thompson to the Department of State, ibid., pp. 148–52.

15. December 11, 1958 memorandum of conference with Eisenhower, ibid., pp. 172–77.

16. See December 13, 1958 memorandum of U.S. delegation conversation, during Ministerial Meeting of the North Atlantic Council, ibid., pp. 193–96; also December 17, 1958 memorandum of conversation between French and American delegations, ibid., pp. 218–19.

17. December 17, 1958 telegram from North Atlantic Council meeting to State Department, ibid., p. 212.

18. Memorandum of December 13, 1958 U.S. delegation conversation, cited in note 16, above, p. 195.

19. Memorandum of January 22, 1959 NSC meeting, FRUS 3 (1958–60): 174, 178.

20. Burr points out ("Avoiding the Slippery Slope," p. 201) that in many respects this was the last major policy meeting upon which Dulles was able to exert his influence. This may be true, but he certainly gave it another good effort when Macmillan, Lloyd, and Eisenhower visited him in his room at Walter Reed hospital in March. See pp. 100–101, below.

21. Undated Dulles paper, "Thinking Out Loud," FRUS 8 (1958–1960): 293; January 26, 1958 telegram from Dulles to NATO mission, ibid., p. 295.

22. Memorandum of January 29, 1959 conference with Eisenhower, p. 301, ibid. For another account of this meeting, see Burr, "Avoiding the Slippery Slope," pp. 200–201.

23. FRUS 8 (1958–1960): 302.

24. Ibid., pp. 302–303.

25. Ibid., pp. 304–305.

26. Dulles memorandum of February 8, 1959 conversation between U.S. and West German delegations, ibid., p. 347.

27. Memorandum of February 9, 1959 conference between Twining and Eisenhower, FRUS 3 (1958–60): 182. The reference to new Soviet ICBM capability may refer to a report Eisenhower received from Allen Dulles the previous August, during the second Quemoy-Matsu crisis. A new NIE, Dulles reported, indicated direct evidence of nine missile systems, and ten operational ICBMs, available to the Soviets sometime in 1959. The heavier of these weapons, Dulles noted, "might produce a 4-megaton explosion." See Editorial Note on August 27, 1958 NSC meeting, ibid., pp. 135–36.

28. See February 23, 1959 MacMillan message to Eisenhower, and February 23, 1959 Eisenhower message to Macmillan, ibid. pp. 385–87.

29. March 4, 1959 memorandum from Herter to Eisenhower, FRUS 8 (1958–1960): 413.

30. On Dulles's courageous performance at Geneva, see Marks, *Power and Peace*, pp. 142–43.

31. Memorandum of March 5, 1959 special meeting of the NSC, FRUS 8 (1958–1960): 424.

32. Ibid., p. 425; Tusa, *The Last Division: A History of Berlin, 1945–1989* (Reading: Addison-Wesley, 1997), p. 159.

33. Memorandum of March 6, 1959 conference with Eisenhower, FRUS 8 (1958–1960): 428–37.

34. Dean Acheson, "Wishing Won't Hold Berlin," *Saturday Evening Post* 231 (March 7, 1959): 33.

35. Ibid., p. 85. On Acheson's critique, also see Bundy, *Danger and Survival*, pp. 372, 375–76.

36. Taylor Testimony before the Preparedness Investigating Subcommittee of the Senate Committee on Armed Services, March 11, 1958, FRUS 8 (1958–1960): 450.

37. Ibid., p. 451. I have added the emphasis, which the reader, if willing to imagine Taylor testifying in his Kansas City drawl, must allow.

38. March 11, 1959 memorandum from Twining to McElroy, p. 454. On Twining's Cold War views, also see Trachtenberg, *History and Strategy*, pp. 106–7.

39. March 11, 1959 Eisenhower Press Conference, *Public Papers of the President 1959* (Washington, 1960), p. 245.

40. Ibid., p. 252.

41. See FRUS 8 (1958–60): 441–44, especially Footnote 1, p. 441. Also see, for a slightly different record of this recommendation, *DDC 1995*, number 1896.

42. Memorandum of March 17, 1959 conference with Eisenhower, FRUS 8 (1958–1960): 492–95.

43. Memorandum of March 17, 1959 conference with Eisenhower, NSA number 988, p. 4. This segment of the conference was not included in the FRUS account.

44. Dulles memorandum of March 20, 1959 conference, FRUS 8 (1958–1960): 515.

45. See Eisenhower's *Waging Peace*, p. 354, and Harold Macmillan, *Riding the Storm, 1956–1959* (New York: Harper and Row, 1971), p. 645.

46. Memorandum of March 20, 1959 conversation, FRUS 8 (1958–60): 520–21.

47. Ibid.

48. Historians who take Eisenhower's opposition to a summit at face value have to explain why he suddenly gave in to Macmillan's demands. Tusa, for example,

argues that Eisenhower had "no sympathy" for Macmillan's position (*The Last Division* p. 160), yet then relates two pages later, without explaining, that Eisenhower agreed to the British demand.

49. Memorandum of April 23, 1959 special NSC meeting, ibid., FRUS 8 (1958–1960): 629, 631.

50. According to a draft NSC memorandum, the President signed on to a contingency plan at a "special meeting" held before the regular NSC one on April 23. But one of the several "caveats," as the memorandum read, was that "any advance planning regarding the alternative uses of force would necessarily be subject to review and decision in the light of circumstances as they develop." In other words, this contingency plan meant nothing. See *DDC 1995*, number 2471.

51. As British Foreign Secretary Selwyn Lloyd, like Clay partial to the *fait accompli*, described it. See memorandum of March 31, 1959 Tripartite Foreign Ministers' conversation, FRUS (1958–1960): 549.

52. June 15, 1959 Eisenhower telegram to Khrushchev, pp 901–03; undated (June 15 or 16) Macmillan message to Eisenhower, pp. 906–8; June 17 Eisenhower telegram to Macmillan, pp. 908–10; all ibid.

53. Undated (June 23, 24, or 25) Macmillan message to Eisenhower, ibid., pp. 938–40.

54. See James G. Richter, *Khrushchev's Double Bind: International Pressures and Domestic Coalition Politics* (Baltimore: Johns Hopkins University Press, 1994), p. 119; and Tusa, *The Last Division*, pp. 173, 175.

55. June 25, 1959 conversation between Averell Harriman and Khrushchev, as related in June 25, 1959 Thompson telegram to Herter, FRUS (1958–1960): 941–43.

56. Herter memorandum of June 25, 1959 conversation with Eisenhower, ibid., pp. 943–44.

57. Herter memorandum of July 1, 1959 conversation with Eisenhower, p. 962; memorandum of July 9, 1959 conference between Herter and Eisenhower, pp. 971–73; memorandum of July 10, 1959 conference with Eisenhower, pp. 976–77; all ibid.

58. July 21, 1959 Eisenhower telegram to Herter, pp. 1026–27, ibid.

59. There is no record of such a plan.

60. Memorandum of July 22, 1959 morning conference with Eisenhower, ibid., p. 1030.

61. Memorandum of July 22, 1959 afternoon conference with Eisenhower, ibid., pp. 1030–33.

62. Ibid. Murphy spoke with Menshikov on the evening of July 23 and told him that Khrushchev's visit would go much smoother if "reasonable progress could be achieved at Geneva." In other words—to translate the diplomatic language—

progress was no longer necessary, despite what Eisenhower had told the Soviet ambassador two days earlier. See FRUS 8 (1958–60): footnote 5, p. 1033.

63. On July 9 Eisenhower had made Murphy the State Department's "Czar" on Berlin.

64. Richard Neustadt, *Presidential Power and the Modern Presidents*, 5th ed. (New York: Free Press, 1990), p. 33 and passim.

7. Intermission, July 1959–January 1961

1. Eisenhower, *Waging Peace*, p. 411. Here is another example from his memoirs where Eisenhower exaggerates his toughness.

2. July 2, 1959 conference with the president, FRUS 3 (1958–60): 228–35.

3. NSC 5906/1, in *DDC 1983*, number 1305; memorandum of July 15, 1959 White House conversation, *DDC 1985*, number 2142. On these debates also see Roman, *Eisenhower and the Missile Gap*, pp. 80–82.

4. NSC 5906/1, in FRUS 3 (1958–60): 295–96.

5. Ibid., footnote 1.

6. Bundy, in *Danger and Survival* (esp. pp. 543–44), argues that the Triad was the invention of the Kennedy administration, but as Roman (pp. 64, 108–9) shows, it really originated in the last years of Eisenhower's term. Also see Rosenberg, "The Origins of Overkill," pp. 48–51.

7. See Gaddis, *Strategies of Containment*, pp. 166–69.

8. On this latter point see Bundy, *Danger and Survival*, p. 354. Also see Trachtenberg, *History and Strategy*, p. 225. On Eisenhower and the SIOP itself see Roman, *Eisenhower and the Missile Gap*, pp. 104–5; and Gaddis, *We Now Know*, p. 258.

9. Lawrence Freedman calls this group "a collection of Democrats, soldiers, sailors, and a growing band of academic specialists in defence." See his *The Evolution of Nuclear Strategy* (New York: St. Martin's Press, 1981), chapters 7 and 8. The quotation is from page 96.

10. For a brief discussion of these RAND analysts see ibid., pp. 230–39.

11. Kissinger, *Nuclear Weapons and Foreign Policy*, p. 131.

12. Ibid., p. 19.

13. Ibid., p. 87.

14. Ibid., p. 175.

15. Ibid., p. 185.

16. Ibid., p. 186.

17. Maxwell Taylor, *The Uncertain Trumpet* (New York: Harper, 1959), p. 137.

18. Ibid., pp. 146, 173.

19. Kennedy, "The Missile Gap," August 14 speech delivered to the U.S. Senate, reprinted in John F. Kennedy, *The Strategy of Peace* (New York: Harper, 1960), p. 38.

20. Kennedy, "Conventional Forces in the Atomic Age," speech given at Lake Charles, Louisiana, on October 16, 1959, ibid., p. 184. In this speech he also discussed his support for a major buildup of conventional forces. On Kennedy's inclination to "above all, do something," also see Gaddis, *Strategies of Containment*, p. 199.
21. I owe this assessment to Robert Divine, *Eisenhower and the Cold War*, p. 154.
22. Insufficient attention seems to be paid to Eisenhower's "Veblenian" feelings about American capitalism. His derogation of the military-industrial complex, together with his adamant opposition to national debt, appear both to stem from a traditional (and from the perpective of the 1990s, prescient) belief that societies can no more withstand unproductive spending than can individuals. To mention another example: in a January 1960 NSC meeting, Allen Dulles noted that the Soviets devoted about twice as much of their GNP to defense than did the United States. Eisenhower reminded the council that this figure was misleading, because the U.S. GNP contained a number of items not included in the Soviet economy, "such as advertising." Discussion of January 21, 1960 NSC meeting, FRUS 3 (1958–60): 368.
23. Memorandum of May 10, 1960 conference with Eisenhower, NSA number 1890, p. 2.

8. Berlin Looms Again, January–July 1961

1. Indeed, many traditional interpretations have the Kennedy administration basically inventing American nuclear policy out of nothing. For an example of this approach, see Michael Mandelbaum, *The Nuclear Question: The United States and Nuclear Weapons, 1946–1976* (Cambridge, England: Cambridge University Press, 1979), chapter 4.
2. Though, as I will discuss in the epilogue, McNamara did attempt this in 1962.
3. As Khrushchev himself pointed out to Kennedy, at the fateful Vienna Summit; see memorandum of June 4, 1961 conversation between American and Soviet delegations, FRUS 14 (1961–63) "Berlin Crisis, 1961–62" p. 89.
4. On Ulbricht's role in the 1961 crisis, see Hope M. Harrison, "Ulbricht and the Concrete 'Rose': New Archival Evidence on the Dynamics of Soviet-East German Relations and the Berlin Crisis, 1958–1961," *Cold War International History Project working paper no. 5* (Princeton, 1993), pp. 37–51.
5. Adenauer was particularly afraid that NATO would choose in the end to let West Germany fall rather than build up sufficient forces to match the Warsaw Pact in Central Europe. Serious NATO nuclear forces would prevent NATO members from arguing that it was militarily impossible to defend West Germany. In a four-power meeting in March Adenauer thus spoke of "the necessity of its [NATO] having nuclear capability." See March 8, 1961 memorandum from Averill Harriman to Secretary of State Dean Rusk, in FRUS 1961–63 volumes

13, 14, and 15, microfiche supplement [hereafter FRUS 14 (1961–63), *supplement*]. On this point also see Trachtenberg, *History and Strategy*, pp. 180–91.

6. On de Gaulle's attitudes about Berlin see Richard Challener, "Dulles and De Gaulle," in Robert O. Paxton and Nicholas Wahl, eds., *De Gaulle and the United States: A Centennial Reappraisal* (Providence, 1994), pp. 163–66.

7. On Soviet internal politics leading up to the 1961 crisis, see Robert M. Slusser, *The Berlin Crisis of 1961: Soviet-American Relations and the Struggle for Power in the Kremlin, June–November 1961* (Baltimore, 1973), esp. chapter 1; and Vladislav M. Zubok, "Khrushchev's Motives and Soviet Diplomacy in the Berlin Crisis, 1958–1962," a June 1994 "Soviet Union, Germany, and the Cold War, 1945–1962" conference paper, pp. 12–27.

8. See William J. Tompson, *Khrushchev: A Political Life* (New York: St. Martin's Press, 1995), p. 224; and Tusa, *The Last Division*, p. 203.

9. March 10, 1961 telegram from Thompson to State Department, FRUS 14 (1961–63): 19; March 16, 1961 telegram from Thompson to State Department, ibid., pp. 30–31.

10. The most egregious example of disrespect toward Kennedy I have found comes from a memorandum written by McGeorge Bundy. In late August, as preparations for a possible confrontation over Berlin mounted, Bundy wrote a preparatory note for the president outlining an upcoming meeting on political strategy. "This is a complex subject," Bundy began, "and the most important one you have. So be patient with a complex memorandum." Imagine Gordon Gray or even Dulles saying this to Eisenhower. See August 28, 1961 memorandum from Bundy to Kennedy, FRUS 14 (1961–63), *supplement*, p. 1.

11. See Tompson, *Khrushchev*, and January 28, 1961 letter from Rusk to Kennedy, FRUS 14 (1961–63), p. 4.

12. Catudal, *Kennedy and the Berlin Wall Crisis*, p. 45. Rusk's proposal may have originated in a memorandum sent to him in January by Walt Rostow, the Deputy Special Assistant for National Security Affairs. See ibid., p. 47.

13. On February 8 Kennedy asked Acheson to chair his advisory committee on NATO; sometime in March (I have been unable to find the precise date) Acheson was named "Special Consultant" on Berlin and Germany. See Douglas Brinkley, *Dean Acheson: the Cold War Years 1953–71* (New Haven: Yale University Press, 1992), p. 117.

14. March 29, 1961 memorandum for the President, *DDC 1993*, number 2372, p. 5.

15. Acheson did not disguise his disdain for the President. In July, for example, he told colleagues that this "nation is without leadership." Catudal, *Kennedy and the Berlin Wall Crisis* p. 182n. Also see Tusa, *The Last Division*, pp. 234–35.

16. April 3, 1958 memorandum from Acheson to Kennedy, FRUS 14 (1961–63), *supplement*, pp. 1–2. On Acheson's 1959 article, see chapter 6, above.

17. Memorandum of April 5, 1961 Kennedy-Macmillan meeting, FRUS 14 (1961–63), pp. 37–38. Catudal (pp. 54–56) argues that the British viewed Acheson's plans with "horror," but this is not really correct. Though Macmillan and Foreign Secretary Alec Home opposed Acheson's general belligerence over Berlin, insofar as Acheson emphasized conventional over nuclear force in defending that city, the British supported him.

18. Though the Kennedy administration continued to compose BNSP in 1961 and 1962, the president expressed his policy wishes more conspicuously in "action memoranda."

19. Reference to NSAM 41 is made in Bundy's April 17, 1961 memorandum to McNamara, FRUS 14 (1961–63), *supplement.*

20. May 5 memorandum from McNamara, FRUS 14 (1961–63): 62.

21. Ibid., pp. 62–63.

22. May 20, 1961 telegram from the JCS to Norstad, FRUS 14 (1961–63), *supplement*, pp. 1–2.

23. This was the U.S.-supported invasion of Cuba, by Cuban expatriates and CIA operatives, which was easily repelled on the beaches by Castro's army. Kennedy's decision not to provide the invaders with American air support led to the ignominious defeat. The president's apparent indecisiveness led Khrushchev to believe that Kennedy was a weak figure who would be easy to manipulate at a summit. See Michael Beschloss, *The Crisis Years: Kennedy and Khrushchev 1960–1963* (New York: Burlingame Books, 1991), p. 149.

24. Though with the successful French atomic test in 1960 de Gaulle was beginning to think differently.

25. Memorandum of May 31, 1961 early afternoon conversation between Kennedy and de Gaulle, FRUS 14 (1961–63), p. 83.

26. Memorandum of late afternoon conversation between Kennedy and de Gaulle, ibid., p. 85. Also see Kenneth P. O'Donnell and David F. Powers, with Joe McCarthy, *"Johnny, We Hardly Knew Ye": Memories of John Fitzgerald Kennedy* (Boston: Little, Brown, 1970), p. 291.

27. Memorandum of June 4, 1961 conversation between Kennedy and Khrushchev, FRUS 14 (1961–63), pp. 87–88; Beschloss provides a lively account of the Summit in *The Crisis Years*, chapters 8 and 9.

28. FRUS 14 (1961–63), pp. 94–96.

29. Indeed, Khrushchev's ultimatum came as no surprise to Kennedy: on May 23 the Soviet leader had told Thompson he would issue one. See Tusa, *The Last Division*, pp. 237–38.

30. Memorandum of June 4, 1961 afternoon conversation between Kennedy and Khrushchev, ibid., pp. 96–98.

31. On Kennedy's dependence upon various pain-killing drugs, see Beschloss, *The Crisis Years*, pp. 186–93.

32. Quoted in Nikita Khrushchev, *Khrushchev Remembers: The Last Testament*, Strobe Talbott, trans. (Boston: Little, Brown, 1974), 500–501.

33. Record of June 5, 1961 conversation between Macmillan and Kennedy, FRUS 14 (1961–63), p. 99; Kennedy speech reprinted in *Public Papers of the President of the United States, 1961* (Washington: GPO, 1962), pp. 441–46.

34. On Kennedy's wishful thinking, also see Beschloss, *The Crisis Years*, p. 176.

35. June 10, 1961 memorandum from Bundy to Kennedy, FRUS 14 (1961–63), pp. 107–9.

36. June 12, 1961 memorandum from Bundy to McNamara, FRUS 14 (1961–63), *supplement*; Editorial Note, FRUS 14 (1961–63), pp. 135–36.

37. Many Europeans suspected that Mansfield was speaking for the administration. I have found no evidence to substantiate, or refute, this claim; all that can be said is that in mid-June Kennedy had not made up his mind about Berlin. He did tell the Italian Prime Minister, Amintore Fanfani on the 12th that the free city idea "might have a great deal of appeal to the unsophisticated." See memorandum of June 12, 1961 conversation between Kennedy and Fanfani, FRUS 14 (1961–63), *supplement*. Mansfield's speech is reprinted in the *Congressional Record*, 87th Congress, 1st session, volume 107, pp. 10328–34.

38. Notes on June 13, 1961 NSC meeting, DDC 1993, number 3447, p. 1.

39. Record of June 16, 1961 meeting of the Interdepartmental Coordinating Group on Berlin Contingency Planning, FRUS 14 (1961–63), p. 121.

40. Ibid., pp. 119–20. Also see Beschloss, *The Crisis Years*, pp. 258–59n.

41. Report from the JCS to McNamara, attached to a June 26, 1961 memorandum from Nitze to Bundy, FRUS 14 (1961–63), *supplement*, pp. 4–5.

42. Memorandum for the Record of June 29, 1961 NSC meeting, FRUS 14 (1961–63), pp. 160–162; NSAM 58, ibid., 162–65.

43. July 6, 1961 memorandum from Bundy to Kennedy, FRUS 14 (1961–63), *supplement*. Two weeks earlier Bundy said that he, Bundy, was "the President's principal adviser on Berlin." June 22, 1961 State Department memorandum, ibid.

44. July 7, 1961 memorandum from Schlesinger to Kennedy, FRUS 14 (1961–63), pp. 173–76; July 7, 1961 covering note on Henry Kissinger's memo on Berlin, NSA number 2144; July 7, 1961 memorandum from Kissinger to Bundy, FRUS 14 (1961–63), *supplement*. Also see Schlesinger's own account in A *Thousand Days* (New York: Houghton Mifflin, 1965), pp. 386–88.

45. See Schlesinger, A *Thousand Days*, pp. 387–88; Beschloss, *The Crisis Years*, pp. 246–47; Catudal, *Kennedy and the Berlin Wall Crisis*, pp. 160–63.

46. July 13, 1961 memorandum from Bundy to Kennedy, FRUS 14 (1961–63), *supplement*, p. 4.

47. Memorandum of July 13, 1961 NSC discussion, FRUS 14 (1961–63), p. 194.

48. Memorandum of July 17, 1961 meeting on Berlin, ibid., pp. 209–12.

49. Memorandum of July 18, 1961 meeting on Berlin, ibid., p. 215. This memorandum was written by McNamara.

50. July 19, 1961 memorandum from Bundy to Kennedy, ibid., pp. 216–18. Bundy's memorandum also suggests that Kennedy was not particularly aware of the issue at hand.
51. Memorandum of July 19, 1961 NSC meeting, ibid., pp. 219–20. On this meeting also see Catudal, *Kennedy and the Berlin Wall Crisis*, pp. 180–83.
52. Rusk's paper is reprinted in FRUS 14 (1961–63), pp. 207–9.
53. See Editorial Note, ibid., p. 224.
54. Kennedy's speech is reprinted in *Public Papers 1961*, pp. 533–40. Another way the United States had conveyed the new approach to the Soviet Union was simply to ensure that certain agencies in Britain and France were made aware of it, as they were known to be infiltrated with Soviet spies. See Trachtenberg, *History and Strategy*, pp. 224, 282.
55. On this point also see Bundy, *Danger and Survival*, pp. 368–69.
56. The proceedings of these meetings are not available, although it would seem that Kohler and Nitze were able to dominate the U.S. delegation; Bundy complained to Kennedy on August 2 that the delegation was "less ready to think of new positions" than even Acheson.
57. Memorandum of August 6, 1961 Quadripartite Ministerial Conversations on Berlin, FRUS 14 (1961–63), pp. 301–2. The entire record of the ministerial meetings, as relayed by Rusk, covers ibid. pp. 269–323.
58. Ibid., p. 279.
59. August 8, 1961 conversation between Rusk and de Gaulle, ibid., 312–16.
60. July 21, 1961 memorandum from Bundy to Kennedy, *DDC 1995*, number 3087, p. 2. Parentheses in original.

9. The Wall and the Prospect of War, August-October 1961

1. Editorial Note, FRUS 14 (1961–63): 325; Tusa, *The Last Division*, ch 10.
2. See Tusa, *The Last Division*, pp. 232–33; Tompson, *Khrushchev*, pp. 235–36.
3. August 14, 1961 memorandum from Bundy to Kennedy, FRUS 14 (1961–63): 330–31; August 14, 1961 memorandum from Kennedy to Rusk, ibid., p. 332.
4. Minutes of August 15, 1961 Berlin Steering Group meeting, ibid., pp. 333–34; Rusk telegram to American Embassy in Germany, ibid., 337–39.
5. Catudal, for example, ends his *Kennedy and the Berlin Wall Crisis* in August.
6. Brandt letter enclosed in August 16, 1961 telegram from U.S. Berlin mission to Department of State, FRUS 14 (1961–63): 345–46.
7. See August 18, 1961 memorandum from Taylor to Kennedy, FRUS 14 (1961–63), *supplement*.
8. August 25, 1961 memorandum from McNamara to Kennedy, ibid., pp. 2–3.
9. Department of State memorandum of August 26, 1961 Four-Power Ambassadorial Group conversation, *DDC 1993*, number 1945, p. 4; cf. Trachtenberg, *History and Strategy*, p. 222. August 25, 1961 memorandum from McNamara

to Kennedy, FRUS 14 (1961–63), *supplement*, pp. 2–3; August 28, 1961 telegram from Rusk to Norstad, ibid., pp. 2–3. Rusk's language also seems influenced by the works of Thomas Schelling. More on Schelling's relation with the Kennedy administration can be found in the epilogue.

10. August 28, 1961 telegram from Norstad to Lemnitzer, ibid. In this telegram Norstad also urged that Clay not be sent to Berlin. On the intense rivalry between Clay and Norstad, see Jean Edward Smith's *Lucius D. Clay* (New York: Holt, 1990), pp. 656–58.

11. Memorandum of September 7, 1961 Berlin Steering Group meeting, FRUS 14 (1961–63): 395–98.

12. Ibid. Bundy's thinking here reflected the ideas of his aide Robert Komer, who argued back in July that Khrushchev "may well interpret our remarks and preparations [about conventional war] as meaning that we are in fact afraid to use nuclears in the clutch." July 20, 1961 memorandum from Komer to Bundy, FRUS 14 (1961–63), *supplement*, p. 1.

13. NSAM 92, issued September 8, 1961, FRUS 14 (1961–63): 398–99.

14. September 11 memorandum from McNamara to Kennedy, FRUS 14 (1961–63), *supplement*, pp. 3–4.

15. September 18, 1961 memorandum from McNamara to Kennedy, NSA number 2484, p. 3.

16. Appendix A to September 11 memorandum from McNamara to Kennedy, cited above, note 14.

17. Nitze analysis attached to October 2, 1961 memorandum from Kohler to Rusk, FRUS 14 (1961–63), *supplement*, pp. 2–7; memorandum of October 2, 1961 meeting with Norstad and the JCS, ibid., pp. 2, 5.

18. October 3, 1961 memorandum from Bundy to Kennedy, ibid., pp. 1–3. Taylor's recommendations were included in Bundy's memo.

19. Memorandum of October 3, 1961 White House conversation, ibid., pp. 2–3.

20. Ibid., pp. 4–5.

21. Editorial Note, FRUS 14 (1961–63): 462; Paul Nitze, *From Hiroshima to Glasnost* (New York: Weidenfeld and Nicolson, 1989), pp. 202–03.

22. Nitze, ibid., pp. 203–5; minutes of October 10, 1961 meeting, FRUS 14 (1961–63): 487–89.

23. Ibid.

24. Nitze did offer Kennedy another alternative. Instead of launching limited nuclear strikes after the failure of conventional war in Europe, he said, "it would be best for us, in moving toward the use of nuclear weapons, to consider most seriously the option of an initial strategic strike of our own." A pre-emptive nuclear strike, Nitze argued, could give the United States a chance for military victory impossible to achieve with conventional war or spasmodic second-strike retaliation. McNamara, however, rejected this. See minutes of October 10, 1961

meeting, FRUS 14 (1961–63): 487–89. Nitze does not mention offering this alternative in his memoirs.

25. August 18, 1961 letter from Kennedy to Brandt, ibid., pp. 352–53; August 24, 1961 memorandum from McNamara to Kennedy, ibid., p. 369; memorandum of August 30, 1961 White House conversation, ibid., p. 382n.

26. This was something Bundy had predicted on the 28th. Reminding Kennedy of the struggle between Truman and MacArthur in Korea, he warned that "Clay will be a burden to you if he takes a line more belligerent than yours." August 28, 1961 memorandum from Bundy to Kennedy, FRUS 14 (1961–63), *supplement* .

27. On Clay's wall-destruction see Garthoff, "Berlin 1961," p. 147.

28. For Clay's side of the story, see Smith, *Lucius D. Clay*, chapter 29.

29. September 28, 1961 telegram from Clay to Rusk, FRUS 14 (1961–63): 441–43; the September 29 message is recorded in footnote 2, ibid., p. 443.

30. October 5, 1961 telegram from Clay to Rusk, FRUS 14 (1961–63), *supplement*, pp. 1–2.

31. October 4, 1961 telegram from Rusk to Clay, FRUS 14 (1961–63): 467–68; October 8, 1961 letter from Kennedy to Clay, ibid., pp. 484–86.

32. October 18, 1961 letter from Clay to Kennedy, ibid., pp. 509–13.

33. NSAM 107, issued October 18, 1961, FRUS 14 (1961–63), *supplement*, pp. 1–2.

34. Khrushchev's reasons for doing this remain unclear, but it is likely that he was hoping to give the Americans an out, as he tried to do with the proposal for a Summit in 1959. See Garthoff, "Berlin 1961," p. 146, and Tompson, *Khrushchev*, pp. 236–37.

35. October 20, 1961 memorandum from Bundy to Kennedy, FRUS 14 (1961–63), *supplement*, pp. 1–2.

36. Memorandum of October 20, 1961 meeting, FRUS 14 (1961–63): 517–18.

37. Ibid., p. 517.

38. October 20, 1961 letter from Kennedy to Norstad, FRUS 14 (1961–63): 520–21.

39. Ibid., p. 521.

40. Gilpatric speech summarized in *The New York Times*, October 22, 1961, pp. 1, 6.

41. Ibid., p. 6.

42. Gilpatric left Washington immediately after his speech to coordinate military planning with the West Germans. Also see Gaddis, *We Now Know*, pp. 256–57.

43. October 23, 1961 telegram from Lightner to Department of State, ibid., pp. 524–25; Gelb, *The Berlin Wall*, pp. 250–53.

44. To his profound regret, Clay had not seen combat in either World War. Friedrichstrasse was his last chance to command forces in the field. On this see Tusa, *The Last Division*, p. 127.

45. Clay explains his motivations in Smith, *Lucius D. Clay*, pp. 660–61. I see no reason to doubt them.
46. October 25, 1961 telegram from Norstad to Lemnitzer, FRUS 14 (1961–63), *supplement*.
47. October 26, 1961 telegram from Rusk to Clay, FRUS 14 (1961–63): 539–41.
48. See October 27, 1961 telegram from Watson to Norstad, which relates Clay's compliance with Kennedy's order. FRUS 14 (1961–63), *supplement*.
49. Clay's call to Kennedy is recorded in footnote 1, telegram from Clay to Rusk, ibid., p. 543. Gelb describes the unusual, even "postmodern" scene around the showdown in *The Berlin Crisis*, p. 256.
50. Quoted in Smith, *Lucius D. Clay*, p. 661. Also see Beschloss, *The Crisis Years*, p. 334.
51. Robert Kennedy had begun to communicate with the Kremlin on a regular basis by meeting with Georgi Bolshakov, a Russian attache and KGB agent. On the Bolshakov connection, see Garthoff, "Berlin 1961," p. 145, and Tusa, *The Last Division*, pp. 336–37.
52. October 27, 1961 telegram from Rusk to Clay, FRUS, 1961–63):14, pp. 544–45. Similar instructions were conveyed from the JCS to Norstad: see October 27, 1961 telegram from Lemnitzer to Norstad, FRUS 14 (1961–63), *supplement*, pp. 1–2.
53. I will discuss the "collapse" of flexible response in the epilogue.

Epilogue

1. In making the following stab at understanding Schelling I have been helped by reading Trachtenberg, *History and Strategy*, chapter one; Freedman, *The Evolution of Nuclear Strategy*, chapter fourteen; and Robert Jervis, *The Meaning of the Nuclear Revolution* (Ithaca, 1989), chapters 1–3.
2. Thomas Schelling, *Strategy of Conflict* (Cambridge: Harvard University Press, 1960).
3. Schelling (pp. 189–90) sees Eisenhower's cavalier references to nuclear war during his first term in this light.
4. Schelling is ambiguous about whether the initial nuclear strike should happen after a war has begun or while a crisis is still peaceful.
5. Ibid., pp. 190–93.
6. Ibid., pp. 195–99.
7. Ibid., p. 196, emphasis in the original.
8. Ibid., pp. 239–42.
9. Schelling, "Nuclear Strategy in Europe," *World Politics* 14 (April 1962), p. 424.
10. Ibid., pp. 425, 427–28.
11. Indeed, much of this paper is reprinted verbatim in the 1962 article.

12. Again, Schelling here obfuscates an otherwise clear argument by introducing the conditional "if they must be used."

13. July 5, 1961 Paper Prepared by Thomas C. Schelling, FRUS 1961–63: 14, pp. 170–71. Emphasis in original.

14. This brief overview of McNamara's new strategy relies upon Desmond Ball, "The Development of the SIOP, 1960–63," in Ball and Jeffrey Richelson, eds., *Strategic Nuclear Targeting* (Ithaca: Cornell University Press, 1986); Sagan, *Moving Targets*, pp. 28–31; and William Kaufmann, *The McNamara Strategy* (New York: Harper and Row, 1964). Ball writes that as soon as he took office "McNamara was an immediate convert" to the no-cities strategy. See "Development of the SIOP," p. 62.

15. Ball, "Development of the SIOP," pp. 63–64.

16. Quoted in Kaufmann, *The McNamara Strategy*, pp. 74–75. See also May 5, 1962 Address by McNamara at Ministerial Meeting of North Atlantic Council, FRUS 8 (1961–63), pp. 275–79.

17. Cf. Schelling: "Control over nuclear weapons in Europe must be tight and centralized." (Schelling paper, op. cit., p. 172).

18. Quoted in Kaufmann, *The McNamara Strategy*, pp. 116–17, emphasis added.

19. June 22, 1962 Basic National Security Policy draft, FRUS 8 (1961–63): 314.

20. Freedman, *The Evolution of Nuclear Strategy*, p. 236.

21. See Ball, "Development of the SIOP," p. 57.

22. Ibid., pp. 67–68.

23. Obviously this is not the place for any kind of detailed account of the Cuban crisis. I owe my understanding of McNamara's role in it to my friend and colleague Phil Nash.

24. For an authoritative account of the deal on the Turkish missiles, see Philip Nash, *The Other Missiles of October: Eisenhower, Kennedy, and the Jupiters, 1957–1963* (Chapel Hill, 1997), chapter 5.

25. See Richard New Lebow and Janice Gross Stein, *We All Lost the Cold War* (Princeton, 1994), pp. 119–123.

26. October 18, 1962 memorandum for file of meeting with the President, in Mary S. McAuliffe, ed., *CIA Documents on the Intelligence agency* 1992, p. 185. Again I thank Phil Nash for sharing this document.

27. Bundy, Kennan, McNamara, and Smith, "Nuclear Weapons and the Atlantic Alliance," *Foreign Affairs* 60 (Spring 1982); McNamara, *Blundering into Disaster: Surviving the First Century of the Nuclear Age* (New York, 1986).

28. Schelling has also written more recently on the calamity of nuclear war, but he has failed to reconcile this position with his arguments of the early 1960s. For example, he ends his article on proliferation, in the inaugural issue of *International Security*, with a section entitled "And Now for the Good News," in which he notes how shocking it would have been for someone to predict in 1951 that

weapons would spread to many nations, that the superpowers and other nuclear states would experience numerous showdowns, that the number of nuclear bombs produced by these states would reach the tens of thousands, and that yet "not a single one of these bombs will go off accidentally." But that is not the only shocking news: "And most important of all," Schelling concludes his article, "there will have been no nuclear weapons fired in warfare." Schelling, "Who will have the Bomb?" *International Security* 1 (Summer 1976), pp. 90–91. He reiterates this argument in *Foreign Affairs*, stating that "I like the notion that . . . civilization depends on the avoidance of military aggression that could escalate to nuclear war." Schelling, "What went wrong with arms control?" *Foreign Affairs* 64 (Winter 1985–86), p. 233. Suffice it to say that in 1960 he did not like that notion.

29. See Paul Fussell, editor's introduction to *The Norton Book of Modern War* (New York: Norton, 1991), pp. 18–25.

Bibliography

1. Archival and Manuscript Collections

Dean Acheson Papers, Yale University
George F. Kennan Papers, Princeton University
Dwight D. Eisenhower Library, Abilene
John F. Kennedy Library, Boston
National Security Archive, Washington D.C.

2. Interviews

Robert S. McNamara, July 1991, June 1993, Washington D.C.

3. Official Documents

Declassified Document Collection, 1983–97

Public Papers of the Presidents:
  Harry S. Truman, 1945–53
  Dwight D. Eisenhower, 1953–61
  John F. Kennedy, 1961–62
U.S. Department of Defense. *Public Statements of the Secretary of Defense,* 1961–62
U.S. Department of State. *Bulletin,* 1954–62
————. *Foreign Relations of the United States,* 1945–1963
————. *Foreign Relations of the United States, microfiche supplement,* 1958–63

————. *Germany, 1947–49, The Story in Documents*
————. *Documents on Germany, 1944–1985*

4. Books

Acheson, Dean. *Power and Diplomacy*. Cambridge: Harvard University Press, 1958.
Alexander, Charles, *Holding the Line: The Eisenhower Administration*. Bloomington: Indiana University Press, 1975.
Ambrose, Stephen. *Eisenhower and Berlin, 1945: the Decision to Halt at the Elbe* New York: Norton, 1967.
————. *Eisenhower* volumes 1 and 2. New York: Simon and Schuster, 1983/84.
Aron, Raymond. *The Great Debate: Theories of Nuclear Strategy*. Garden City: Doubleday, 1965.
————. *Peace and War: A Theory of International Relations*. Garden City: Anchor Press, 1973.
————. *Clausewitz, Philosopher of War*. Englewood Cliffs: Prentice-Hall, 1985.
Ausland, John, *Kennedy, Khrushchev, and the Berlin-Cuba Crises, 1961–1964*. Oslo: Scandinavian University Press, 1996.
Ball, Desmond. *Politics and Force Levels: The Strategic Missile Program of the Kennedy Administration*. Berkeley: University of California Press, 1980.
————, and Jeffrey Richelson, eds. *Strategic Nuclear Targeting*. Ithaca: Cornell University Press, 1986.
Beschloss, Michael. *Mayday: Eisenhower, Khrushchev, and the U-2 Affair*. New York: Harper and Row, 1986.
————. *The Crisis Years: Kennedy and Khrushchev 1960–1963*. New York: Burlingame Books, 1991.
Betts, Richard. *Soldiers, Statesmen, and Cold War Crises*. Cambridge: Harvard University Press, 1977.
————. *Nuclear Blackmail and Nuclear Balance*. Washington: Brookings Institution, 1987.
Billings-Yun, Melanie. *Decision Against War: Eisenhower and Dien Bien Phu, 1954*. New York: Columbia University Press, 1990.
Bischof, Gunter, and Stephen Ambrose, eds. *Eisenhower: A Centenary Assessment*. Baton Rouge: Louisiana University Press, 1995.
Boyer, Paul. *By the Bomb's Early Light: American Thought and Culture at the Dawn of the Atomic Age*. New York: Pantheon, 1985.
Brands, H. W., Jr. *Cold Warriors: Eisenhower's Generation and American Foreign Policy*. New York: Columbia University Press, 1988.
Brendon, Piers. *Ike: His Life and Times*. New York: Harper and Row, 1986.
Brinkley, Douglas. *Dean Acheson: the Cold War Years 1953–71*. New Haven: Yale University Press, 1992.

Bibliography

Bibliography

Brodie, Bernard. *Sea Power in the Machine Age.* Princeton: Princeton University Press, 1942.

———. *Strategy in the Missile Age.* Princeton: Princeton University Press, 1959.

———, ed. *The Absolute Weapon: Atomic Power and World Order.* New York: Harcourt, Brace and Co., 1946.

Bundy, McGeorge. *Danger and Survival: Choices About the Bomb in the First Fifty Years.* New York: Random House, 1988.

Callahan, David. *Dangerous Capabilities: Paul Nitze and the Cold War.* New York: Harper and Row, 1990.

Catudal, Honoré. *Kennedy and the Berlin Wall Crisis: A Study in U.S. Decision-Making.* Berlin: Berlin-Verlag, 1980.

Chang, Gordon H. *Friends and Enemies: The United States, China, and the Soviet Union, 1948–1972.* Stanford: Stanford University Press, 1990.

Christensen, Thomas J. *Useful Adversaries: Grand Strategy, Domestic Mobilization, and Sino-American Conflict, 1947–1958.* Princeton: Princeton University Press, 1997.

Clarfield, Gerald H. and William M. Wiecek. *Nuclear America: Military and Civilian Nuclear Power in the United States, 1940–1980.* Philadelphia: Harper and Row, 1984.

Clay, Lucius D. *The Papers of General Lucius D. Clay,* Jean Edward Smith, ed.,. Bloomington: Indiana University Press, 1974.

Cutler, Robert. *No Time to Rest.* Boston: Little, Brown, 1965.

Davison, W. Phillips. *The Berlin Blockade: A Study in Cold War Politics.* New York: Arno Press, 1980.

Divine, Robert. *Eisenhower and the Cold War.* New York: Oxford University Press, 1981.

———. *The Sputnik Challenge.* New York: Oxford University Press, 1993.

Dockrill, Saki. *Eisenhower's New Look National Security Policy, 1953–1961.* New York: St. Martin's Press, 1996.

Dulles, John Foster. *War or Peace.* New York: MacMillan, 1950.

Eisenhower, Dwight D. *The White House Years: Mandate For Change, 1952–56.* Garden City: Doubleday, 1963.

———. *The White House Years: Waging Peace, 1956–61.* Garden City: Doubleday, 1965.

Eisenhower, John. *Strictly Personal.* Garden City: Doubleday, 1974.

Enthoven, Alain, and K. Wayne Smith. *How Much is Enough? Shaping the Defense Program, 1961–69.* New York: Harper and Row, 1971.

Etzold, Thomas, and John Lewis Gaddis, eds., *Containment: Documents on American Policy and Strategy.* New York: Columbia University Press, 1978.

Feaver, Peter. *Guarding the Guardians: Civilian Control of Nuclear Weapons in the United States.* Ithaca: Cornell University Press, 1992.

Forrestal, James. *The Forrestal Diaries*, Walter Millis, ed.,. New York: Viking Press, 1951.

Freedman, Lawrence. *The Evolution of Nuclear Strategy*. New York: St. Martin's Press, 1983.

Fussell, Paul. *The Great War and Modern Memory*. New York: Oxford University Press, 1975.

———. *Thank God for the Atom Bomb, and Other Essays*. New York: Summit Books, 1988.

———, ed. *The Norton Book of Modern War*. New York: Norton, 1991.

Gaddis, John Lewis. *The United States and the Origins of the Cold War, 1941–47*. New York: Columbia University Press, 1972.

———. *Strategies of Containment: A Critical Appraisal of Postwar American Security Policy*. New York: Oxford University Press, 1982.

———. *The Long Peace*. New York: Oxford University Press, 1987.

———. *The United States and the End of the Cold War*. New York: Oxford University Press, 1992.

———. *We Now Know: Rethinking Cold War History*. New York: Oxford University Press, 1997.

Gallie, W. B. *Philosophers of Peace and War*. Cambridge: Cambridge University Press, 1978.

Gardner, Lloyd. *Architects of Illusion: Men and Ideas in American Foreign Policy*. Chicago: Quadrangle Books, 1970.

Garthoff, Raymond L., ed. *Sino-Soviet Military Relations*. New York: F. A. Praeger, 1966.

Gelb, Norman. *The Berlin Wall*. New York: Times Books, 1986.

George, Alexander L. and Richard Smoke, *Deterrence in American Foreign Policy: Theory and Practice*. New York: Columbia University Press, 1974.

Gilpin, Robert. *War and Change in World Politics*. Cambridge: Cambridge University Press, 1981.

Graebner, Norman, ed. *Ideas and Diplomacy: Readings in the Intellectual Tradition of American Foreign Policy*. New York: Oxford University Press, 1964.

Greenstein, Fred I. *The Hidden-Hand Presidency: Eisenhower as Leader*. New York: Basic Books, 1982.

———, ed. *Leadership in the Modern Presidency*. Cambridge: Harvard University Press, 1988.

Guhin, Michael A. *John Foster Dulles: A Statesman and His Times*. New York: Columbia University Press, 1972.

Halberstam, David. *The Best and the Brightest*. New York: Random House, 1972.

Halperin, Morton. *Limited War in the Nuclear Age*. New York: Wiley Press, 1963.

Hamby, Alonzo. *Man of the People: A Life of Harry S. Truman*. New York: Oxford University Press, 1995.

Harlow, Giles D. and George C. Maerz, eds. *Measures Short of War: the George F. Kennan Lectures at the National War College of 1946–47*. Washington: National Defense University Press, 1990.

Herken, Gregg. *The Winning Weapon: The Atomic Bomb in the Cold War, 1945-50*. New York: Knopf, 1980.

———. *Counsels of War*. New York: Knopf, 1985.

Hewlett, Richard and Francis Duncan. *Atomic Shield: A History of the United States Atomic Energy Commission, volume 2, 1947-52*. University Park: Pennsylvania State University Press, 1962.

Hietala, Thomas. *Manifest Design: Anxious Aggrandizement in Late Jacksonian America*. Ithaca: Cornell University Press, 1985.

Hixson, Walter. *George F. Kennan, Cold War Iconoclast*. New York: Columbia University Press, 1989.

Holloway, David. *The Soviet Union and the Arms Race*. New Haven: Yale University Press, 1983.

———. *Stalin and the Bomb: The Soviet Union and Atomic Energy, 1939–1956*. New Haven: Yale University Press, 1994.

Hoopes, Townsend. *The Devil and John Foster Dulles*. Boston: Little, Brown 1973.

Hunt, Michael H. *Ideology and U.S. Foreign Policy*. New Haven: Yale University Press, 1987.

Immerman, Richard H., ed. *John Foster Dulles and the Diplomacy of the Cold War*. Princeton: Princeton University Press, 1990.

Isaacson, Walter, and Evan Thomas. *The Wise Men: Six Friends and the World They Made*. New York: Simon and Schuster, 1986.

Jervis, Robert. *The Illogic of Nuclear Strategy*. Ithaca: Cornell University Press, 1984.

———. *The Meaning of the Nuclear Revolution: Statecraft and the Prospect of Armageddon*. Ithaca: Cornell University Press, 1989.

Kahn, Herman. *On Thermonuclear War*. Princeton: Princeton University Press, 1960.

———. *Thinking About the Unthinkable*. New York: Horizon Press, 1962.

Kaplan, Fred. *The Wizards of Armageddon*. New York: Simon and Schuster, 1983.

Kaufmann, William, ed. *Military Policy and National Security*. Princeton: Princeton University Press, 1956.

———. *The McNamara Strategy*. New York: Harper and Row, 1964.

Keegan, John. *The Face of Battle*. New York: Penguin, 1976.

Kennan, George F. *American Diplomacy, 1900–1950*. Chicago: University of Chicago Press, 1951.

———. *Russia, the Atom, and the West*. New York: Harper, 1959.

———. *Memoirs, 1925–1950*. Boston: Little, Brown, 1967.

———. *Memoirs, 1950–1963*. New York: Pantheon, 1983.

————. *The Nuclear Delusion: Soviet-American Relations in the Atomic Age.* New York: Pantheon, 1983.

————. *Around the Cragged Hill: A Personal and Political Philosophy.* New York: Norton, 1993.

Kennedy, John F. *The Strategy of Peace.* New York: Harper, 1960.

Keohane, Robert, ed. *Neorealism and its Critics.* New York: Columbia University Press, 1986.

Khrushchev, Nikita. *Khrushchev Remembers: The Last Testament,* Strobe Talbott, trans. Boston: Little, Brown, 1974.

Kinnard, Douglas. *President Eisenhower and Strategy Management.* Lexington: University Press of Kentucky, 1977.

Kissinger, Henry. *A World Restored.* Boston: Houghton Mifflin, 1954.

————. *Nuclear Weapons and Foreign Policy.* New York: Harper, 1957.

————. *The Necessity for Choice: Prospects of American Foreign Policy.* New York: Harper, 1960.

Kistiakowsky, George B. *A Scientist at the White House: The Private Diary of President Eisenhower's Special Assistant for Science and Technology.* Cambridge: Harvard University Press, 1976.

Kolko, Joyce, and Gabriel Kolko. *The Limits of Power: The World and United States Foreign Policy, 1945–54.* New York: Harper and Row, 1972.

Lasby, Clarence G. *Eisenhower's Heart Attack: How Ike Beat Heart Disease and Held on to the Presidency.* Lawrence: University Press of Kansas, 1997.

Lebow, Richard Ned and Janice Gross Stein. *We All Lost the Cold War.* Princeton: Princeton University Press, 1994.

Leffler, Melvyn. *A Preponderance of Power: National Security, the Truman Administration, and the Cold War.* Palo Alto: Stanford University Press, 1992.

Liddell Hart, Sir Basil. *Strategy, The Indirect Approach.* New York: Praeger, 1954.

Lilienthal, David E. *The Journals of David E. Lilienthal: The Atomic Energy Years, 1945–1950.* New York: Harper and Row, 1964.

Luard, Evan, ed. *The Cold War: A Re-appraisal.* New York: Praeger, 1964.

Macmillan, Harold. *Riding the Storm, 1956–59.* New York: Harper and Row, 1971.

————. *Pointing the Way, 1959–61.* London: MacMillan, 1972.

Mandelbaum, Michael. *The Nuclear Question: The United States and Nuclear Weapons, 1946–1976.* Cambridge: Cambridge University Press, 1979.

————. *The Nuclear Revolution: International Politics Before and After Hiroshima.* Cambridge: Cambridge University Press, 1981.

Marks, Frederick W., III. *Power and Peace: The Diplomacy of John Foster Dulles.* Westport: Praeger, 1993.

Mayers, David. *George Kennan and the Dilemmas of US Foreign Policy.* New York: Oxford University Press, 1988.

McCormick, Thomas J. *America's Half-Century: United States Foreign Policy in the Cold War*, 2nd ed,. Baltimore: Johns Hopkins University Press, 1995.

McNamara, Robert. *Blundering into Disaster: Surviving the First Century of the Nuclear Age*. New York: Pantheon, 1986.

McNeill, William H. *The Pursuit of Power: Technology, Armed Force, and Society since A. D. 1000*. Chicago: University of Chicago Press, 1982.

Medhurst, Martin J., *Dwight D. Eisenhower: Strategic Communicator*. Westport: Greenwood Press, 1992.

Melanson, Richard A., and David Mayers, eds. *Reevaluating Eisenhower: American Foreign Policy in the 1950s*. Urbana: University of Illinois Press, 1987.

Miscamble, Wilson. *George F. Kennan and the Making of American Foreign Policy, 1947–1950*. Princeton: Princeton University Press, 1992.

Morgenstern, Oskar. *The Question of National Defense*. New York: Random House, 1959.

Morgenthau, Hans. *Scientific Man vs. Power Politics*. Chicago: University of Chicago Press, 1946.

———. *Politics Among Nations*, 1st ed. New York: Knopf, 1948.

Moss, Norman. *Men Who Play God: The Story of the Hydrogen Bomb and How the World Came to Live With It*. New York: Harper and Row, 1968.

Murphy, Robert. *Diplomat Among Warriors*. Garden City: Doubleday, 1964.

Naimark, Norman N. *The Russians in Germany: A History of the Soviet Zone of Occupation, 1945–1949* Cambridge: Harvard University Press, 1995.

Nash, Philip. *The Other Missiles of October: Eisenhower, Kennedy, and the Jupiters*. Chapel Hill: University of North Carolina Press, 1997.

Neustadt, Richard. *Presidential Power and the Modern Presidents*, 5th ed. New York: Free Press, 1990.

Newhouse, John. *War and Peace in the Nuclear Age*. New York: Knopf, 1989.

Niebuhr, Reinhold. *The Children of Light and the Children of Darkness*. New York: Charles Scribner's Sons, 1944.

Ninkovich, Frank. *Germany and the United States: The Transformation of the German Question Since 1945*. Boston: Twayne Publishers, 1988.

———. *Modernity and Power: A History of the Domino Theory in the Twentieth Century*. Chicago: University of Chicago Press, 1994.

Nitze, Paul. *From Hiroshima to Glasnost: At the Center of Decision*. New York: Weidenfeld and Nicolson, 1989.

O'Donnell, Kenneth P., and David F. Powers, with Joe McCarthy, *"Johnny, We Hardly Knew Ye": Memories of John Fitzgerald Kennedy*. Boston: Little, Brown, 1972.

Osgood, Robert E. *Limited War: The Challenge to American Strategy*. Chicago: University of Chicago Press, 1957.

Palmer, Gregory. *The McNamara Strategy and the Vietnam War: Program Budgeting in the Pentagon, 1960–68*. Westport: Greenwood Press, 1978.

Paret, Peter. *Clausewitz and the State*. Princeton: Princeton University Press, 1985.

———. *Understanding War: Essays on Clausewitz and the History of Military Power*. Princeton: Princeton University Press, 1992.

Parmet, Herbert. *Richard Nixon and His America*. Boston: Little, Brown, 1990.

Paxton, Robert O. and Nicholas Wahl, eds. *De Gaulle and the United States: A Centennial Appraisal*. Providence: Berg, 1994.

Pickett, William B. *Dwight D. Eisenhower and American Power*. Wheeling: Harlan Davidson, 1995.

Posen, Barry. *The Sources of Military Doctrine: France, Britain, and Germany between the World Wars*. Ithaca: Cornell University Press, 1984.

Prados, John.. *The Soviet Estimate: U.S. Intelligence Analysis and Russian Military Strength*. New York: Dial Press, 1982.

———. *The Keepers of the Keys: A History of the National Security Council from Truman to Bush*. New York: W. Morrow, 1991.

Pruessen, Ronald. *John Foster Dulles: The Road to Power*. New York: Free Press, 1982.

Qiang Zhai. *The Dragon, the Lion, and the Eagle: Chinese/British/American Relations, 1949–58*. Kent: Kent State University Press, 1992.

Quester, George H. *Nuclear Diplomacy: The First Twenty-Five Years*. New York: Dunellen, 1970.

Rhodes, Richard. *Dark Sun*. New York: Simon and Schuster, 1995.

Richardson, Elmo, and Chester J. Pach, Jr. *The Presidency of Dwight D. Eisenhower*. Lawrence: University Press of Kansas, 1992.

Richter, James G. *Khrushchev's Double Bind: International Pressures and Domestic Coalition Politics*. Baltimore: Johns Hopkins University Press, 1994.

Roman, Peter J. *Eisenhower and the Missile Gap*. Ithaca: Cornell University Press, 1995.

Rosenberg, Emily. *Spreading the American Dream: American Economic and Cultural Expansion, 1890–1945*. New York: Hill and Wang, 1982.

Rosenthal, Joel. *Righteous Realists: Political Realism, Responsible Power, and American Culture in the Nuclear Age*. Baton Rouge: Louisiana State University Press, 1991.

Rusk, Dean. *As I Saw It*. New York: Norton, 1990.

Sagan, Scott, *Moving Targets: Nuclear Strategy and National Security*. Princeton: Princeton University Press, 1989.

———. *The Limits of Safety: Organizations, Accidents, and Nuclear Weapons*. Princeton: Princeton University Press, 1993.

Schelling, Thomas. *The Strategy of Conflict*. Cambridge: Harvard University Press, 1960.

———. *Arms and Influence*. New Haven: Yale University Press, 1966.

———. *Choice and Consequence*. Cambridge: Harvard University Press, 1984.

Schick, Jack. *The Berlin Crisis, 1958–62*. Philadelphia: University of Pennsylvania Press, 1971.

Schilling, Warner R., Paul Y. Hammond, and Glenn Snyder. *Strategy, Politics, and Defense Budgets*. New York: Columbia University Press, 1962.

Schlesinger, Arthur, Jr. *A Thousand Days: John F. Kennedy in the White House*. Boston: Houghton Mifflin, 1965.

Shapley, Deborah. *Promise and Power: The Life and Times of Robert McNamara*. Boston: Little Brown, 1993.

Sherry, Michael S. *The Rise of American Air Power: The Creation of Armageddon*. New Haven: Yale University Press, 1987.

———. *In the Shadow of War: The United States since the 1930s*. New Haven: Yale University Press, 1995.

Shlaim, Avi. *The United States and the Berlin Blockade: A Study in Crisis Decision Making*. Berkeley: University of California Press, 1983.

Slusser, Robert M. *The Berlin Crisis of 1961: Soviet-American Relations and the Struggle for Power in the Kremlin, June-November 1961*. Baltimore: Johns Hopkins University Press, 1973.

Smith, Jean Edward. *Lucius D. Clay: An American Life*. New York: Holt, 1990.

Snyder, Glenn. *Deterrence and Defense: Toward a Theory of National Security*. Princeton: Princeton University Press, 1961.

Sorenson, Theodore C. *Kennedy*. New York: Harper and Row, 1965.

Stephanson, Anders. *Kennan and the Art of Foreign Policy*. Cambridge: Harvard University Press, 1989.

Strauss, Lewis. *Men and Decisions*. Garden City: Doubleday, 1962.

Taylor, Maxwell. *The Uncertain Trumpet*. New York: Harper, 1959.

Teller, Edward with Allen Brown. *The Legacy of Hiroshima*. Garden City: Doubleday, 1962.

Tompson, William J. *Khrushchev: A Political Life*. New York: St. Martin's Press, 1995.

Trachtenberg, Marc. *History and Strategy*. Princeton: Princeton University Press, 1991.

Truman, Harry S. *Memoirs of Harry S. Truman: Volume Two, Years of Trial and Hope*. Garden City: Doubleday, 1956.

Tusa, Ann. *The Last Division: A History of Berlin, 1945–1989*. Reading: Addison-Wesley, 1997.

Tusa, Ann and John. *The Berlin Airlift*. New York: Atheneum, 1988.

Van Dusen, Henry P., ed. *The Spiritual Legacy of John Foster Dulles*. Philadelphia: Westminster Press, 1960.

Wallerstein, Immanuel. *Geopolitics and Geoculture*. Cambridge: Cambridge University Press, 1992.

Waltz, Kenneth. *Man, the State and War*. New York: Columbia University Press, 1959.

———. *Theory of International Politics*. Reading: Addison-Wesley, 1979.

———. *The Spread of Nuclear Weapons: More May Be Better*. London: International Institute for Strategic Studies, 1981.

———, and Scott Sagan. *The Spread of Nuclear Weapons: A Debate*. New York: Norton, 1995.

Walzer, Michael. *Just and Unjust Wars*. New York, 1977.

Wampler, Robert A. *NATO Strategic Planning and Nuclear Weapons, 1950–1957*. College Park: University of Maryland Press, 1990.

Weart, Spencer. *Nuclear Fear: A History of Images*. Cambridge: Harvard University Press, 1988.

Weigley, Russell. *The American Way of War: A History of United States Military Strategy and Policy*. New York: Macmillan, 1973.

———. *Eisenhower's Lieutenants: The Campaign of France and Germany, 1944–45*. Bloomington: Indiana University Press, 1981.

Williamson, Samuel R., and Steven L. Rearden, *The Origins of United States Nuclear Strategy 1945–1953*. New York: St. Martin's Press, 1993.

Wyden, Peter. *Wall: The Inside Story of Divided Berlin*. New York: Simon and Schuster, 1989.

York, Herbert. *The Advisors: Oppenheimer, Teller, and the Superbomb*. San Francisco: W. H. Freeman, 1976.

———. *Making Weapons, Talking Peace: A Physicist's Odyssey from Hiroshima to Geneva*. New York: Basic Books, 1987.

Zhang Shu Guang. *Deterrence and Strategic Culture: Chinese-American Confrontations, 1949–1958*. Ithaca: Cornell University Press, 1992.

6. Articles

Acheson, Dean. "The Illusion of Disengagement." *Foreign Affairs* 36 (April 1958).

———. "Wishing Won't Hold Berlin." *Saturday Evening Post* 231 (March 7, 1959).

Arneson, Gordon R. "The H-Bomb Decision." *Foreign Service Journal* 46 (May 1969).

Brands, H. W. "The Age of Vulnerability: Eisenhower and the National Insecurity State." *American Historical Review* 94 (October 1989).

Brodie, Bernard. "Nuclear Weapons: Strategic or Tactical?" *Foreign Affairs* 32 (January 1954).

———. "Strategy Hits a Dead End." *Harper's* 211 (October 1955).

Burr, William. "Avoiding the Slippery Slope: The Eisenhower Administration and Berlin." *Diplomatic History* 18 (Summer 1994).

Cumings, Bruce. "The End of the 70-years' Crisis: Trilateralism and the New World Order." *World Policy Journal* 8 (Spring 1991).

Deudney, Daniel. "Nuclear Weapons and the Decline of the *Real*-State." *Daedalus* 124 (Spring 1995).

Dulles, John Foster. "A Policy of Boldness." *Life*. May 19, 1952).

———. "The Evolution of Foreign Policy." *Department of State Bulletin* 30 (January 25, 1954).

———. "Policy for Security and Peace." *Foreign Affairs* 32 (April 1954).

———. "Challenge and Response in the United States Policy." *Foreign Affairs* 36 (October 1957).

Griffith, Robert. "Dwight D. Eisenhower and the Corporate Commonwealth." *American Historical Review* 87 (January 1982).

Harrison, Hope M. "Ulbricht and the Concrete 'Rose': New Archival Evidence on the Dynamics of Soviet-East German Relations and the Berlin Crisis, 1958–1961." *Cold War International History Project working paper no. 5*. Princeton 1993).

Hoffmann, Stanley. "An American Social Science: International Relations." *Daedalus* 106 (Summer 1977).

Immerman, Richard. "Confessions of an Eisenhower Revisionist." *Diplomatic History* 14 (Summer 1990).

Kennan, George. "Russia, the Atom, and the West, 1959." *The Listener* 42 (October 29, 1959).

———. "A Proposal for Western Survival." *New Leader* 42 (November 16, 1959).

Kissinger, Henry. "American Policy and Preventive War." *Yale Review* 44 (March 1955).

———. "Military Policy and Defense of the 'Grey Areas' " *Foreign Affairs* 33 (April 1955).

Lebow, Richard Ned. "The long peace, the end of the cold war, and the failure of realism." *International Organization* 48 (Spring 1994).

Maranell, Gary M. "The Evaluation of Presidents: An extension of the Schlesinger Polls." *Journal of American History* 57 (June 1970).

McMahon, Robert J. "The Study of American Foreign Relations: National History or International History?" *Diplomatic History* 14 (Fall, 1990).

Metz, Steven. "Eisenhower and the Planning of American Grand Strategy." *Journal of Strategic Studies* 14 (Winter 1991).

Morgenthau, Hans. "Death in the Nuclear Age." *Commentary* 32 (September 1961).
———. "Truth and Power." *Commentary* 32 (January 1962).
———. "Four Paradoxes of Nuclear Strategy." *American Political Science Review* 58 (March 1964).
Rabe, Stephen G. "Eisenhower Revisionism: A Decade of Scholarship." *Diplomatic History* 17 (Winter 1993).
Rosenberg, David Alan. "American Atomic Strategy and the Hydrogen Bomb Decision." *Journal of American History* 66 (June 1979).
———. "The Origins of Overkill: Nuclear Weapons and American Strategy, 1945–60." *International Security* 7 (Spring 1983).
Schelling, Thomas. "Who Will Have the Bomb?" *International Security* 1 (Summer 1976).
Soman, Appu K. " 'Who's Daddy' in the Taiwan Strait? The Offshore Islands Crisis of 1958." *Journal of American-East Asian Relations* 3 (Winter 1994).
Vandercook, Wm. F. "Making the Very Best of the Very Worst." *International Security* 11 (Summer 1986).
Waltz, Kenneth. "War in Neorealist Theory." *Journal of Interdisciplinary History* 18 (September 1988).
Weber, Steve. "Realism, detente, and nuclear weapons." *International Organization* 44 (Winter 1990).
Woodward, C. Vann. "The Age of Reinterpretation." *American Historical Review* 66 (October 1960).

Index